The New Canadian Poets

1970–1985

The New Canadian Poets 1970–1985

EDITED BY

Dennis Lee

McClelland & Stewart Inc.
The Canadian Publishers
481 University Ave., Toronto, Ontario M5G 2E9

Canadian Cataloguing in Publication Data

Main entry under title:

The New Canadian poets, 1970–1985

Includes bibliographies.
ISBN 0-7710-5216-2

1. Canadian poetry (English) – 20th century. *
I. Lee, Dennis, 1939–

PS8293.N48 1985   C811′.54′08   C85-098243-X
PR9195.7.N48 1985

The publisher makes grateful acknowledgment to the
Ontario Arts Council and the Canada Council for their
assistance.

Every effort has been made to ascertain ownership and
acknowledge copyright for reprinted material.
Information would be welcomed that would enable the
publisher to rectify any error.

Set in Sabon by The Typeworks, Vancouver
Printed and bound in Canada by Gagné Ltd.

Contents

Introduction

This is an anthology of English Canadian poets who published their first books between 1970 and 1985. They make up a wonderfully eclectic generation, unprecedented in its diversity and depth. For many readers it will come as a welcome shock to discover the quality of their work, which has been gathering force, virtually unheralded beyond their immediate circles, in the last fifteen years.

Before exploring the poetry itself, we might examine the conditions from which it emerged. These are extra-literary, of course, but the general situation of new poets in this period is intriguing, and provides a useful backdrop to their writing.

Consider the matter of numbers – which are mind-boggling. Throughout the sixties there had been a gradual but steady escalation in poetic debuts. In 1959, three first books of poetry appeared in English Canada; in 1964 there were eight; in 1965, twelve; in 1967, seventeen.[1] And after 1970, the deluge! No one can keep accurate count any longer, but one conservative estimate is that from seven hundred to a thousand poets started publishing in book form between 1970 and 1985 – an average of sixty a year.[2] And that is only a small proportion of the poets who were publishing their first work in magazines at the same time. The country had erupted in new poets, from sea to sea.

Yet these numbers, startling as they are, reveal only part of a larger transformation in the literary milieu – which leads to the second unique feature of the period. When I started reading for this anthology, one discovery in particular took me aback. Many of the best new poets were unfamiliar with one another's work. Not only that: often they were unaware of each other's *names*. For better or worse, this had never been true before in

Canadian poetry. Through previous decades, a worthwhile collection that appeared in Vancouver one January would be assimilated, by December, all the way to Halifax. Even at its most prolific, as in the flurry of new poets during the late sixties, Canadian poetry had always been something one person could keep in focus – particularly a younger poet, searching out peers in hope and trepidation.

After 1970, all that changed. For one thing, the avalanche had begun; who can read sixty first books a year? The rise of regional presses was another factor, since many of their titles were never seen outside their home province. As well, book prices were going up; building a personal library became more difficult. And unlike their immediate predecessors, few of the strong new poets of the seventies and eighties appeared in an early blaze of lyric glory. Whatever the reason, many developed more slowly, hitting their stride in their late twenties, their thirties, even their forties. So even when readers did catch up with them, their talent was not always immediately evident.

The result of all these developments was that the "poetry community" dissolved during the seventies into a series of blurry sub-communities, which seldom overlapped. Across the country, emerging poets were more isolated and less visible than ever before – to each other as much as to the reading public. The effect of the explosion of numbers in our poetry was a drastic reduction in the visibility of new poets.

A further change in the situation of new poetry involves the background of the poets. Forty per cent of the writers in this anthology were born outside Canada, and another ten per cent are children of immigrants.[3] Individual cases are so tangled and so various that no conclusions can be drawn *a priori* about their work. But about the phenomenon itself there can be no doubt. In terms of national origins, sense of place, cultural and ethnic identity, this is far and away the most cosmopolitan generation in our history.

Questions of number, visibility, and background have more to do with the sociology of poetry than with poetry itself, and I'll leave the explanation of these developments to the social sciences. But they serve as a dramatic reminder: this is a distinct new generation, which deserves to be read in its own right.

•

What does the poetry of these people have in common?

The first artistic fact about this generation is the neck-wrenching variety in its assumptions about what a poem is. There are recognizable schools and tendencies. But if you take a step back and survey the range of what new poets have been doing, the pattern is one of exhilarating variety, of many incompatible models of excellence. The period has been called "eclectic"; provided it's not taken to mean that individual poets write eclectically, the term is apt.

To put such eclecticism into perspective, we should consider the manner in which this generation came of artistic age. There have been as many paths as poets, of course. But most of these writers have one thing in common: while they were working through their apprenticeship – in the late sixties, or during the seventies [4] – they had to reckon with a dramatic model of how a new generation does things. This was furnished by the slightly older poets who had appeared in a rush after 1965: Atwood, bissett, Bowering, MacEwen, Newlove, Nichol, Ondaatje, for instance. Within a very short time those newcomers had stormed into prominence; between 1966 and 1972, they collected the Governor General's Award for poetry no fewer than seven times. This was quite an act to follow.

It is not just the youthfulness and talent of the sixties poets which matter here; it's the collective impression they gave, of overturning traditional apple-carts left, right, and centre. That was the model of "new poetry" with which the poets who followed them had to deal. You were now expected to chant the poem, it appeared; to set fire to it; make visual designs from it; breathe it and serialize it and concretize it. You had to spend nights on Black Mountain, and cross-pollinate genres. And the preferred mood was hard-edged *extremis*. A spirit of iconoclastic innovation prevailed, even if only some of the new writers exemplified it fully. The essence of literature lay in its radical novelty; each generation, by implication, was obliged to rebuild poetry from the foundations up, if it was serious about poetry at all.

In fact, not every new poet of the sixties would have urged non-stop experimentation as the only proper path, in all times and places. But that is by the bye. After 1970 or so, those poets were *there;* they were highly innovative; and they were good. For a younger poet, still groping to find his or her voice, the prestige conferred upon "radical innovation" by their example was very great.

This presented the same danger, for the younger poets, as would any other orthodoxy. The model of the poet as perpetual iconoclast and innovator had not emerged, with a struggle, from *their* own needs and practice; it was presented to them, by circumstance, as a *fait accompli.* It would have been a temptation to follow that model out of timidity or opportunism, rather than conviction. Reproducing avant-garde gestures could become a panacea, a way of avoiding their own necessary odysseys. They might drift into a hectic, faddish pseudo-experimentalism, which aped the externals of their predecessors' work but had no grounding in any serious artistic vision of their own. . . . And in the early seventies, it must be said, a number of emerging poets went through the motions of being experimental simply because "experimental" was in fashion. The results, though occasionally flashy, were as dismal as you might expect.

This puts in its proper light the eclecticism which finally emerged as the hallmark of the period. In a great many cases, the pattern followed by stronger poets was one of standing back from the sixties poets, and hunkering down for an extended apprenticeship elsewhere; spending a decade or more in private obscurity, while new paths and possibilities took shape; and then emerging with a voice and preoccupations which had a momentum of their own, whether traditional, experimental, or whatever. Sometimes poets coalesced into groupings configured along quite different lines from anything the sixties had envisioned. And many are finally consolidating their long period of independent growth by issuing a Selected; a third of the poets here have recently done so.

That is to say: this new generation – poet by poet, and with little or no public discussion of the strategy – did the only thing a self-respecting new generation can. It ignored the hard-earned wisdom of its elders, and found its own way ahead. It has plundered much from its predecessors, here and abroad: but on each poet's own terms, not as a procession of clones. The final result is the confident and exuberant variety of the poetry here – the work of an eclectic generation.

•

Putting together an anthology from such a fertile period has been a challenge. The main question was, how to do justice to individual writers, and also to the period as a whole? Representing a dozen poets, say, would misrepresent the bursting-at-the-seams quality of the period. But printing a couple of poems by each of a hundred writers would simply leave the reader's head spinning.

The solution I arrived at is this. I have chosen twenty poets for intensive coverage, with up to fifteen pages apiece. These are writers whom I could not conceive of presenting in shorter compass, because of the quality and scope of their achievement. And I've sought more extensive treatment of the period by presenting another twenty-five poets at three or four pages apiece. I've tried to present them at their characteristic best; however, my primary aim has been to represent – as far as space permits – the wider range of endeavour in the period. Each of these poets deserves to be read independently and in greater depth – as do several dozen others I've been unable to include, but who would be welcome additions here. It saddens me that limits of space have made such rigorous guidelines necessary.

Eclecticism calls for an editorial policy as well; mine has been to follow the grain of the period and be equally eclectic. That is, I've attempted to represent conflicting schools and tendencies by their best work (including cases where they are schools of one), rather than screening out groupings *a priori*. Readers may mentally edit a slimmer version of *The New Canadian Poets* for themselves; I welcome this, while pointing out that readers of other persuasions will do the same, with very different results. A whole series of sub-anthologies is contained here, kicking and fighting between the covers.

Another policy decision derives from the fact that this anthology is part of a series.[5] Its immediate predecessor, Eli Mandel's *Poets of Contemporary Canada* (1972), dealt with poets who reached maturity during the sixties. Understandably, Mandel did not include a dozen or more poets of that generation who now look very good, but whose strongest work began after his collection appeared. It was a temptation to represent those late-blooming poets here. I've decided against it, however. Poets of the sixties have generally been well treated by anthologists and critics, while the subsequent generation is still waiting for a first round of serious attention. This policy has meant interpreting the starting-date in draconian fashion; no poet who published a book before 1970 has been considered.

The other end of the period was problematic too. I have had to pass over many poets—mostly in their twenties and thirties—whose work is, in the best sense of the hackneyed term, promising. It will be up to the next anthology in this series to represent them as they'll soon deserve.

What you'll find here, then, are forty-five Canadian poets who published their first book after 1970. Most were born between 1945 and 1955, and so were in their thirties when this selection was made.[6]

•

In the sections that follow, I have drawn four sketch-maps of the terrain. They indicate patterns found in the period, each of which applies to some but not all of the poets here. They focus in turn on *content, voice, image,* and *phenomenological stance*. While these afford ways of finding coherence in this very heterogeneous body of work, they are relevant to the poetry of other times and places as well; there is no suggestion that they reveal something unique to this generation alone. And other approaches would turn up further patterns of coherence, which would enrich those investigated here. The ones I've chosen reveal common-denominator aspects of the poetry, rather than going deeply into poems or poets who are singular.

But at this point you may want to turn directly to the poetry, and consider what follows as though it were an Afterword.

&

I

A first way of sorting the period is by looking at "schools of content." These are not simply themes a critic might choose to trace, such as "the relation of parents and children," or "the threat of nuclear holocaust." They are conscious, deliberate groupings among poets who share an obsession with some urgent body of experience, often one which had not been taken as a fit subject for poetry before. On the basis of that shared concern, poets have come together to found presses and magazines, write manifestos, compile anthologies, and the like.

Perhaps a third to a half of these poets have been involved in a school of content, or write at times from a sense of common cause with one. None of them can be read solely in terms of participation in such a group. But the period as a whole begins to take on more coherence when you recognize the presence of these schools.

•

The first is that of the *Prairie documentary*. There were already precedents in the work of Anne Marriott, Dorothy Livesay, John Newlove; the touchstone figure in this generation has been Andrew Suknaski. In 1973, his *Wood Mountain Poems* established a normative range of subjects for the genre: autobiography, family politics, small-town lives and yarns, immigrant experience, native life, Canadian history, the relation between folk art (such as pub talk) and poetry – all focused from a consciously Prairie perspective. And the book found a normative voice for such material: the anecdotal vernacular. While few of the poets who responded directly to the new centre of gravity of *Wood Mountain Poems* are represented here, there are independent approaches to the central material in poems by Leona Gom, Gary Hyland, Robert Kroetsch, Kim Maltman, Monty Reid, Dale Zieroth.[7]

It has been striking to watch a communal Prairie story itching itself into poetry. But then – to widen the focus briefly – the Prairie-documentary poets have been doing something which is incumbent on some poets all the time: that is, to explore, challenge, and confirm the spirit of place. While this is decidedly a time of regionalist poetry, there have been no comparably developed "schools of place" outside the Prairies during the period. But the same impulse can be felt – in very different modes – in works like Christopher Dewdney's "A Natural History of Southwestern Ontario," Don Domanski's sequence *Heaven,* Charles Lillard's "Rivers Were Promises," Al Pittman's Newfoundland vignettes. In fact you could probably find the impulse in every poet here, if not always in the poems I've selected. Love of one's own, as Plato observed, is how a human being first approaches love of the good. On the Prairies as elsewhere.

•

A second conscious school of content is the *feminist.* The term means many things to many people; I'm using it here in a broad way, to refer to poetry which manifests any of the concerns or approaches raised in the women's movements of the last few decades. One type of feminist poem takes established political topics, such as male chauvinism or experiences unique to women, as its explicit content. Jeni Couzyn's "The Red Hen's Last Will and Testament . . . " is an example. Another type investigates wider subjects from within a clearly feminist consciousness – Bronwen Wallace's "Reminder," for instance.[8]

I have the impression that no one Canadian poet of this generation has established norms of feminist poetry to which others are now responding. (Insofar as older poets have influenced this school, they include Sylvia Plath, Margaret Atwood, Adrienne Rich. But many of the deepest influences have not been poets at all.) That said, a central figure is certainly Bronwen Wallace; exploring human experience from a female and feminist perspective seems to flow naturally with the grain of her imagination. Strong feminist poems come also from Mary di Michele, Robyn Sarah, Anne Szumigalski, among others.

Again, we can broaden the focus to consider several related points. Not every poem written by a woman is "feminist," obviously, nor is every poem on the subject of men and women. There was a recurring poem in the fifties and sixties, which dealt with sex and was written by a man; the counterpart now is a poem about the sexes, usually though not always written by a woman. And in man-and-woman poems such as these, the central point is not the author's stand on feminist issues. I think of Roo Borson's "Talk," Pier Giorgio Di Cicco's "Relationships" (though not his "Male Rage Poem," which does take the feminist agenda as crucial), Judith Fitzgerald's "Past Cards 21," Diana Hartog's "The Common Man."

Something striking in poems by women here – feminist or not – is how broad a range of roles and speaking stances they claim. In fact, several poems by Lorna Crozier, Paulette Jiles, Susan Musgrave, Sharon Thesen are likely to provoke a double-take in the reader – partly, at least, because it is still startling to read a poem in which a woman is forthrightly angry or aggressive. Or in which she deliberately speaks from within one of the stereotypes that have been off-limits as personae, being considered too unflattering: as vamp, for instance, or as bitch, jailbait, blues momma. Crozier's "This One's for You" or Thesen's "Dedication" are no more shocking than were earlier poems by Layton or Cohen. But they are no less shocking, either; they confront social/poetic stereotypes just as vigorously (even if the stereotypes they challenge are different), force us either to reject the poem out of hand or to re-group our reading assumptions.

What's intriguing is not just the breaking of taboos, though. Once you've assimilated that, you notice that other good poems by the same writers enact impulses which should stereotypically be excluded by anger or aggression – playfulness, intellectual rigour, nurturing, joy. To react to the "taboo" poems alone would miss the larger point: that these poets seek to articulate as full a range of being human as possible.

•

The common theme in the third grouping is the experience of *being an immigrant, or the child of immigrants*. This grouping shows only some of the attributes of a conscious and fully self-defined school. True, there have been anthologies of immigrant poetry. And beyond that, a good many poets have written about immigrant experience. But there is less of a sense than with other groupings of poetic energies consciously coming together, or of poetry itself being recast by the experience whose pressure the poets share. These writers seem like individuals who have dealt with comparable content in varying ways; when they do come together, it seems more after-the-fact.

Be that as it may, there are many such poets writing. Here they include Pier Giorgio Di Cicco, Mary di Michele, Raymond Filip, Leona Gom, Kristjana Gunnars, Andrew Suknaski, Dale Zieroth. As their surnames suggest, it is when the dislocation of emigrating to Canada has been most severe that poetry on the subject has been most vital. Literal displacement is seldom a subject for British or American immigrants.

One thing these poets have in common is a sense of loss that is attached to a specific place abroad – however mythic it may have become in memory, lore, or fantasy. This can lock into the here-and-now as well. Andrew Suknaski's elegiac perspective, for example, whether it is illuminating the experience of native peoples, Chinese railway workers, or small-town personages, resonates with his own sense of a holy communal place in the Ukraine, lost by his immigrant forbears before he was born. Something comparable is true of many immigrant poets.

•

A fourth conscious school of content takes *daily work* as its subject. A good many poets have identified centrally or occasionally with this school; two of them are represented here. Tom Wayman is the leading exemplar and spokesman; he has edited several thoughtful anthologies of work poetry, and has made the vernacular voice a provocative medium for the subject. And Howard White, with an ear and vision of his own, focuses on macabre, tall-tale elements in the lore of lumbering, fishing, and truck-driving.

Perhaps because this tendency had roots in left-wing analysis, it began by taking blue-collar work as the subject of choice, along with frontier-job experience. Latterly the emphasis seems to have shifted to work as the daily lot of most human beings, whatever their class.

•

It goes without saying that there is as much "content" in the other poets here as in the ones cited above. Moreover, there are thematic concerns – destruction of the environment, for instance – which can be traced in poet after poet across the period. But as far as I know, these four cases are the only ones where poets themselves have formed "schools of content." A reader interested in other themes, such as relationships, ecology, peace and war, will want to track them through the poetry for him or herself.

A final thought: not on schools of content, but on the convictions that may give rise to such schools, and that often play a contentious part in poetry. I find several of these poets compelling when they write most directly from ideological conviction – to which (a reader is bound to assume) they subscribe in daily life, and in whose service the poem speaks. Common wisdom in contemporary English-speaking letters has it that doctrinal poetry is invariably bad poetry. But while I certainly recognize the pitfalls of versified ideology, the maxim strikes me as no more sensible than saying that all poetry about daffodils, mothers, or God is bound to be bad. There are reams of sentimental dreck on those subjects. But you can write badly about anything; recognizing that says nothing about the possibility of writing about it well.

And when I follow the trajectory of Brian Fawcett's determination to "slime the Beautiful with facts"; or feel stirred by the passion for social justice in Tom Wayman's sermons and curses; or (in a different vein) track with bemused pleasure through some elaborately propositional ramble by David Donnell or Robert Kroetsch – then I find myself unwilling to accept the dictum that doctrine must always and only kill poetry. Mind you, I'm usually in a tug-of-war with these poems. I'm never sure if I trust their rhetorical stance (which seems so much more *certain* than I'm usually able to feel); at the same time, they leave me questioning my own moral and aesthetic commitments. But when a poem is making life uncomfortable for me in that way – as in any other – I usually end up cherishing the experience, however gingerly, and respecting the poem.

II

A second way of sorting the period is by trying to *hear* it, by tuning in to the range of voices found in the poetry. And across the whole period – though possibly not across this anthology – the most commonly heard single voice is one I think of as the *vernacular*. A minority of poets here write in vernacular all the time; others do so selectively; others, not at all. A vernacular poem may be addressing a beloved, recalling an incident from the past, issuing a political denunciation. But we need to examine the voice itself, not the uses to which it is put.

This is a sturdy, flexible tone, which draws on the resources of daily speech in Canadian English. During this period the

strongest vernacular influence has been the poetry of Al Purdy.
But that doesn't imply a purely native genesis; the impulse to
cast literary baggage aside and write in a way that approx-
imates daily speech has often arisen before. Think of Villon,
Chaucer, Donne, Wordsworth, Pound, Frost. The range of
what can be accomplished in vernacular is broader than you
might expect; the following is a brief sampling from this
volume.

Vernacular can be absolutely bald – as in Andrew Suknaski's
work, where the poet tries simply to get out of the way and let a
story that matters come through:

> in 1914
> [philip] well and my father walked south from moose jaw
> to find their homesteads
> they slept in haystacks along the way
> and once nearly burned to death . . .

Taking that relatively neutral tone as a point of reference,
you can then see one branch of vernacular swerving away into
a racy, substandard "folk" diction. Consider Howard White's
sardonic:

> Used to be in the woods all you had to
> watch out for was junkies nodding off
> getting caught with their ass in the bight
> now it's these Christly poets . . .

In the same direction, vernacular can reproduce the speech
conventions of a sub-culture, as in Gary Hyland's audition of
teenage English:

> Okay so I'm crazy, but I could be rich
> with acne clinics all across Canada
> cause I developed a surefire treatment
> scarless, painless, and inexpensive . . .

In a similar vein, Paulette Jiles can move vernacular towards the idiom of song lyrics:

> Honey, you know when you talk like that
> you're the only man I'll ever love.
> Just keep talking.
> That's what you're good for ...

And Lorna Crozier can catch a comparable honkytonk idiom:

> Hey, big talker,
> waited all my life
> for a man like you.
> Come my way, I'll blow
> the fuses in your big machine,
> short all your circuits ...

These examples work with slangy or "substandard" English (using the term to describe their diction, not to judge it). And that is not an easy thing to do well, as one can discover by trying.

There is sometimes a quality of *jeu d'esprit,* for a highly literate poet, in writing in "substandard vernacular." But usually it is not just a playful exercise. The refusal of correctness implies, in the hands of a poet of substance, at least, a conscious stance on matters of social or personal importance, one which the reader is tacitly invited to share. It may suggest, "Ordinary people's lives are considered sub-poetic – but you and I know they have a passion, savvy, and dignity that make most 'poetry' feel insulated from real life." Or the implicit stance may involve the speaker's own feelings; it may convey, for instance, "I don't know any Officially Certified Poetry in which feelings as direct and subversive as mine have been expressed. But I'll write an *un*-certified poem – and we can go ahead and enjoy their tang and reality anyway." These unstated ver-

nacular attitudes can be as potent as anything in the poem
itself.

•

Vernacular poetry is not just poetry in slang, however. It can
also be poetry that sounds like the relaxed conversation of a
literate person; we could call it "literate vernacular." And that
recognized, it's clear that casual diction and syntax (perhaps
the most striking stylistic features of substandard vernacular)
are only part of what vernacular poets are drawn to. They are
really taking a whole set of conventions, a logic of coherence
for poems, from the model of the speaking voice engaged in
conversation.

The conventions of literate vernacular include the following.
The speaker can be roughly identified with the writer (though
it may or may not be helpful to do so). He or she addresses the
reader conversationally on some subject of mutual interest.
The poem covers as much ground – both in exploration of sub-
ject matter, and in progress of insight or emotional intensity –
as might be traversed in a good conversation of somewhat
greater length. And the whole thing is organized by the logic of
conversation; thus there are no wild syntactic innovations,
self-conscious literary tropes, or highly burnished effects of
verbal music.

Listening to the poetry of the period, it's striking what a high
proportion is written in literate vernacular. This is true of
work from the United States, Britain, and Australia as well as
from Canada; consider a few examples from this anthology.

I had a very strong desire
to kiss a lemon.
No one was watching.
I kissed a lemon.

So much for that.
(Robert Kroetsch)

There was something
I thought I should remember
this morning ...
>   (Marilyn Bowering)

Emily, these baubles that people your world
have no desires of their own,
baby woman, what can I tell you to try to be
without being wrong?
>   (Mary di Michele)

I will hitch-hike out of here one day
with my hair in my eyes and a good breeze blowing
and cause a little confusion I'm sure–
>   (Artie Gold)

There was never gentleness.
All this romantic bullshit
about growing up on farms.
All I remember
are the pain and death.
>   (Leona Gom)

Is that last passage in "substandard" or "literate" vernacular? It hardly matters; the categorization will depend, I suppose, on whether one knows literate people who say "bullshit" readily. What does matter is that, once again, the rhetorical organization of the poem is based on the model of conversation.

•

Poets who choose to write in vernacular begin by eschewing a wide range of poetic effects, often with the implication that "effects" are all they are. But how do they keep the poem from just lying there on the page – flat, prosy, superficial, and un-resonant?

The first answer, alas, is that many vernacular poets are unable to keep that from happening; some don't even seem to realize it's a danger. But good vernacular poets have developed unobtrusive resources of craft, which they deploy within the conventions of conversational English. These have to do with shifts in level of diction, the use of line-breaks to point emphases, and a whole further range of moves, many concerned with pacing and rhythm – which by a kind of unspoken agreement among vernacular poets are the area of craft in which technique can be consciously deployed without violating the canons of plain speech.

By way of example, consider a little piece by Tom Wayman, where he's describing a moment of mundane elation.

> South-east of Edmonton, on the road that leads
> to Vermilion, Lloydminster, and the Saskatchewan
>   border
> I feel coming into me again like
> a song about a man born in the country
> the joy of the highway . . .

Notice how the syntax and rhythm crest in the fifth line – after the litany of place-names, and the mild syntactic delays – when the meaning finally completes itself. That cresting momentum wells up under the formulaic words "the joy of the highway," gives them a greater resonance than they might have had on their own, and makes the affirmation of joy the more credible.

The poem is powered by the mystique of the commonplace; it would have been contradictory to break into high-falutin' poetic gestures. Nonetheless the poem finds unobtrusive ways of its own to pace, heighten, and point the experience it's recreating.

•

The literate-vernacular stance also carries an unspoken message. Usually, I believe, it's an invitation to trust the speaker's sincerity. "There's nothing up my sleeve," it seems to say. "I'm not trying to score literary points. The unadorned directness of my words shows they're reaching for true things; whatever they find, they'll find straightforwardly, non-trickily."

Despite this candour, which does indeed come across in much of the poetry, it's worth noting that vernacular conventions still *are* one set of conventions: one possible grid of seeing and saying, as real and as artificial as any other. And vernacular has its own set of built-in dangers – chiefly, I believe, that it may agree to settle for too little, accept too low a ceiling on poetry. The resources of an honest conversational voice do not exhaust the full resources of a human being, nor of the world. Pitching one's voice exclusively in that register can make it difficult to find access to broader or deeper things for which a poem may equally hunger.

From that standpoint, it's intriguing to listen to poets who write in a vernacular voice – and then break all the rules, pursue goals very different from those of "conversation." I think of David Donnell or Don McKay. Or August Kleinzahler, whose work often relies on an acute ear for grungy vernacular – and then turns out to be a contemporary recasting of themes (such as the loss of a golden age of heroism) as classically Poetic as anything in Vergil:

> The racket, man
> in that arcade – those slobs
> at toy war go unh, unh night and day....
> Birds just shot through
> the arch
> screaming,
> Jeeeeeezuz, my feathers
> my pretty little bones...
> I remember
> where was that
> in Troy I think –
> or some dry hill
> out west.
> It's years now.

And Robert Kroetsch's vernacular stance is equally deceptive. His literate, plainspoken, sometimes jokey voice invites us into one kind of poem. But when we get there we discover we've arrived some place different: a hall of mirrors in which the poem keeps disappearing up its own most intimate apertures, snickering at the spectacle of itself *being* a poem and raising questions about the way the imagination knows the world.

By the same token, it's interesting to watch poets who claim the freedom to write both in and out of vernacular: Don Coles, for instance, or Pier Giorgio Di Cicco, Don Domanski, Sharon Thesen. Consider these examples of a poet doing both.

> Such giants we are and so hardly
> here, mere shapes in the dust and our
> deaf hands yelling so loud,
> the diaphanous blood, the diaphanous
> bone, and the truth so small as it crumbles it swims
> in and out of the intestine,
> floats through the ear's net, the eye's net,
> the sieve of the palm.
>
>   (Robert Bringhurst)

> These poems, these poems,
> these poems, she said, are poems
> with no love in them . . .
>   These are the poems of a man
> like Plato, she said, meaning something I did not
> comprehend but which nevertheless
> offended me. . .
>
>   (Robert Bringhurst)

> When I see her flesh budding I am eviscerated
> with cool hollow hands, agile in theiyr nervous
> evacuation of digestion. She is Hungry Hollow,
> the memory succubus with her twelve-year-old
> grace.
>
>   (Christopher Dewdney)

When it's raining cats and dogs you've got to cut corners
because you could get your eyes peeled. You must come
to grips with yourself until you fly off the handle & then
if you're not fit as a fiddle you'll spill the beans. . . .
(Christopher Dewdney)

(The latter is another instance of using vernacular to sabotage
vernacular, of course; the speaker rattles on for two pages
without once emerging from this cocoon of dead metaphors.)
Part of the fascination of the period lies in watching the strat-
egies, dead-ends, overlaps, and permutations which a volatile
vernacular tradition has been creating.

•

I spoke earlier of tuning in to the range of voices in this period.
But once you recognize the vernacular, both substandard and
literate, and perceive how it draws organizing energy from the
conventions of conversation, I don't know how much further
you can get with "voice" as a basis for sorting the period.
This is not because vernacular is the only voice you'll hear;
far from it. As the last quotations suggest, some of the highly
distinctive achievements of the period have come in non-verna-
cular voices. But most of them are one of a kind; what calls for
discussion is not their general resemblance to one another, but
their unique resemblance to themselves.
Needless to say, this is not the place to investigate them in-
dividually. But to suggest their variety, let me give a few more
examples of non-vernacular voice:

O mouse on the telephone! dunk your biscuit static!
O tapioca from Oka tango!
O chrome shimmy of blackfly blood!
O dill to pistachio!
(Peter van Toorn)

Epigrammatic Frenchmen say,
   if temperate or staid,
that 'reculer pour mieux sauter'
   explains the retrograde.
       (David Solway)

my granddaughters are combing out their long hair
   sitting at night
on the rocks in Venezuela   they have watched their
   babes
falling like white birds from the last of the treetop cradles
they have buried them in their hearts where they will
   never forget
to keep on singing them the old songs
       (Colleen Thibaudeau)

s ss s ss s ss s s
s tonn tonn tonn tonn tonn tonn tonn
s tt s tt s tt s t
s nonn nonn nonn nonn nonn nonn nonn
       (Paul Dutton)

I don't know for the world
why the soul does not darken
to remember them quick, and how
swiftly they fled – courage and strength
gone over to the far shore,
all mortal kindness sunk in hollow skull.
       (Jon Furberg)

III

It's striking how many poets of this generation turn to *the image* as a way of exploring the world, and of allowing a richness, even a pre-rational wildness, into the poem. The tend-

ency is found in vernacular and non-vernacular writers alike.
Exploring it lets us discern another common feature in many
poems of the period, though it won't reveal everything there is
to know about any one writer.

All poetry works with imagery, of course. I'm referring
to something more distinctive: first, to poets who take "the
image" as the fundamental imaginative unit with which to
parse the world; and second, to poets who turn to surreal im-
ages, or "deep images" (in Robert Bly's term) – to images from
well beyond whatever would be predictable at a given point –
to deepen, clinch, extend, redirect what is happening. I don't
suggest that poets have never done this before. But it is a fre-
quent resource for a considerable minority of this generation.

Among poets who construe the world through images, the
purest case must be that of Roo Borson. In her work, arresting
visual images such as,

> Everywhere you go: the incurable beauty
> of the earth. The sunsets like an armful
> of dying flamingoes.

or,

> Among branches
> a bird lands fluttering,
> a soft grey glove
> with a heart.
>
> The land at twilight.
> Swamps of black mist.
> A first planet. A swordtip.
> The bird chanting
> in a jail of darkness . . .

are ubiquitous – but not as decoration. Borson *thinks* in im-
ages. They have the same force as a physicist's reports on mass,

position, and velocity, or a mapmaker's stylized squiggles:
that is, they constitute a direct reading of the world, in the
terms which are fundamental to this particular reader.

Paulette Jiles has a comparable image-intelligence. Watch
her finding her way through a complex emotional situation by
means of imagery:

> Later I can lie on a hospital bed
>   and think about
> things.
> I have a stunning concussion.
> We are small, small I tell you,
>   among all these animals.
> We can be thrown great distances,
> we bounce when we hit.
>   You stand several miles away at
> the bedside and grip my hand . . .

There are so many more examples – not just of "memorable
images," but of "thinking by image" – that I'm not sure where
to stop. But consider two. Kim Maltman takes a different tack
than Jiles or Borson. Rather than following a series of brief im-
ages that become a step-by-step advance through the world,
the entire poem often articulates a single, literal image with
which it can construe the world, around which it can organize
some of the world's density and energy. The process can be
observed here in a poem like "Tina," though one needs to read
a number of his poems to catch the full drift of it.

Erin Mouré often proceeds by an uprush of surprising im-
ages, which she usually anchors in the literal process-of-feeling
of an agitated speaker. In "White Rabbit," however, she comes
at the matter differently. She gives us one bizarre image – of a
rabbit suspended sadistically from a third-storey window by
some man in her life, and left to dangle just off the ground –
which we're unsure whether to interpret as literal, surreal, sym-
bolic, or just what. Then she wings through a whole bitter roll

of feeling and stocktaking, propelled by the negative energy in that one discomfiting image. Again, it is a distinctive way of bringing the speaker's situation into focus through imagery.

•

Some of these poets use images in a bolder way still. Whether or not they are consistently "image-thinkers," they often come up with a single, dramatically unexpected image as a way of turning a crucial corner in a poem, or as a way of ending it. The image is then to be "heard," I believe, in something like the way a transitional or resolving chord is heard in music. It gathers or releases meanings which might not find any other avenue of entry into the poem.

Consider the way David Donnell's intricately counterpointed meditation on "Emily Dickinson's Horses" is resolved with this unexpected, surreal image:

> ... these horses
> these 4-year-olds restrained by carriage traces
> released from box stalls
> let loose on dirt roads
> these wild-eyed responders with a single rose between
> their teeth

Some of the challenge to the reader is simply to come to that with the right form of concentration – to be prepared for a poem to shift gears this way, swerving at the point of climax into a single rich image for contemplation. (Re-reading the examples of surreal or deep images here, I realize I've inadvertently chosen four instances involving flowers. The coincidence is gratuitous; we're not seeing the emergence of a new horticultural school.)

Pier Giorgio Di Cicco does something comparable in resolving a bittersweet poem about his father:

>   . . . it is this man who will sit
> on his front lawn, after the fifth hemorrhage, having
> his last picture taken
> because he drank too much.
>
> It is this man who will sit under his mimosa
> by the highway, fifty pounds underweight, with no
> hospital, and look
>
> there are great white roses in his eyes.

Or consider a poem by Robert Priest, which begins "The kiss I just missed giving you wound up later on another mouth," and ends:

> Indelible. Indelible. Wants to go finally to the
> graveyard of old kisses, each one with its denied
> rose strolling ghostly over. Each one with its sun-
> set nova quenching in amber on its headstone. O
> each of its stopped explosions driven down to juice
> in some white withering berry there.

And Roo Borson, along with her capacity for moving through a recognizable lifescape by means of images, can open out a poem with an arresting, discordant image such as this:

> The other men loll against the outsides of buildings,
> looking up at the stars,
> inconsequential.
>
> One of them bends down to smell a flower.
> There are holes in his face.

Other poets are doing intriguing things in this area: Don Domanski, for instance, or Marilyn Bowering, A. F. Moritz, Susan Musgrave.

•

The poets I cited in the last section have frequently set themselves to school with a rich tradition of "the image," often of a neo-surrealist cast, which developed among a variety of foreign poets during this century. (In fact, the widespread shift of allegiance from Black Mountain to South American surrealism – to over-generalize wildly – is one of the things that make 1970 a genuine watershed.) It's helpful to identify this tradition of the image, which has been interacting with other traditions in recent Canadian poetry. For the writing which results has goals and sources of momentum of its own, which cannot be interpreted adequately through other poetics.

There are no simple genealogies of influence to be drawn, and no list can be complete. But from the United States, Robert Bly and James Wright have been important mentors for some. From South America, Pablo Neruda and César Vallejo have been even more influential. (When I enquired among contributors about "influences," the non-Canadian name that came up most frequently was Neruda's – in perhaps a quarter of the instances where people responded.) And there are a number of European poets who have had a strong presence for the "image-poets" of this generation; the names of Rilke and Cesare Pavese recur – neither one a surrealist, but each preoccupied with the image.

•

The matter of "influences" can be considered in more general terms; it's an area in which this generation is quite distinct from its predecessors. Individual poets have chosen mentors and ancestors from abroad, as Canadians have always done; in addition to the poets mentioned above, contributors to this anthology spoke of their debt to poets as various as Chaucer, Rimbaud, Olson, Larkin, Milosz, Tranströmer. Yet at the same time they have drawn, with equal un-self-consciousness, from Purdy and Atwood and Ondaatje, to cite the pre-eminent Canadian influences on this generation.

And that brings me up short. I can remember the sense of blank futility I got around 1960, as an apprentice poet, reading Lampman and D. C. Scott and Pratt and realizing there was nothing there for me beyond the examples of personal artistic courage. I also remember the sense of virtually breaking a taboo when I did discover energy sources in my own time and place. So it is moving to read a generation for whom none of that is an issue to begin with. Of course there are poets to learn from in Canada; there are poets to learn from abroad; what's the big deal? It is a nice irony that our most foreign-born and blurrily dispersed generation is the first to be (in this respect) so uncomplicatedly indigenous, so fully at home in Canada.

IV

There are many other approaches one could take to the poetry of the period, and each would reveal something of interest in it. The last one I'll suggest here is somewhat unconventional. It involves an impulse that has driven a number of these poets, which I can only call *phenomenological*. (To see what I'm pointing to, you don't need to know the history of that contentious philosophical term.) This is an impulse to make the poem recreate a two-way process, in which the world is known by consciousness and consciousness knows the world.

Poets of this persuasion are nudged into a series of idiosyncratic innovations in the way their poems proceed, in order to catch the minute local disturbances that arise when world and consciousness interact. I haven't seen this tendency discussed anywhere; I don't believe it's a self-conscious movement.[9] And the innovations vary so much from poet to poet, in fact from poem to poem, that you can discern their continuity only by gazing through them to the common impulse beneath. It's one that has surfaced in other times and places; I'm simply struck by its unheralded vitality here and now. Let me give some examples.

Don McKay has developed a voice in which we can meet both the birds and beings to which the speaker devotes his attention, and also the teasing play of his consciousness *as* he attends to them – frequently (or so we're led to believe) shooting past them, tripping up, pausing to snicker ruefully at his own mishaps, then pelting ahead again to spend himself in wonder on the sheer *this*-ness of a heron or a child.

The casebook example is also the broadest example, which makes it a good place to begin. Here's McKay being wakened in the middle of the night by a *something,* a noise he can't at first identify. The initial ten lines enact the churning of his consciousness as it passes from deep sleep to wide-awake in half a second, riffling through a series of preposterous associations in an attempt to place the sound. It's only in the second stanza that consciousness and world come into sync.

Waking JESUS sudden riding a scream like a
train braking metal on metal on
metal teeth receiving signals from a dying star sparking
off involuntarily in terror in all directions in the
abstract incognito in my
maidenform bra in an expanding universe in a where's
my syntax thrashing
loose like a grab that like a
look out like a
live wire in a hurricane until

until I finally tie it down:
it is a pig scream
a pig scream from the farm across the road

McKay doesn't usually prolong the freefall of consciousness this much, the space of time in which he's not fully absorbed into the world. But it's instructive to see, since it prepares us for his more usual habit of giving us world and consciousness at once, as they move in and out of phase with one another.

Here he is, trying to get away from the house on a cold morning:

> Breath grows mossy, visible
> cliché. My car
> also wishes it were dead, repeats
> were dead, were dead
> before it kicks and runs.

In that repeated "were dead, were dead" we hear the double chug of a car engine that is refusing to catch, while the speaker huddles over the steering column in the cold and keeps turning the key, wishing the day itself had never started. The whole out-there scene is called up by the words. But at the same time we get the exasperated play of the speaker's consciousness itself, as it converts – quite uselessly, irrelevantly, and humanly – the double chug into an absurd, vindictive death-wish on the part of the goddam car, which is clearly out to sabotage his last vestiges of sanity. . . . Ridiculous? Of course; but how true to the way we dwell in the world.

Time and again, in a series of improvised and unrepeatable little coups, McKay contrives to give us both the world and consciousness knowing the world.

•

Here's the beginning of Dale Zieroth's "Father," in which the speaker is recalling two moments of childhood terror:

> Twice he took me in his hands and shook
> me like a sheaf of wheat, the way a dog shakes
> a snake, as if he meant to knock out my tongue
> on the kitchen floor. I never remembered
> what he said. . .

Listen to the way the rhythms move, creating two antithetical impressions at once. Read as prose, the opening sentence is well-proportioned, flowing, almost periodic; it implies a calm authority in the speaker, who is able to marshal these vignettes before our mind's eye with understated eloquence. But the line-breaks, which at first seem clumsy in the extreme, undercut that detachment; they instigate a series of off-balance, juddering lurches. For the poem is in fact reliving the experience it describes, of being shaken violently back and forth.

That double rhythmic effect – of calm and of lurching – conveys the precise emotional condition of the adult speaker as he relives his childhood terror. And it does so more convincingly than would any mere statement *about* his condition, such as, "I have a degree of emotional perspective on my childhood, but remembering certain episodes can still make me quake with fear." A description of that kind would remain detached from the speaker's state; Zieroth's poem *embodies* its own ambivalent condition, coaxes us to relive it ourselves.

It's that willingness in the poet to which I'm pointing – a willingness to keep the poem open to any move that will help enact the phenomenological texture of conscious experience. Zieroth's line-breaks may be quite unlike McKay's "were dead, were dead." But they respond to a comparable necessity; in each case the poet is recreating both an experience and the funny galumphs and murmurs of consciousness as it embraces the experience. He is honouring the intricate cross-pressure of observer and observed – a consort which apparently wants to be celebrated as an imperfect marriage, a willing yet perpetually incomplete union. Consciousness adheres as faithfully as it can to the specificity of world. Sometimes knower and known are perfectly matched; at other times consciousness goes banging about extraneously on its own, or is not up to union with the world – which then remains opaque, is glimpsed across a divide.

•

I think too of a poem by Don Coles, "Codger," which portrays a sturdy, narrow, unshakably self-righteous old gent, ready to rehearse at a moment's notice the pathetically sparse justification his life has found in a span of seven or eight decades.

Here's the beginning:

> Think what we like of him, dim old dawdler,
> Main Street gazer, birdy shuffler –
> Stiff-collared, shiny-shoed, liver-spotted –
> Or say it, his peace won't budge. He'll summon
> Our dead betters in dozens to smile us down . . .

And here's how it ends:

>   And one or two
> Girls, never mind them, when he was a stripling,
> Before Clara. But he remembers a woman
> Getting out of a car in winter, must be
> Forty years ago, looked straight at him when he
> Came up. He kept right on walking, of course,
> But boy, that was a look!

Notice what has happened to the speaking consciousness in the course of the poem. At the outset the speaker exhibits the codger at arm's length, like an exotic specimen – which he undeniably is: a specimen of southern-Ontario small-town puritanism, preserved in the defiant pathos of old age. And the speaker has no hesitation about fixing him with quick labels – "dim old dawdler, Main Street gazer, birdy shuffler" – even though the note of superiority in his own compacted verbal cleverness may be, in its way, as distasteful as the codger's plodding, unassailable provincialism.

By the end, the speaker's idiom has changed completely. He has moved to an almost complete identification – first of all with the codger's turn of phrase (which seems to ease the studied, constricted quality in his own phrase-making). But it is an identification we experience as a deeper acceptance: of the old man, and of the culture he comes from, on their own life-terms. This is no longer the voice of a clever boy from the codger's hometown, who grew up, went away to university, and has come back to patronize the quaint, embarrassing folkways he's mercifully outgrown. It's the voice of a more chastened further maturity, which can accept and celebrate (wryly, perhaps) what is four-square and upstanding in that terribly limited version of being human. The old man is repressed and narrow; yet he has stood up for things that matter, and even kept alive a dream of passionate transcendence.

In that movement of consciousness – enacted first in the movement of idiom – we are again given a dance of world and self interacting. Coles gives us the codger; he also gives us the process of reconciliation in which the speaker listens to the old man and begins to *hear* him, identifying with him empathetically.

•

This impulse is compelling, to speak words that are neither purely subjective (the lyrical ego making its cry) nor purely objective (the arm's-length specification of a world of neutral facts) – but that will somehow transcend that artificial division, which has been with us in one form or another for centuries.

Many more poets here would repay a phenomenological reading. Without knowing exactly what would turn up, I'd want to explore the work of Robert Bringhurst, Christopher Dewdney, Pier Giorgio Di Cicco, David Donnell, Judith Fitzgerald, Diana Hartog, Robyn Sarah, Sharon Thesen, Colleen Thibaudeau, John Thompson, Bronwen Wallace.

If you know the period already, you'll recognize that there is much more to be said about these poets, one by one. Some of the most challenging writers, in particular, need to be investigated more deeply in light of the challenges each has set him or herself. But it is time now to desist, with a few last editorial remarks.

While I spoke at the beginning about editing in a spirit of eclecticism, that shouldn't be confused with editing by quota. I have taken quality as the criterion throughout. I'm as interested as anyone else to see how these selections divide up – by region, gender, genre, colour, or creed. But that is after the fact. Within the limitations of one editor's judgment and time, the selections reflect what I found in the new poetry – not what statistics said should be there, nor what I chose to impose.

Constraints of space make it difficult to include long poems in an anthology, and they have led to the usual scamping of the form here. Perhaps someone will do for recent examples what Michael Ondaatje accomplished in *The Long Poem Anthology* (1979). By the same token, it would be grand to see a series of partisan anthologies (of which a few have already appeared), each dedicated to a particular slant or tendency in the new poetry. Or some works of poetics or criticism which taught us to read these poets more fully on their own terms.

The alphabetical sequence is meant as a neutral framework. A disadvantage is that a poet with a quiet voice sometimes lands between more stentorian poets, and could be drowned out. I trust the reader will adjust his or her set accordingly.

In preparing this volume, I have picked the brains of so many people across Canada that a list would read like a short telephone directory. Foregoing specific credits, let me offer heartfelt thanks to each.

One consultant deserves special mention. Donna Bennett also took on cruel and unusual responsibilities with the material at the end of the book. The accuracy is hers; any remaining bloopers are mine.

•

The best poetry of the next fifteen years may well come from a published poet who is not represented here, but who will catch fire the week this anthology goes to press. *The New Canadian Poets* is dedicated to that man or woman.

Dennis Lee

Introduction

Notes on the Text

* Most of these poets are highly conscious of lining, layout, spelling, and the like. Where conventions vary in the course of this book, they reflect each author's intent. (The one consistent exception is that of run-on lines. Ideally, no long lines would be broken; where that was unavoidable, the run-on portion has been indented by a standard measure in every case.)

* There are brief notes at the end, accompanying the biography of the relevant poet, on poems which might remain inscrutable without some preliminary leads. More local points within a poem have not been annotated.

* The biography of each poet mentions one or two collections that are currently available. Full bibliographies for all poets appear in a separate section.

Footnotes

1. These figures come from George Woodcock, "On the Resources of Canadian Writing," in *Background Papers,* ed. Ontario Royal Commission on Book Publishing, Toronto: Queen's Printer, 1972, p. 77. He is quoting a 1969 article by Louis Dudek in *Canadian Literature*. It must be recognized that the figures are indicative, but undoubtedly not precise.

2. This estimate is by Beth Appeldorn of the Longhouse Bookshop in Toronto, which attempts to carry every Canadian trade book in print. It was made in private conversation in August 1984.

   The pattern is of an explosion of first books and chapbooks in the early and mid-seventies, tapering off more recently. If the current level continues, the next ten or fifteen years will see far fewer poetic debuts than in 1970–1985 and the last fifteen years will appear as a temporary anomaly.

   Since the figure given is only an estimate, I'll treat "a thousand poets" as a graphic way of saying "a great many poets."

3. In giving a profile of these New Canadians, "place of birth" is the simplest indicator, though it sometimes oversimplifies things. In

any event, exactly half the eighteen newcomers were born in the United States; others were born in England, Germany, Holland, Iceland, Italy, South Africa. Among second-generation Canadians there are additional roots in Ireland, Lithuania, Poland, Russia, Scotland, and the Ukraine.

While immigration has undoubtedly been a major factor in this literary generation, the figures here can't be extrapolated uncritically; I can't believe that forty per cent of all new poets in this period have been New Canadians, for instance. And even taking this anthology as representative of a smaller group, the numbers remain provisional; alternative choices could validly have been made in Part Two, and each would produce a different set of figures.

Two immigrants who lived and wrote here during the period (Jeni Couzyn and August Kleinzahler) have now returned to other homelands. Though they retain Canadian ties, it seemed appropriate to consider them only for Part Two.

4. As the sixth footnote will suggest, the age of several contributors makes the following discussion irrelevant to their artistic maturation. Colleen Thibaudeau, for example, had found her voice well before 1965. For a few of the immigrant poets, equally, Canadian poets of the sixties may not have presented the challenge I describe.

5. *Poets of Contemporary Canada* presented ten poets who came to maturity between 1960 and 1970. While that in turn established the starting-date for this collection, the date has a cogency of its own. By 1970 the poets anthologized by Mandel – Atwood, Newlove, Ondaatje, Purdy, for instance – had themselves become normative; newer poets wrote as they did, in part, because the generation of the sixties was there to react to. So the date "1970" corresponds with a real, if somewhat elusive, line of demarcation.

Applying the starting-date rigorously means excluding many strong poets who published their first book in the sixties, but were not selected for Mandel's anthology. Their number explains why the policy was necessary: they include Victor Coleman, Frank Davey, Doug Fetherling, Gail Fox, David Helwig, George Jonas, Joy Kogawa, Patrick Lane, Dennis Lee, Pat Lowther, David McFadden, Stuart MacKinnon, Barry McKinnon, Daphne Marlatt, Tom Marshall, bp Nichol, Stephen Scobie, Peter Trower, Fred Wah, J. Michael Yates.

The only exceptions to this rule, David Donnell and David Solway, have such idiosyncratic bibliographies that it will be clear why they have been treated as "new poets."

6. All the exceptions are older, though generally by only a few years. But there is one anomaly which has strained my brain, and which serves as a reminder that an anthologist's tidy categories are never more than conventions.

Four of the new poets I wanted to include (Coles, Kroetsch, Szumigalski, Thibaudeau) are significantly older than the others – yet they did publish their first collections after 1970. Would their presence blur the generational focus? I wondered. . . . Eventually, the anomaly of leaving them out seemed more serious than the anomaly of putting them in, and in they went. But a reader investigating "generational" matters should remember that these poets came of artistic age by different rhythms than the others.

I have referred to these poets collectively as "a generation" throughout this introduction. The term needs to be used with caution, however. It usually implies a cohesiveness, and a widespread sharing of assumptions, which by definition can't be taken for granted in an "eclectic generation."

7. This list, like others to follow, points to relevant poems in the anthology. Robert Kroetsch is listed because of "Stone Hammer Poem"; Lorna Crozier is not mentioned at all, despite her many Prairie poems, since none are represented here. In cases where a complete list would be absurdly long – such as two paragraphs below, with "poems of place" – I have listed only enough examples to illustrate the point being made.

8. A third type of feminist poem has been pioneered in France and Quebec; it attempts a fundamental re-imagining of language itself, to see if words and syntax – along with the more amenable domain of imagery – can be made to articulate the world in terms compatible with female experience. Though Canadian poets like Daphne Marlatt and Lola Tostevin have explored the field, I have not found examples to include here.

9. The closest analogy in contemporary poetics is the "post-modernist" poem, which is aware of itself *as* a poem and reflects the process of its own making in various jumps and asides. George Bowering has written thoughtfully about the aesthetic; in this volume, Robert Kroetsch is an exemplar. But while the approach is comparable to that of "phenomenological" poetry, there's a strategic difference. In the latter case, the speaker is understood to be reflecting from the midst of a literal situation: waking up at night,

trying to start a car, remembering being punished by his father. And the moments of self-reflexive consciousness illuminate the inner processes of the person in that situation – not the process by which "a poem" is being composed by "a poet." The conventions resemble one another, but their import is radically different. Generally speaking, Canadian writers of a post-modernist cast are somewhat older than the generation represented here.

Part One

Roo Borson

TALK

The shops, the streets are full of old men
who can't think of a thing to say anymore.
Sometimes, looking at a girl, it
almost occurs to them, but they can't make it out,
they go pawing toward it through the fog.

The young men are still jostling shoulders
as they walk along, tussling at one another with words.
They're excited by talk, they can still see the danger.

The old women, thrifty with words,
haggling for oranges, their mouths
take bites out of the air. They know the value of oranges.
They had to learn everything
on their own.

The young women are the worst off, no one has bothered
to show them things.
You can see their minds on their faces,
they are like little lakes before a storm.
They don't know it's confusion that makes them sad.
It's lucky in a way though, because the young men take
a look of confusion for inscrutability, and this
excites them and makes them want to own
this face they don't understand,
something to be tinkered with at their leisure.

FLOWERS

The sunset, a huge flower, wilts on the horizon.
Robbed of perfume, a raw smell
wanders the hills, an embarrassing smell,
of nudity, of awkward hours on earth.
If a big man stands softly, his wide arms
gentled at his sides, women dissolve. It is the access
to easy violence that excites them.

The hills are knobbed with hay,
as if they were full of drawers about to be opened.
What could be inside but darkness?
The ground invisible, the toes feel the way,
bumping against unknown objects
like moths in a jar, like moths
stubbing themselves out on a lamp.

The women sit in their slips,
scattered upstairs through the houses
like silken buds.
They look in the mirror,
they wish they were other than they are.
Into a few of the rooms go a few of the men,
bringing their mushroomy smell.

The other men loll against the outsides of buildings,
looking up at the stars,
inconsequential.

One of them bends down to smell a flower.
There are holes in his face.

JACARANDA

Old earth, how she sulks,
dark spin-off
wielding wings and swords,
mountain ranges, centuries,
our eyes with their impurities.

Dusk. Planets like spilled mercury
and the stars exuding
loneliness, the old battle
for which there are no medals.

Often I look in that mirror
in which things happen over again.
Useless. Or I look
to the teasing water full of days
and clouds that drift like smoke,
and hours when the head sleeps,
an inn for strange guests. If only
we were easier creatures.

But the jacaranda reclines
like a wise thing,
stars crystallizing
beyond its dusky plumes.
Here in the amethyst air of early autumn,
the dryness a talisman,
the moon the egg of a luminous bird,
the jacaranda's wand-like branches
command each thing to be.

The jacaranda with its feathery leaves
blooms clusters of amethysts,
and its winged boxes
lilt toward the green plains bearing

an imploded formula
for jacarandas.

This is the endless catechism of beasts,
each a question and an answer,
on which time
in luminous drops
is raining down.

GREY GLOVE

Among branches
a bird lands fluttering,
a soft grey glove
with a heart.

The land at twilight.
Swamp of black mist.
A first planet. A swordtip.
The bird chanting
in a jail of darkness.

This is the last unclassified bird,
the one one never sees,
but hears when alone, walking.

You can see how far I've gone
not to speak of you.
Birds have made a simple bargain
with the land.

The only song I know
is the one I see with my eyes,
the one I'd give up my eyes
in order for you to hear.

THE MIDWEST IS MADE OF APPLEBLOSSOMS

At evening whole trees drift ghost-like through the fields.
A few gophers and I witness the launching of the moon
over the far treetops, as if we were one family.
What do you think of that? It is a night for discovering
the limits of things, the air is that calm.
For a moment the midwest is made of appleblossoms.
They settle like fog. Ambiguous man that I love,
you have lived in so many bodies, inserted yourself
behind so many pairs of eyes,
do you do it just to confuse me? Sometimes it's not easy
to follow you, would you always take on another body
to find me again?
Man of blue eyes,
how can I even say these words to you? As if
you would be offended by something true.
But I have moved through the bodies of so many women
just to get here with you.

NOW AND AGAIN

Night should be fuller than this.
Lying on our backs in scratchy twigs,
there aren't enough stars in this place,
the brightest lights are the distant buildings

in a circle around us. Two people
without a thing to say to one another, or things
that can't be said. Right beside us:
whole societies of frogs and insects,
and we in ours.
I don't want to be made of words and feelings.
I don't want to be a body that craves.
We get up and stumble through bushes,
back toward civilization. Who are we
to be holding hands? The pond gives back
the reflections of two creatures a little startled
at being brought up to date
on their own existence.
How old can a person get?
Now and again it seems like it's time
to pass the baton and let somebody else
run their little way into the future.

AT NIGHT
YOU CAN ALMOST SEE THE CORONA OF BODIES

I

In the twilit grasses: beasts
like a billion implications.
Through impeccable air they look up
but their eyes are not tools.

Past this planet and moon chasing each other
lurk the huge spaces
we're about to break loose into,
and the stars seep out

like those unfelt tears that gather
at the edges of the eyes in a big wind.

Turning back to our lovers
for a final look that will last perhaps
another fifty years
before our eyes are irrevocably altered,
what can we do or say?
The conflicting scale of things.

At rush hour
there are a billion people walking away forever.
They come at me
with the face of a herd
bound for extinction.

II

Men walk around, dressed
from the neck up in memories.
If you look in their eyes
sometimes their lives are showing.
Sometimes the imploded faces
of dead men.

At times a word can amplify the twilight,
but in talking the tongue moves
like a puppet or a shadow.

Placing yourself in that slight peril,
like a hero, an athlete of existence,
will not save you.

Everywhere you go: the incurable beauty
of the earth. The sunsets like an armful
of dying flamingoes.

III

Ocean of failed wings,
cypresses that grope into shapes of wind:
girls homely enough to have secrets
lean here and there in every landscape
as quietly as brooms.

Over the mills
strands of smoke test their wingspread
and are pulled apart in the beaks of wind.

How is it possible that young girls
sit by the firelight and daydream of dying?
Not yet fearing anything.

The wharves lean like dark waterbirds, ankleted with light.
The invisible outer planets sit in the palm trees;
grief, the bird, flies to and fro in the great
shadowy combs. Between rows of crates
sealed for trade, the moon, a frozen heartbeat.
Laughter dispersing like smoke.

Dusty men spend night along the docks, smoking,
looking out to sea, which is full of answers.
On the grassy promenade
dark-clothed men lead women sheathed in twilight,
who offer only
open, frightened faces.

IV

Snow that sparkles like fresh-laid concrete,
pines exhaling an odor of mint and sweat,
I wake up every day, not even knowing where the earth is.
Why should I speak?

The animals' eyes are full of nuance,
but that is only the look of being alive.

Men injected with this restlessness, to them
the cool hills knotted with trees,
the animals and plants smell of a thousand repetitive
    processes.
The chasm between stars, godless,
neither night nor day nor point of view,
a place where light travels
invisibly until it hits, dreamless,
a deep sleep among the movements of bodies.

v

The white rain of oncoming cars
slides down the pane of this continent, this hour.
History we make up to go to sleep by. That way
the hugeness of space
does not damage us.

In the twilit air where men lie
side by side with spirits,
beasts alternately hunt and sleep.
It is hard to know the depths of things,
even of our own eyes, but the earth
is speakably lovely, its confetti
of snow, jungles of costumed birds,
lapis, seas, pyrite,
every kind of weather fused
into this planet, over whose night horizon
the moon lifts like the face of a man coming to in battle,
the earth at his cheek,
seeing nothing but the open sky.

Roo Borson

BY FLASHLIGHT

Camped out here once, much younger,
with Paul – his muscles all awake beneath the shirt –
whom none of us would touch. Betsy, Jan, and I
lying wide apart in the clearing
like freshly branded cattle,
wet grass at the edges of our eyes.
The icy heat, the paralysis, the wish . . .

the stars so far apart up there
you could see between them

but trusted ourselves even less
and so lay there
knowing only what we felt:
those who ministered to "the real world"
were full of empty threats.

The firs jut three feet farther
into the sky-map now.
The flashlight leads us back,
you, my favorite remembered friends: for this we need
one set of legs to share, my eyes, and the flashlight,
grazing frictionless over the ground, as guide.

For my part, I come back
every few years to take a turn through these woods,
our piece of luck for a summer, eight acres
of redwood and huckleberry,
papery skulls embedded in the forest floor, the bulkier bones
we could never assemble: of deer, or stray cattle, or some
    other animal
we never saw alive.
Which of you keeps up the breadbaking, in memory

of that first laughable sunken loaf? Which of you
still moons at fourteen-year-old boys for us all?

Sitting by the fire, muscles tired
from carrying all three of us around.
Funny how little I've learned, when everyone else
has grown taller around me, like the fir trees,
shutting out a little more light.
The taste of coffee, deep at night, when nobody could care.
The bat that sweeps at eye-level through the twilit house.
The hidden inhabitants, the unknown guests.
Huge forests, fostered on neglect.
The sensuous, probing spiders.
Lights that get left on all night.
The sudden attack of rain on the roof, any time.

LOYALTIES

Old shoes,
where are you taking me now?
You who've spent a night in the Pacific
farther out than I dared to go –
and I found you again, bedraggled in the morning,
separated from each other by fifty feet of beach,
salt in all your seams, and sand, and seaweed.
That time I thought you were lost for good.
Old shoes, the first my grown feet accepted
without the deep ache that comes
of trying on what others have meant for me. Don't worry,
it's me they're laughing at, those who find us unfashionable.
Our last day upright on the earth
we'll fit each other still.
Don't let them trick you into sorrow.
If they stow you in a box that's too small

in the depths of some unfamiliar closet, remember
the walks we took, the close
companionship of shoes and feet.
Remember the long
mouthwatering days, each place
we rested, just taking it in. We took it in
for a reason, for the time when they'll stow us away
where there is nothing to see, to do, to feel.
And when you've relived it all as much as you need,
when you tire of standing still,
remember the imperceptible holes, how they tore and grew,
the socks, pair by pair, those soft
kittens that came between us, playful, how soon
the walking wore them down.

BEFORE THE FIRST BIRD THINKS TO BEAR ITS
WEIGHT FROM THE BRANCH

Each day before dawn comes a false dawn. It fools even the
birds. They come flying, still asleep, to take up their places
along the phone lines and relieve them of that unresolved
talk. Such chaotic chirping! And then, sleep-flying back to
their branches, falling silent for another four hours.

Cobwebs caught in the bushes: grandiose ruins of an
obscure architecture. Meadow mists, siphoned and beckoned
out of earth and air, blown and meandered. A lone spider,
severed hand of winter, stringing up yet another grand,
withering snowflake. But the thing I meant to show you,
what this little walk through the woods is for: see it, under
that bush. Still lying there, new to death, giving off a faint
negative charge. Look how the wind flickers its fur in a
parody of running. How wind enters its mouth, but not as
breath. And the eyes, gelled in a line of sight snapped

sideways, invisible as the beam of a flashlight left on at dawn.

The wind keeps coming from different sides as if, not the wind, but the directions themselves were changing. I needed to show you this. Maybe you'll explain what it means to tell us, lying there like that, after whatever took place in the dark. Lying on the loosely braided needles, the little silver roses fallen from the pines. In the off-light before sunrise, before the first bird thinks to bear its weight from the branch.

Marilyn Bowering

ARMISTICE

There was something
I thought I should remember
this morning,
when the single cannon at the harbour
was fired,
belling starlings and crows from the oak trees
in a feint of wings,
and the silence settled ash-like on the branches.

There was something to remember,
but those who would help me are dead,
and the old uncles won't talk of it.
No one wants, really, to remember,
and now we have no one to help us
conjure star-bright eyes and dim bodies
that lie brined in death-salted fields.

There was something there this morning,
and it was not a celebration with flowers,
and it was not the music of the bands
whose tunes are Lethe for the killing.
It was something about rivers
that I wanted to recall.
Not the boatman
and his ferry,
or the flowers – the poppies,

asphodel, and rose-open mouths
of the dead –
but the sloping through mountains and valleys,
and the river dividing with the sea.

And maybe it was the sea,
calming the continents,
or the clouds, thick with warm rain;
or was it just to remember,
as we remember the dead,
and to pray them out of their tragedy?
And maybe this is why,
to remember a few of the thousands,
so that in some year
we may have enough prayers,
and meanwhile, no time to go making new dead,
no time or prayers to spare for that,
for we are occupied praying,
praying the renewal of the rivers
and the sea;
and it was this,
that until we have counted the bodies,
and the praying for them is done,
we shall be hungry and thirsty,
and no digging and covering up,
no sprouting or reaping in the salted fields,
will nourish us.

WISHING AFRICA

There's never enough whiskey or rain
when the blood is thin and white,
but oh it was beautiful,
the wind delicate as Queen Anne's lace,

only wild with insects
breeding the sponge-green veldt,
and bands of white butterflies
slapping the acacia.
The women's bodies were variable as coral
and men carried snakes on staves.

It would do me no good
to go back,
I am threaded
with pale veins,
I am full with dying,
and ordinary;
but oh if there was a way
of wishing Africa.

When there was planting,
when there was harvesting,
I was not far behind
those who first
opened the ground.
I stitched in seed,
I grew meat in the earth's blond side.
I did it all with little bloody stitches.
What red there was in me
I let out there.
The sun stayed forever
then was gone.

I am scented with virus,
I breed flowers for the ochre
my skin was.
There is no sex in it.
I am white as a geisha,
my roots indiscriminate
since my bones gave way.

It is a small, personal pruning
that keeps me.
I had a soul,
and remember how it hurt
to be greedy and eat.

WELL, IT AIN'T NO SIN TO TAKE OFF YOUR SKIN
AND DANCE AROUND IN YOUR BONES

I heard bones clacking last night
in the bed.
It was dreams, and not sleeping –
could it be a cold future?
There was snow on the morning ground.

I could hear skin, loose and naked
as it sloughed, layer by layer:

I liked its shape and hair and the pads
of its fingers,

but I could dance, I could dance with the bones.

Little lamb on the hillside,
you were drowning in snow,
and your ewe and shepherd danced over a stone:
warm rivers ran from those dancing feet
(black hooves and toes).

I slept badly last night,
listening to bones move like ancient wheels
over a slippery road.
They made a sound, chattering
like pebbles dropping down a mountain,

like hot streams bubbling from lava,
like a long time ago,

when there was you dancing, and me dancing.

RUSSIAN ASYLUM

One of the difficulties is in being
alone, not one with anything or one,
not even a dog or witness.
One of the difficulties is in not being able to move,
or breathe or speak –
to do anything, that is.
One of the difficulties is that you are always
going under when they come; you are fogged and weathered
with lack of sleep.
One of *them* fits something in your vein –
your vein swallows it, questionless.

One of the women takes your lover away.
She is kind and
feeds you when you can't hold a spoon.

You're awake all through it, but it doesn't last long.
Be reassured, brother,
believe there is nothing serious, nothing in it.

They walk you along the sea,
they ask after your family. They offer food and when you
push it away, it's you who look foolish,
yes, you do. Your reasons do not pass outside your brain,
not from eyes to speech –
and even if they did, what good would that be?

You're alone, and they help it along
with something good for you – something
painless and sweet.
   Over the official's desk applications roll in;
there are lives, happy lives, and people behind them.
   You could have been any of them,
then.
Oh, it's harrowing this – going under, going down,
writing out love like this.

NIGHT TERRORS

The stars are peep-holes God looks through,
the hydra-headed creature who holds
the universe together, an eye at each hole
for his pleasure.

I'm afraid. I'm afraid.
Disease spiders the blankets,
and you are dead, dead – not at my side moaning
through your dreams of war,
but gone;

and I am drowning
behind a car door that won't open underwater.
There are babies in the backseat
howling for mother.

The eye at the hole blinks.

Christ is dead. Jesus my Savior is dead.
When I lie down there is no sleep.
When I lie down I am afraid.

I count, like little blinds over each star-eye –
wind, faithful as a parent,
the clean sea,
the arrangement of trees, shadow, trees,
and everyone who swore never to leave me
and never did –

these are enough,

but still I struggle with panic.
The car door is locked from the outside.
The water rises –
such a small window to crawl through –
and the babies are in the back
floating like bleach bottles,
little flotsam lives not lived out.
Oh, they can't be left, no.

You awaken enough to put out an arm, a foot, a raft.
But you are slippery with sweat,
your body bruised by the hands of those who grasp at you
for dear life.

You too are under observation.

The eye blinks.
I cover you up.

Jesus my Lord is dead. And never rose.
Jesus wept.

The eye at the hole blinked twice.
I slept.

I sleep now, my love, and keep you dearly.

TOO HAPPY

after George Faludy

I

Are you a true animal?
Your face melts into the semi-darkness of daybreak,
you sniff yourself all over like a flower.

I touch open the star in the centre of
your belly, a little wound,
and drink you up.

Like God, do you love me still?
I would not be afraid
to wake up like this each dawn.

2

I have seen myself, shaped like an insect,
preying on you.

My tongue drills open your brain,
my mouth drinks you up,

and you revive me.

That is not what I wanted.

It is you who should take me and draw me
between your teeth like a cat a fish,
so that only the bones are left, so that
a dry skeleton falls like a leaf.

Perhaps you love me still.
I grow so strong on you that I could grind
the planet itself to pieces.

God knows this isn't my wish.

I am too happy.

GRANDANGEL

Grandmother, grandangel,
you carry a black briefcase.
It spills you as you hurry along.
Drop me something warm,
undamaged as a uterus,
promise me blood.

Don't let the goods slip,
bring me business, get me things –
your eighty late breakfasts
and change of rings.

Promise me, granny, a whole hog:
draw your skirts up, beat the doctor –
I have the cat tied, the hens fed –
granny, granny, take up my bed.

ST. AUGUSTINE'S PEAR TREE

The pear tree drops its fruit –
yellow stones ripe as olives –

not a fall out of love,
but a ripened fruit,
over over over
into the world.

In each act is separateness,
not accident.

The wind knocks at the branches,
the link is broken.

Think of overbloomed poppies, thick as paint
in the dust,
or the pear tree white with drought,

or when the self takes its scissors out
and cuts the cord,

heading towards light,

and so, falling inwards,
is born.

Robert Bringhurst

THESE POEMS, SHE SAID

These poems, these poems,
these poems, she said, are poems
with no love in them. These are the poems of a man
who would leave his wife and child because
they made noise in his study. These are the poems
of a man who would murder his mother to claim
the inheritance. These are the poems of a man
like Plato, she said, meaning something I did not
comprehend but which nevertheless
offended me. These are the poems of a man
who would rather sleep with himself than with women,
she said. These are the poems of a man
with eyes like a drawknife, with hands like a pickpocket's
hands, woven of water and logic
and hunger, with no strand of love in them. These
poems are as heartless as birdsong, as unmeant
as elm leaves, which if they love love only
the wide blue sky and the air and the idea
of elm leaves. Self-love is an ending, she said,
and not a beginning. Love means love
of the thing sung, not of the song or the singing.
These poems, she said. . . .
                        You are, he said,
beautiful.
            That is not love, she said rightly.

DEUTERONOMY

The bush. Yes. It burned like they said it did,
lit up like an oak in October – except
that there is no October in Egypt. Voices
came at me and told me to take off my shoes
and I did that. That desert is full of men's shoes.
And the flame screamed *I am what I am.*
I am whatever it is that is me,
and nothing can but something needs to be
done about it. If anyone
asks, all you can say is, I sent me.

I went, but I brought my brother to do
the talking, and I did the tricks – the Nile
full of fishguts and frogs, the air opaque
and tight as a scab, the white-hot hail,
and boils, and bugs, and when nothing had worked right
we killed them and ran. We robbed them of every
goddamned thing we could get at and carry
and took off, and got through the marsh at low tide
with the wind right, and into the desert. The animals
died, of course, but we kept moving.

Abraham came up easy. We took
the unknown road and ate hoarfrost and used
a volcano for a compass. I had no plan.
We went toward the mountains. I wanted, always,
to die in the mountains, not in that delta.
And not in a boat, at night, in swollen water.
We travelled over dead rock and drank dead water,
and the hoarfrost wasn't exactly hoarfrost.
They claimed it tasted like coriander,
but no two men are agreed on the taste

of coriander. Anyway,
we ate it, and from time to time we caught quail.

Men and half-men and women, we marched
and plodded into those hills, and they exploded
into labyrinths of slag. The air licked us
like a hot tongue, twisting and flapping and gurgling
through the smoke like men suffocating or drowning, saying
An eye for an eye, and on certain occasions
two eyes for one eye. Either way, you model me
in thin air or unwritten words, not in wood,
not in metal. I am gone from the metal when the metal
hits the mold. You will not get me into any image
which will not move when I move, and move
with my fluency. Moses! Come up!

I went, but I wore my shoes and took a waterskin.
I climbed all day, with the dust eating holes
in my coat, and choking me, and the rock cooking me.
What I found was a couple of flat stones
marked up as if the mountain had written all over them.
I was up there a week, working to cool them,
hungry and sweating and unable to make sense of them,
and I fell coming down and broke both of them.
Topping it all, I found everybody down there drooling
over Aaron's cheap figurines, and Aaron chortling.

I went up again to get new stones
and the voices took after me that time and threw me
up between the rocks and said I could see them.
They were right. I could see them. I was standing right
    behind them
and I saw them. I saw the mask's insides,
and what I saw is what I have always seen.
I saw the fire and it flowed and it was moving away
and not up into me. I saw nothing

and it was widening all the way around me.
I collected two flat stones and I cut them
so they said what it seemed to me two stones
should say, and I brought them down without dropping
   them.

The blisters must have doubled my size, and Aaron said
I almost glowed in the dark when I got down.
Even so, it seemed I was pulling my stunts
more often then than in Egypt. I had to,
to hold them. They had to be led to new land,
and all of them full of crackpot proverbs and cockeyed
ideas about directions. Aaron and I
outbellowed them day after day and in spite of it
they died. Some of weakness, certainly, but so many of them
died of being strong. The children stood up to it
best, out of knowing no different – but with no
idea what to do with a ploughshare, no
idea what a river is. What could they do
if they got there? What can they even know how to
   wish for?
I promised them pasture, apple trees, cedar,
waterfalls, snow in the hills, sweetwater
wells instead of these arroyos, wild grapes. . . .

Words. And whatever way I say them, words only.
I no longer know why I say them, even though
the children like hearing them. They come when I call them
and their eyes are bright, but the light in them is empty.
It is too clear. It contains . . . the clarity only.
But they come when I call to them. Once I used to sing them
a song about an eagle and a stone, and each time
I sang it, somehow the song seemed changed
and the words drifted into the sunlight. I do not
remember the song now, but I remember
that I sang it, and the song was the law and the law

was the song. The law is a song, I am certain. . . .
And I climbed to the head of this canyon. They said
I could look down at the new land
if I sat here, and I think it is so, but my eyes
are no longer strong, and I am tired now of looking.

DEMOKRITOS

I

Bearing children is even more dangerous,
said Demokritos, than buying a mirror,
yet this wealth strangely easy to come by –
a bed and two books,
bread and fruit and a strong pair of shoes.
In spite of bad government there was good weather,
but after the heart the first thing
to sour is always the water.
The demon's summerhouse is the soul.

II

What is is no more than what isn't;
the is, no advance on the isn't. Is
is isn't with rhythm.
Touching and turning the isn't is is.
Not being is basic. As silence is,
isn't is – during, before and after the sound.
Isn't is everywhere. In you. Outside.
Presence is absence keeping time.

III

That which splits off from the edgeless has edges.
It dries into light, it ignites into fire.

Fire and mind I believe to be
round, though knowledge is always
lopsided, like elm leaves.
Nose, eyes, ears, tongue
and fingers are fingers – all fingers
groping for imprints in the intermittent air.

IV

Such giants we are and so hardly
here, mere shapes in the dust and our
deaf hands yelling so loud,
the diaphanous blood, the diaphanous
bone, and the truth so small as it crumbles it swims
in and out of the intestine,
floats through the ear's net, the eye's net,
the sieve of the palm.

V

A man must be ready for death
always, as sound must always be ready
for silence. There are of course contrary yearnings,
called information and music, but call it
laughter or call it
beatitude, a good joke is the most you can ask.

VI

The uncountable rhythms uncountable
worlds – more in some places than others.
Motion, on closer inspection, appears
to be limited to reverberation and falling.
Never look down without turning.
Never live with your back to the mountains.
Never mend net with your back to the sea.

VII

Thus the earth goes south each summer.
The mind moults in the north like a widgeon
and rises, hunting or grazing, in autumn,
riding the gale,
the stain of the voice like a handprint at intervals
in the unravelling rigging.

VIII

Incidentally, you may notice,
said Demokritos,
the eagle has black bones.

LEDA AND THE SWAN

for George Faludy

Before the black beak reappeared
like a grin from in back of a drained cup,
letting her drop,
she fed at the sideboard of his thighs,
the lank air whitening in the sunrise,
yes. But no, she put on no knowledge
with his power. And it was his power alone
that she saved of him for her daughter.
Not his knowledge.
No.
He was the one who put on knowledge.
He was the one who looked down out of heaven
with a dark croak, knowing more
than he had ever known before,
and knowing he knew it:

knowing the xylophone of her bones,
the lute of her back and the harp of her belly,
the flute of her throat,
woodwinds and drums of her muscles,
knowing the organpipes of her veins;

knowing her as a man knows mountains he has hunted
naked and alone in –
knowing the fruits, the roots and the grasses,
the tastes of the streams
and the depths of the mosses,
knowing as he moves in the darkness he is also
resting at noon in the shade of her blood –
leaving behind him in the sheltered places
glyphs meaning mineral and moonlight and mind
and possession and memory,
leaving on the outcrops signs meaning mountain
and sunlight and lust and rest and forgetting.

Yes. And the beak that opened to croak
of his knowing that morning creaked like a re-hung
door and said nothing, felt nothing. The past
is past. What is known is as lean
as the day's edge and runs one direction.
The truth floats
down, out of fuel,
indigestible, like a feather. The lady
herself, though, whether
or not she was truth – or untruth, or both, or was neither –
she dropped through the air like a looped rope,
a necklace of meaning, remembering
everything forwards and backwards,
and lit like a fishing skiff gliding aground.

That evening, of course, while her husband, to whom
she told nothing, strode like the king
of Lakonia through the orchestra

pit of her body, touching
this key and that string in his passing,
she lay like so much
green kindling,
fouled tackle and horseharness under his hands
and said nothing, felt
nothing, but only
lay thinking
not flutes, lutes and xylophones,
no: thinking soldiers
and soldiers and soldiers and soldiers
and daughters,
the rustle of knives in his motionless wings.

THE STONECUTTER'S HORSES

I, Francesco, this April day:
death stirs like a bud in the sunlight, and Urban
has got off his French duff and re-entered Rome
and for three years running has invited me to Rome,
over the bright hills and down the Cassia,
back through Arezzo one more time,
my age sixty-five and my birthday approaching,
the muggers on the streets in broad daylight in Rome,
the hawks and the buzzards. . . .
                                        Take this down.

No one has thought too deeply of death.
So few have left anything toward or against it.
Peculiar, since thinking of death can never be
wasted thinking, nor can it be come to
too quickly. A man carries his death with him
everywhere, waiting, but seldom thinking
of waiting. Death is uncommonly like the soul.

What I own other than that ought to fall
of its own weight and settle. But beggars and tycoons
and I are concerned with our possessions,
and a man with a reputation for truth
must have one also for precision.
                                        I leave
my soul to my saviour, my corpse to the earth.
And let it be done without any parades.
I don't care very much where I'm buried,
so it please God and whoever is digging.
Still, you will ask. You will badger me.
If I am dead you will badger each other.
But don't lug my bones through the public streets
in a box to be gabbled at and gawked at and followed.
Let it be done without any parades.

If I die here in Padova, bury me here
near the friend who is dead who invited me here.
If I die on my farm, you can use the chapel
I mean to build there, if I ever build it.
If not, try the village down the road.

If in Venezia, near the doorway.
If in Milano, next to the wall.
In Pavia, anywhere. Or if in Rome...
if in Rome, in the center, of course, if there's room.
These are the places I think I might die in
in Italy.
                Or if I happen to be in Parma,
there is a cathedral of which, for some reason,
I am the archdeacon. But I will avoid
going to Parma. It would scarcely be possible,
I suppose, in Parma, not to have a parade.

At any rate, put what flesh I have left
in a church. A Franciscan church if there is one.

I don't want it feeding a tree from which
rich people's children swipe apples.

Two hundred ducats go to the church in which
I am buried, with another hundred to be given
out in that parish to the poor, in small doses.
The money to the church, let it buy a piece of land
and the land be rented and the rental from the land
pay for an annual mass in my name.
I will be fitter company in that sanctuary
then, present in spirit and name only,
than this way, muttering to the blessed virgin
through my hemorrhoids and bad teeth. I should be glad
to be rid of this sagging carcass.
                                    Don't write that.

I have cleared no fields of their stones. I have built
no barns and no castles. I have built a name
out of other men's voices by banging my own
like a kitchen pan. My name to the Church
with the money it takes to have it embalmed.
Very few other things. My Giotto to the Duke.
Most men cannot fathom its beauty. Those
who know painting are stunned by it. The Duke
does not need another Giotto, but the Duke knows painting.

To Dondi, money for a plain ring to remind him
to read me.
            To Donato – what? I forgive him
the loan of whatever he owes me. And I
myself am in debt to della Seta. Let it
be paid if I haven't paid it. And give him
my silver cup. Della Seta drinks
water. Damned metal ruins the wine.

To Boccaccio, I am unworthy to leave
anything, and have nothing worthy to leave.

Money then, for a coat to keep himself warm
when he works after dark, as he frequently does,
while the river wind stutters and bleats at his window,
and his hand-me-down cordwood fizzles and steams.

My lute to Tommaso. I hope he will play it
for God and himself and not to gain fame
for his playing.
                    These are such trivial legacies.

Money to Pancaldo, but not for the card table.
Money to Zilio – at least his back salary.
Money to the other servants. Money to the cook.
Money to their heirs if they die before I do.

Give my Bible back to the Church.
                        And my horses . . .
my horses.
            Let a few of my friends, if they wish to,
draw lots for my horses. Horses
are horses. They cannot be given away.

The rest to my heir and executor, Brossano,
who knows he is to split it, and how he is to split it,
and the names I prefer not to put into this
instrument. Names of no other importance.
Care for them. Care for them here in this house
if you can. And don't sell off the land to get money
in any case. Selling the earth without cause
from the soul is simony, Brossano. Real-estate
hucksters are worse than funeral parades.
I have lived long enough in quite enough
cities, notwithstanding the gifts
of free lodging in some of them, long enough, Brossano,
to know the breath moves underfoot in the clay.
The stone quarried and cut and reset
in the earth is a lover's embrace, not an overlay.

The heart splits like a chinquapin pod,
spilling its angular seed on the ground.

Though we ride to Rome and back aboard animals,
nothing ever takes root on the move.
I have seen houses and fields bartered
like cargo on shipboard. But nothing takes root
without light in the eye and earth in the hand.

The land is our solitude and our silence.
A man should hoard what little silence
he is given and what little solitude he can get.

Just the one piece over the mountains
ought, I think, to be given away. Everything
I have ever done that has lasted began there.
And I think my heir will have no need to go there.

If Brossano die before I do,
look to della Seta. And for his part let him
look into that cup. He will know my mind.

A man who can write as I can ought not
to talk of such things at such length. Keep this
back if you can. Let the gifts speak
for themselves if you can, small though they are.
But I don't like the thought of what little there is
spilling into the hands of lawyers through lawsuits.
The law is no ritual meant to be practised
in private by scavengers. Law is the celebration
of duty and the ceremony of vengeance. The Duke's
law has nothing to do with my death
or with horses.
                    Done.
                           Ask the notaries to come over
precisely at noon. I will rewrite it
and have it to sign by the time they arrive.

SARAHA

What is
is what isn't. What isn't
is water. The mind is a deer.
In the lakes of its eyes,
the deer and the water
must drink one another.
There are no others,
and there are no selves.
What the water sees
is – and is not what you think
you have seen in the water.

There is no something, no nothing,
but neither. No is
and no isn't, but neither. Now,
don't defile the thought
by sitting there thinking.
No difference exists
between body and mind, language
and mind, language and body.
What is, is not. You must love,
and let loose of, the world.

I used to write poems,
and like yours, they were made
out of words, which is why
they said nothing.
My friend, there is only one word
that I know now, and I have somehow
forgotten its name.

Don Coles

PHOTOGRAPH

This photograph shows a man
who is smiling
standing beside a woman whose smile
may in this moment be just coming
or just going
in a path between a cedar tree
on their right
and unidentifiable bushes on their left
in bright sunlight.
She is wearing a wide white hat
and a loose dress,
he a dark suit, white shirt
with stiff collar,
and a tie with a large knot –
costumes which, since it is evidently
a hot day in summer,
indicate the picture is not recent.
I'm moved to know that in fact
this summer is seventy years ago
and the man and woman
so seemingly at ease here
are my 30-year-old unencountered
grandparents (who died
three years after this photograph
was taken, as we, outside
the photograph, know,
but inside it they do not: my mother
is perhaps almost inside the photograph,
perhaps just beyond it,

perhaps lying in the shade
of the cedar to their right,
and will soon be one year old),
and to know that my mother
will grow older with persons
not present in this photograph,
and so will not adequately be told of
these smiles, this afternoon
of sunlight on a path
(how, partly shadowed
under the wide white hat,
her eyes moved to the sounds
around them, the cicada
in the high trees, how
the warmth of the afternoon lay
across his shoulders
on the dark cloth), the hot green smell
of cedar moving in the mind.
It reminds me of Villon and other
unrecovered seasons, but better than that
it focuses for me a minute when
changeless, constant things fused with
two people who smiled just then
to invincibly form
a space in time which (as perhaps
in that minute they felt, and so
entered it with great anxiety, but
also with great love) that summer
would not carelessly release
but would continue to offer so that
it might one day be acknowledged,
as I would acknowledge it now,
so that they are still there,
or here,
and may be encountered now
if I can make the afternoon
absolute enough, the smell of cedar

endless enough and green
in its summer heat, if I can make
their smiles turn towards her,
standing, now, and older,
and facing them
in the path between the bushes and the cedar
in the bright sunlight
smiling

SOMETIMES ALL OVER

Sometimes all over
people like me wish
an ineffable meditation
or an unfading girl
announces new times:
always that measureless peace,
always those white arms,
suiting. Already frequently
I have expected, learn always
no. Breathing out,
that held harmony cracks,
old unsurrendered images
peevishly re-engage me;
her eyes or mine
further enquire. It seems likely
this will always be,
but when I try to live
a wiser way and hope for less, I
notice soon my even advancement,
approval of boring friends;
dream I sleep soundly; perceived, once,
a snug & familiar finish.
Scare speedily back then

towards my nearer-drifting (it
may be) harm, my
patient believed fable:
look how I may love simply,
let brightness mend.

CODGER

Think what we like of him, dim old dawdler,
Main Street gazer, birdy shuffler –
Stiff-collared, shiny-shoed, liver-spotted –
Or say it, his peace won't budge. He'll summon
Our dead betters in dozens to smile us down,
They know if we don't who was there in livelier times
And did his share, helped give a shape
To shouts all quiet now, and what's more
They won't change their minds. That time
The railroad almost picked another town,
Meetings all night that week; two wars, one that he
Went to; and everybody's climb, not easy,
When the market bust in '29. And in a pinch,
What about Jack Thwaite, the curling rink that night,
And what *he* said? Spare with his praise,
Jack Thwaite, so everybody listened. They don't come
Any fairer than Jack, he supposes still, and not
On account of those fine sentiments, either.
Felt that way about him for years.
                              And one or two
Girls, never mind them, when he was a stripling,
Before Clara. But he remembers a woman
Getting out of a car in winter, must be
Forty years ago, looked straight at him when he
Came up. He kept right on walking, of course,
But boy, that was a look!

Don Coles

ON A BUST* OF AN ARMY CORPORAL
KILLED ON HIS TWENTY-FIRST BIRTHDAY
DRIVING A MUNITIONS WAGON IN THE BOER WAR

*in Port Elgin, Ontario

Ten feet up atop a slim stone column
His face, neatly bearded, forage cap
Tidily centred, stares out over the town's
Bowling green. His decent demeanour precludes
The phallic reference – Freud's coeval,
He is innocent of much that we have agreed
To know. This summer he has been here
Eighty years. Beneath him, now as in most
Summer evenings all this while, 80-year-olds
In straw fedoras and roomy trousers trundle
Their bowls up & down the trimmed and illuminated
Lawns. Their ages are as unchanging as his,
Their conversations are of the seasons,
Their fashions a matter of apparent obdurate
Conviction. For eighty years their random
Old-folks' wisdom, their windy laughter, their
Thrifty movements have entered his vision,
Risen to his hearing from these murmurous lawns.
Winters some dic, turn, though elsewhere,
To stone as he did, alternates take over.
This summer a few of them might, finally, have been
His children. Late at night he sees them enter
The empty green, hears the suppressed click
Of bowls, the floated discreeter voices. And
Finds it odd, still, those distant, paused horsemen,
That roaring hurt, reins gone slack,
In Africa.

AH! QU'ILS SONT PITTORESQUES,
LES GRANDS JARDINS MANQUÉS

Laforgue can have his trains –
What brings the yearning arrow
On its long arc into me anytime
Is nothing so down the platform dwindling
But is the naming of
The great public gardens of central Europe –
Mirabelle, Prater, Englischer, Krávloká.
These names control entire decades of drifting
Shade and sun, while beyond them
Cars with absurd and tiny accelerations
Fret the historic perimeters:
Salzburg, Vienna, Munich, Prague.
What are they, the great gardens, except
Unhurried and beech-avenued and bronze-
Dignitary-supervised, but
Every now and then in an unselfconscious hour
One of them, Mirabelle, say,
And should Prater or Englischer ever do this
At the same time it is terrible,
Awful, can release into a carefully thought about
Place a woman whose beauty
Seriously stuns a region of the blood
Of any *flâneur* who sees her.
And this of course is why that blood-stunned man
Is here, and why, years ago,
He was in a similar garden in Dresden and
Leipzig too, sometimes with a Russian name
In those far-off and inequitable days
And sometimes French or German
But most often, probably, Austrian (although
This matter of national avocations
Remains of unestablished significance here),
Entering the park in the sunshine

In the early afternoon for the park's own sake
Though bearing his composed expectation
With him, and the park opening itself
To him, its straight avenues and
Its plumes of water chugging thinly upwards
Between the sunlight and his eye,
And its well-raked walks and its oddly complaisant
Rain-simplified horsemen.
And the woman, in the randomly occurring long
Afternoons when one of the women is there,
Turns her unguarded face, her unbearably
Though from our intact points of view blamelessly
Beautiful face almost towards him in some moment
When he has not quite reached
The fountains in the park's centre, and sometimes
He speaks to her
With sublime consequences and sometimes
Her beauty seems to him
Too unmanageable for any words of his
And then he may find instead
A shopgirl showing smooth knees on a bench,
And there are ample reasons for this.
I have been in all of those gardens
I have named,
Although the gardens in Leipzig and Dresden
I have not been in.

Krailling, bei München,
Dez. 1980

MAJOR HOOPLE

A grotesque, I knew.

Vainglorious and logorrhoeac, gassing away
From above his ballooning waistcoat
To lodgers sitting or standing in
Attitudes of decorum-annulling scepticism.

He seemed to have no teeth;
Neither did Martha, dirigible-wife.
Their identical faces were puddings,
Hers was sensible and without illusions.
Two or three times a year
She would almost smile.

His harrumphing and egadding.
His fez. His spats.

The skinny boarders, travelling
Salesmen by the unpremeditated look
Of them. Proofs of their lostness
Were the lengthening cigarette ashes, wilting
Towards rumpled shirts.
They had nobody to warn them.

To what did I compare him?
A home-derived image of man as
Unmockable, the high seriousness
Of middle years. By which standards
He would not do. So gross, so
Unrespected. He verged on

The repellent. He was barely human.
He was appalling.

But now he fills me with longing
For a reliable time where
He meant all those things (and
Age and failure too, star-distant then from me
As those), instead of
A caricatured but incontestable man.

And where beyond him, and beyond
The afternoon paper's large pages,
The smell of newsprint coming up close
As my arms spread wide to begin
The last orderly re-folding,
The lights have just come on in
The dining room. Soon a lost voice will say
Come to supper.

from "Landslides"

Visits to the Gericare Centre

I

As you steadily – startled
Into reverie only when
The spoon nearly misses
Your mouth – munch your way
Through supper,

Strapped up straight & fed
From a mashed bowl,

Your eyes concentrating
As if to force
A devoted, furious someone

To appear,
Far-travelled ransomer
With whom you also soon must be
Far and travelling
(Not as I am,

Shuttered with memory and with
Repeated enterings of this
Room, also with thinking
Of how the staircase
To the parking lot will look,

Of an impending book or recent
Sex – and you *convenable,* soon,
In after-hours stasis,
Unable to turn over but staring out
Over rubbishing years):

     Who, when you go, will
Guard that whole winter I
Never left my bedroom or
The snow my windowledge, kept
Home from school

An endless, unachieving winter
To begin again, out of
Childish muse & dream,
This old, hard business of
Meddling with time?

V

Your face is between two mysteries.
How death will be, your face
In sprinting patches rusts
Towards it, it is wearing out
Towards one mystery.

The other is just before
I was born, I have studied the
Inaccessible sunlight on the verandah
When I was almost there, your face
Watches my sister

Who is three years old and stands
Mildly within the sunlight,
Its prodigious composure
Has always eluded me.
This is the other mystery.

VIII

How human beings are alike
In undefended states!
No knowing how much you've
Heard or understood, but
For an hour now

I have held your hand
And talked to you
Of extreme things
 – Some silences between –
As you, in hours too early

In my life for me to give
Accounting of, surely
With some comparable (unchecked, privately

Soaring) voice lulled or dreamed
Me. As though we had,

Those many years before,
Leaned out to look & found
Both of us (until both
Faded there) listening from some
Stupendous, covenanted

Place to sounds too deep
For remedy. Those sounds are
Burrowing but still audible,
It needs us both to
Let them go.

XII

What does the old chair
In your room, in the house which
I will but you will not
See again, think of you now?
How can your trusted books

Bear another beginning, the surfaces
Of new eyes? Beauchamp in his career,
Lucy Gayheart's footsteps running
Away, those journeyers who
Wandered and for you

Again & again wandered through
Deepening Wessex hedgerows, these go
On, but now surely diminished, surely
Interrupted as if by rain
In the middle

Of a sentence. Those
Hedgecutters who must now

Recollect their craft alone and,
Stiffly in rinsed landscapes,
Start over.

"What is the good of having made
So many dolls?" Michelangelo asked, and
Yet the boundaries of help he spied were
Broad, that record-breaking evidence was
Out in the light.

While you, whose wisdom's shut
And death's sheer edges all around,
Slide traceless. Though there's
A narrow rim of calm. God help us
To our proper use.

XIII

Remembering that line praising "A mind
In full possession of its experience,"
And thinking of you, of all that
Chaos is repossessing behind the
Widening, night-glittering moat,

Sometimes I'll rant, or grieve,
But rather now would sidestep
Eternitywards and glimpse a sort of
Comfort there, out under the stars
Where every man's

In soul-motion,
And know the private life's
Motley and generous
And in its manifoldness flies
Finally above pity,

Its soon-surrendered experience
Full of destructible small glories
Like wings glinting
In odd places under the eaves,
Possessed only as

Rain over a barn's roof is possessed,
As a book shelters a mind
In its brief strength or
A thrilled child laughs even while
Leaves resume their pause,

Shading pressed grass,
All soon restored to time, things
Not important enough for saving,
Images it was sufficient to reflect on
Only a little,

The briefest glance
Towards which may, however,
Deliver us.

Lorna Crozier

ANIMALS OF SPRING

You want to take them in
let them sleep in your bed,
purr on your kitchen counter.
You dip your hand in honey.
Tongues lick your fingers,
tickle your palm. You feed them
cubes of sugar, milk from an eye dropper,
you tie ribbons in their hair.

These are the half-formed,
the helpless, some are blind.
But soon they take their shape,
eyes open, listen to the voice
that stirs inside them. It says
wind, snow. It says meat, mate,
hunt, marrow.

They grow to fill your house
as goldfish fill the space they live in.
But these are not goldfish
trapped in a bowl. These are
the animals of spring, the ones you found
playing in the forest, the teddy-bears
you take to bed, the kittens you tease
with skeins of wool.

One day
when you honey your fingers,
offer the sweetness to be licked,
your hand will disappear.

MARRIAGE: GETTING USED TO

It did not take me long
to get used to his leather
wings, no, they felt good
like an old, much-loved coat
draped over my shoulders
It was his feet I couldn't stand,
his horny feet, ugly as a bird's,
the yellow claws and the pride
he took in them:
> how he oiled the scales
> and saved the clippings
> making me a necklace
> from the broken claws
> sewing flakes of skin
> like sequins in my clothes.

Even his tricks were okay
the way his words turned
to flames at parties
sizzling flies from the air,
lighting cigarettes for ladies
with his tongue. It wasn't that
that bothered me.

It was waking to find him
with a flashlight and a mirror
staring under the covers at his feet.

It was his nails
clicking across linoleum
(he was too vain to wear slippers)
and after he had gone to work,
it was the fallen gold scales
that lay on the sheet like scattered coins.

THIS ONE'S FOR YOU

Hey, big hummer,
who can strut like you?
Crotch-tight jeans, boots
shiny as pool balls, heels
pounding stars into pavement
you call sky.

Hey, big rooster,
who can cockadoodledo
like you do? You raise the
bloody sun from his corner
your voice, brass
bell in the ring.

Hey, prize fighter,
who can screw like you?
Women howl your name,
say no man will take
your place, buzz them
like an electric drill.
You spin the world
on the end of your cock.

Hey, big talker,
waited all my life

for a man like you.
Come my way, I'll blow
the fuses in your big machine,
short all your circuits.
I'll break the balls
you rack on the table,
I'll bust your pool cue.

WE CALL THIS FEAR

We call this fear *love,* this tearing,
this fist, this sharpened tongue
love. I could kill you, I say,
many times. You do not carry
the only pain. There is more
than your world: the drunks
you find bleeding on the tiles,
the women full of holes, the dog
with torn eyes, the poet who has
chewed his tongue.

There is this room,
this woman who brings you food
wears your bruises on her cheeks.
I am tired, so tired.
There is always something wrong.
You spit words at me
like broken teeth and I, stupid
woman, string them into poems,
call them love.

Lorna Crozier

EVEN THE DEAD

Even the dead reach for you
as you walk, so beautiful,
across the earth.

Their fingers turn to flowers
as they break through
the soil, touch the air.

The bouquets in your room
are the hands of the dead,
transmuted. Roses.

Salal. Gladioli.
Scent covers you, a fine dust.
Leaves move in benediction.

Even the dead bless you.
Their blossoms glow
like muted lanterns

lighting your way
as you walk
green paths of sleep.

THE CHILD WHO WALKS BACKWARDS

My next-door neighbour tells me
her child runs into things.
Cupboard corners and doorknobs
have pounded their shapes
into his face. She says

he is bothered by dreams,
rises in sleep from his bed
to steal through the halls
and plummet like a wounded bird
down the flight of stairs.

This child who climbed my maple
with the sureness of a cat
trips in his room, cracks
his skull on the bedpost,
smacks his cheeks on the floor.
When I ask about the burns
on the back of his knee,
his mother tells me
he walks backwards
into fireplace grates
or sits and stares at flames
while sparks burn stars in his skin.

Other children write their names
on the casts that hold
his small bones.
His mother tells me
he runs into things,
walks backwards,
breaks his leg
while she lies
sleeping.

STILLBORN

who
looped the cord
around his fine new neck

who
hanged him
in my bone gallows   my

beautiful son
blue as the blue
in Chinese porcelain

DELIGHT IN THE SMALL, THE SILENT

Delight in the small
those that inhabit
only a corner of the mind
the ones shaped by wind
and a season: a slip of
grass, the nameless flower
that offers its scent
to a small wind

Delight in the silent
the ones that change shape
soundlessly as moons:
the fossil golden bee
caught in amber, the bone
transmuted to stone, the
chrysalis of the gypsy moth

Delight in flesh
that does not turn to
word, the ones without
voice or master. The old dog
who denies name, moves
arthritic legs to whatever
you choose to call him

Weary of men, of words
carved even in the penis
bones of bears, delight
in the small, the silent
whose language lies
in their doing and their
undoing, those who turn
to stone to bone to wing
without a shout of praise
find their perfect form
become imago

CARROTS

[*from "Erotic Chlorophylls"*]

Carrots are fucking
the earth. A permanent
erection, they push deeper
into the damp and dark.
All summer long
they try so hard to please.
Was it good for you,
was it good?

Perhaps because the earth won't answer
they keep on trying.
While you stroll through the garden
thinking *carrot cake,*
carrots and onions in beef stew,
carrot pudding with caramel sauce,
they are fucking their brains out
in the hottest part of the afternoon.

Lorna Crozier

THE FLOWERS OF GEORGIA O'KEEFE

The nasturtium with its round leaves
sucks the bee inside, becomes an O'Keefe
blossom hung on the wall of the sky.
Light spills from each petal, gathers
at the soft, sweet centre. There sits
Sigmund Freud where he's always wanted
to be, whispering secret words as the bee
fills its sack with pollen.

Georgia O'Keefe walks her dog
through mesas where everything blooms.
Somewhere a painting begins.
It makes its first strokes across the canvas,
flowers open their mouths, bees mount stamens.
Freud checks his pocket watch, wonders
what his wife will make for dinner,
whispers *shit, cunt, fuck,* the bee
drowning in pollen. In the desert
Georgia watches the dome of a skull
rising like a moon over the horizon.
Her dog sleeps among succulents. Roses
lift his eyes to heaven.

Freud dreams himself inside a flower,
red and redolent with light.
Somewhere his wife is singing,
he doesn't hear. Too many
flowers in his garden. Too many bees
drunk on pollen. The blooms are hysterical.
They make his head hurt.

SOMETIMES MY BODY LEAVES ME

Sometimes my body leaves me,
goes into another room
and locks the door. There

it bangs about
like an angry thief.
What is it looking for?

Then there are its silences
stretched thin and taut
between us, invisible

as a fishing line
falling through layers
and layers of green.

I don't know what it feels,
if it feels anything;
or what it remembers,
if each cell holds a memory.

I don't know what sounds to make
to call it back.

What does it do when it sits alone
without a book or anything
resembling love?

Christopher Dewdney

from *A Natural History of Southwestern Ontario,* Book 1

This is of two worlds – the one diurnal men know and that other world where lunar mottled eels stir like dreams in shallow forest water. Allowing both these mechanisms to continue operating, we slowly remove and replace theiyr parts with corresponding and interlocking nothings. The glass machinery is equally filled with allusion to our aestive carnality, an infinite part of the pattern which regenerates itself with its own repetitive logic.

Triassic afternoons in early October.

Each huge spring bud a transparent chrysalis pregnant with moth wings unfolding into bats. (Every nuance & cartesian plotted in radar-tunnels.) The secrecy of your voice behind me in a crowd, remoras vacuous and cold that lurk in the eddies of your passing.

The air is water.

The skin, neither moist nor dry, is a permeable membrane of cells dividing the summer landscape into pink and blue. Spring aches in the heart and stomach, the surfacing of women in moist soil and moonlight.

When I see her flesh budding I am eviscerated with cool hollow hands, agile in theiyr nervous evacuation of digestion. She is Hungry Hollow, the memory succubus with her twelve-year-old grace. She supervises wet dreams in Arkona. She is fair, she is dark with leg tendons that pull rock nerves under her soles up into tension brown & flash white into night sky.

In the night sky she composes its entirety of interlocking replicas of herself.

The stars are perhaps mistakes yet to be opaqued in the negative of creation.

A large yellow ochre terraced excavation mound built in a topographic reconstruction of The Coves. There are stone bridges and the dream city is nearby. In the city, which is a composed triad of Kingston, Paris and Dundas, the street cars & trains run almost in confluence with the streets and sidewalks. Pedestrians must sometimes escape to lawns to avoid them. There is a long descent to the river which is wide & a slide much like a long sluice descends this slope. The trestle raises the aquarium river just above its surface, proceeding to the opposite bank where Mattawa stands.

The boulevard homes glitter with stained glass windows depicting vague garden lusts. A hot moist climate engenders palmettos and lush cucumber trees. The streets wind through a labyrinth of small parks, bridges, streams and limestone outcroppings. Small creeks course through concrete seal-pools and oxbows. Earthquakes occur almost as frequently as the ominous roar of flash floods.

We are just a step away from ourselves. Wings of northern alloy clash high in the vaulted & metallic night. Don't turn around if the dark negative figure following you up the stairs isn't yourself. The exoskeleton is a bicycle, striding magnification, snake chains and turgid rubber on asphalt. Gasoline sunsets through smoked glass as slime molds proceed through moist rain-shower humus. There is a universe where what we consider uncanny here occurs almost ten times as frequently.

Stars drip out of the cutaneous erectile velvet blue
bandshell night, a full moon with lavender areola. Accidents
are almost predatory in this universe. Bats investigate houses
as would skin-divers nervously explore peculiar corals.
Cecropia moths flutter on tissue – flitting shadows. The
night air arranges itself in thermal conglomerates of cool &
warm. Stone outcrops replaying the solar dictation.

Wet foliage.

Summer dawn at London airport. The further trees British
camouflage into dream at visual horizon. Glass observation
decks empty of passengers reflect the radar-dish, still in
the morning mists. Aerials glint in the dawn – orange
translucent against Arabic blue.

There is nothing arbitrary in the predestined universe of
the past. Emerald crystal caves in hot black tar. Cloudy
airport haze and warm afternoons. Basement parties &
guests annihilated in gasoline pools that burst into flame.
Moon passing behind fast night clouds. Hot wind and moth
tunnels traced by pheromones. There are conferences to
which we are interminably drawn over which forces other
than human preside.

One hears the nervous tapping of fingers.

I am walking south on Wharncliffe Road, everything is
working by remote control.

Petrolia bathed in a neo-carboniferous glow. Oil and gas
flow from the taps of every household. Tar sands abound,
some with live trapped smilodons snarling & surprisingly
lean. In Petrolia the limestone is so soft farmers ploughing
theiyr fields feel only a slight drag as their blades slice
through boulders. Fossils are dragged through the rock like
crumbs through butter.

Small deserts perhaps an acre across occur throughout
Southwestern Ontario. Prickly pear cacti grow on Pelee

Point – egrets stilting through low glades – crescent dunes in the early evening. The sand is skin. Raccoons swaying in gale force winds high in the beech canopy running over the escarpment's edge.

At noon the exposed limestone of the Paris valley becomes a parabolic reflector of atmospheric space focused inside the stranger's brain. Jewelled sundews at Byron Bog. Pitcher plants & fir with sphagnum moss and an underground lake. Nighthawks vigilant through the awesome stirring folds of night. Our dark luminous stenches. Flashing white bars on theiyr wings, theiyr flight delineating our most habitual routes. The metamorphosis of insects proceeds. Leaves turn into sparrows that fly away at the sound of an approaching train, I am told by a small old man to lie down on the tracks, I must be crushed by the oncoming night train before my dreams can begin. Its light shines dimly around the curve of this hill.

When we enrage the wasps we cannot hide, composite terror batters itself against the screen door seeking only our pain.

The storms follow the valley & the houses at its lip are exploded by lightning. When our foreheads glide through each other's symmetry, as far apart & identical as colliding galaxies, the room breaks into flashing white shards of interstellar nothingness. This being no ordinary storm. It is the dark and solipsistic cranial haze around the tops of spruce in the August Quebec 1958 CNR Niagara-poster moon-light. Yes, we are alone. Alone being totally lonely, totally lovely, totally omniscient. The sweet desert of soul spreading its dark beautiful wings against the stillness & poise of an August night.

Our seasons do not contaminate the constellations.

The sun low and summer softly stabbing you, as if you weren't quite sure when her fingernails had pierced your skin. Forest swamps cellophane green with duckweed floors. Paw-paws rotting into the September soil. The continuum in summer is a mature expectation holding forth its mortality.

Great blue skinks – the waves of Erie on white sand – thick subtropical forest here at the dream's margin. Montreal submerged just beyond Pelee Point. Canals and abandoned fields with cantelope and egrets. I am a certain woman in this she approaches me shyly at the edge of clearing. Barely pubescent my breasts are undeveloped and my penis seeks some feline vagina. The lynx padded forest floor bathed in monsoon stained glass northern mineshaft star cathedral. Two birds suddenly combine in mid-air a suspended vortex of wing and feather.

The mirror evaporates and the human trapped in the other room crouches and begins to approach your opening, his eyes wide with fear.

from "Remote Control": 3 poems

ON ATTAINING REMOTE CONTROL

I am surrounded by am surrounded by silence
conspiring, conspiring.
Not paranoia, not paranoia but the mute and taut faces
    of memory
pressing, pressed at my night window.
The hand that invades my hand invades
touches judgment and unnerves the tracking.
Turns the signposts in a vortex of directions.
I had to build an enclosure surer
than any prison about me.

Now the alternate flickering, now the alternate
  flickering
of my will incandescent and dim
strobes the motion into a clear design.
A cold fire that I can run my invaded hand through
to burn away its polygamy.

And always the two directions knowing damned well
that everything cannot be monitored.
(But O that somehow in the vertigo of knowledge
the equation for a pure random will raise itself
like braille on the bark of these blind elms.)
Listening to waves while parading
blood and miracle before a faceless sky.
The poem is written within the jurisdiction
of remote control. Like the switch on some bed-lamp
that we, in a cold sweat out of sleep, clutch for
half imagining the light actually coming on.

OUT OF CONTROL: THE QUARRY

It is a warm grey afternoon in August. You are in the
country, in a deserted quarry of light grey devonian
limestone in Southern Ontario. A powdery luminescence
oscillates between the rock & sky. You feel sure that you
could recognize these clouds (with their limestone texture)
out of random cloud-photographs from all over the world.
    You then lean over and pick up a flat piece of layered
stone. It is a rough triangle about one foot across. Prying at
the stone you find the layers come apart easily in large flat
pieces. Pale grey moths are pressed between the layers of
stone. Freed, they flutter up like pieces of ash caught in a
dust-devil. You are splashed by the other children but move
not.

Christopher Dewdney

THE SONG OF REMOTE CONTROL

Give yourselves up to Remote Control.
There is no choice, either you come knowing
or not knowing. You come.

Grovel like newborn in total submission
throwing away jewels and watches in
profusion to our sweet robbers.
Give up totally.
Step down from the control tower &
marvel at the jets colliding in brilliant explosions
over the airstrip. Grimace
piss with fear if you like,
then give up.
Give up like a joyful suicide
gracefully from a high building.
Give up like the never-to-be-born are giving up.
Give yourselves over to Remote Control.
We will take care of everything.

Give up.

UNITED

I would walk through the hissing January blizzard.
I would walk through the shimmering mirage
                                        of gas flames
like a flickering blue moss, glowing
beneath my feet.
I would walk down the long hospital corridor
to where you lay.

I would come down small boats in the tiny
tributaries of your national river system.
I would pray to incantations of your wholeness,
your divinity.
I would wait centuries to hold you,
carve through aeons of rock to gaze
at last upon your fossil.
I am demented and the cold & empty nights are
unbearable. I gnaw on the poison
that distils these words. I am ravaged
in the thin plane of the blizzard
just above the horizon.
I am surrounded by unendurable beauty
endless a succession of this truth.
Manifold destiny. May the cradle of the ocean
spawn our likeness in years to come.

HAIKU

My roof was once firm
yet now it cannot even
keep the stars out.

BOREAL ELECTRIC

For my lady, keeper of my wound.
　　　　　　Graffito

She is the twilight intangible, a thin instruction
burning within the envelope generators. Alter
sublime in the cenozoic asylum. And

I am case-hardened. Natty causal an
auto-facsimile. Denoting cold fire.
There is nothing sentimental
about these rocks. I am
the envelope generator growling
in the shifting code facsimiles of night.

Zone trances. Indigo.

I would have her mouth the words
"statutory rape" slowly. Arrested
for intent to denote this line.
This lodestar being visible only
to the discerning eye.

The disconcerting eye.

THE DIALECTIC CRIMINAL:
HAND IN GLOVE WITH AN OLD HAT

When it's raining cats and dogs you've got to cut corners be-
cause you could get your eyes peeled. You must come to grips
with yourself until you fly off the handle & then if you're not fit
as a fiddle you'll spill the beans. That's hitting below the belt
with the short end of the stick, if I can bring the point home,
ladies.

It all started in early 1975, I had an axe to grind during a
blanket freeze. It was no great shakes but I had to go against
the grain, iron out the details. You see, I pulled a few strings &
had to go off the deep end. But I guess I had reckoned without

my host. (That's burning the candle at both ends because this whole thing rings a bell.) The host carried a torch for this chick & now she's praying through the nose. I guess the handwriting was on the wall though.

Anyway, before I got the drop on this I bit the dust and turned the tables. I caught the big shot hanging around by a thread generally laying it on the line. I told him I thought he was right off the wall and it went to his head. He kept it under his hat but greased my palms anyway. Yet I always say strike while the iron is hot and lay low till the heat's off because drawing a line is like splitting hairs. I'd be in the groove now if it wasn't for a bolt out of the blue & even then I got taken to the cleaners. But the whole kit and caboodle is right as rain by my money.

You on the other hand, you put your foot in your mouth & bit off more than you could chew. Now with what's left you put your foot in the door and then accuse *me* of changing my tune? I *had* to change my tune in order to face the music.

I'm going through the motions after bringing the house down because a fly-by-night that held water led me down the garden path. I'm coming on like this because I put one over on you. And now you're out on a limb getting a charge. If you hadn't swapped horses in midstream maybe you could've gotten off. But you've got to keep the ball rolling because we're playing with loaded dice. But then again, who am I to remain on the level?

Anyway back in '75 I was riding a dark horse with a grain of salt up my sleeve. I burned my bridges as I got to them. Everyone around me was starting from scratch because they threw in their towels. I was going like a bat out of hell, I got the drop on it under my skin. A drop in the bucket that is, so now I'm right down your alley because I blew my top. "In hot water?" you ask; no, just flashing. I'm making tracks because this place is definitely nothing by mouth, by word of mouth that is. You see, when you're over your head in a car pool & no one is biting then it's time to break the ice. And break the ice I did, lemme tell you, this bruiser I double-crossed was loaded for bear. I figured it was time to throw a monkey wrench into the works when suddenly he pulled a boner. I didn't waste any time, I hit him below the belt and buried the hatchet. It's a dog's breakfast, lemme tell you, when you're hand in glove with an old hat.

Now I'm letting it all hang out in my old stomping grounds and you can go and take the cake because I've been beating around the burning bush long enough. I've got a stiff upper lip from blowing hot and cold on you bad eggs. I'll never let by-gones become old stand-bys because the leading edge takes the friction.

You're shitting bricks but I'm sweating blood.

from *A Natural History of Southwestern Ontario,* Book 2

GRID ERECTILE

Because of its erotic & cool underparts & the sunset
    emblazoned on its membranous back. Its electric
    litheness.
Because it is a living precipitate of twilight.
Because it is large & soft with external gills.
Because it is tropical and changes colours.
Because the pattern on its back is a thin point.
Because they are so numerous and docile.
Because it whispers through foliage. An animate mobile
    tendril of chlorophyll.
Because it is like an adder, spawning mythology.
Because it is beautiful like a sleek girl with a choker.

For the milk sliding couples beaded with honey.

Because it is large and primitive & therefore closer to the
dinosaurs.

Because they are the only lizards we have.

Because they fly around mercury vapour lamps at night &
alight on suburban screens with their exotic & large
bodies.

Because of their silent glittering black flight.

Because of a summer evening in 1954. It opened its wings &
I received its revelation.

Because of summer nights behind the mosque.

Because it signals the height of summer.

Because of its mathematical precision at the infinite disposal
of curiosity. Because its markings are the summation of
military heraldry, the olive green of the English military.

Because it is a tropical species here in Southwestern Ontario.

Because they are nocturnal, tropical thin points of extreme
beauty. Sculptural perfection in living and dense wood.

Because their chrysalis resembles a vase. Their humming
flight & the insoluble intricacy of their June camouflage.

Because of the size & gothic modelling of their pincers, their
chestnut brown elytra.

Because it is so tiny. (Weighs as much as a dime.)

Because it is pale underneath. Tawny above.

Because it is the eyes of night.

Because it is even larger, like a fox bat.

Because it is our largest and only cat.

Because they are capricious night gliders.

Because it is a predator.

Because of its inky fur. Tunnels twisting around roots.

Because it is a southern species migrating northwards.
Evidence for an inter-glacial warming trend.

Because of their glowing eyes in the driveway at night.
Their rasping marsupial cries.

Because of the caves.

Because of its unearthly face.

Because it is all of night.

Because it is a falcon.

Because it is sub-tropical.

Because it is a stilted & accurate blue mist.

Because it is the north, unwarranted in a shallow pond.

Because it is a tropical species slowly migrating north,
starting at Point Pelee.

Because it is a sub-tropical iridescent metal.

Because it is the arctic migrating at the centre of blizzards.

Because they are astonishing aerialists.

Because the vacuum of space is so near.

Because of a dream.

Because they draw out the soul.

Anticipation. Electric gradients. The irresistible approach of
the arc hammer. Excitation in the ion shadows.

Because they come after you & seem to float in dreams,
the bend sinister.

Because of the storm.

Because of an erotic insularity in the moist almost tropical
wind.

Because they illuminate everything in a grey powdery light
and turn the outside into a surreal theatre of marvellous
intent. The warmth allows the spectators to remove their
clothes.

Lunacy & a saturnalian trance of corporeal clarity.

Because they are tropical.

Because they are both out of place & welcome.

Because they witnessed extinct races of fabulous creatures.

Because it is carnivorous & wet.

Because it is a carnivorous morning jewel in the sphagnum.

Because they are full lips & vulvas & are all of summer.

Because they are a tropical species here in Southwestern
Ontario.

Because it has huge leaves and is tropical with cerise jurassic
fruit.

Because it is fragrant & tropical.

Because its fruits are pungent.

Because the flowers are huge. Night glowing & perfumed.

Because of the pools.

Because their smooth mahogany pebbles are enclosed in vegetable geodes.

Because of fovea centralis.

Because they flowered all of beneath into above and translated it perfectly.

Because it is a living fossil.

Because of the colour & smoothness of its bark, the silence & level loam floor of the beech forest.

Because of the fragrance of its gum.

Because of the wooden petals of their flowers.

Because of the waterfalls & the morning glen.

Because it is the memory capital of Canada.

Because I perceived an order there.

Because the concretions are there.

Because of mid-summer nights, memory steeped in fireflies.

Because it overlooks Lake Huron.

Because the cedar pools are nearby.

For it was once submerged.

Because it is a huge invisible river.

Because of the collections in grey powdery light of Toronto winter afternoons spent in the devonian era.

Because it is a cathedral of limestone.

Because it is awesome.

Because chronology was commenced there.

Because of the black river formation. Last hold-out of the White Elm.

Because of the beech forest & what came after.

Because I got to know Lake Erie & glacial clay there.

Because I grew up beside them & they taught me everything I know.

Because it is a huge & silent underwater predator.

Because it is huge and primitive.

Because it cruises, hovering, long snouted crocodilian.

Because it is primitive.

It is a warm grey day in August. A powdery luminescence oscillates within the patches of night beneath the trees. Nocturnal pools characterized by crickets & day foraging bats. A wind stirs the fissures of the canopy. What is still is expectant. Bat's dusky membranes envelop the writhing coils of a small snake, theiyr standoff illuminated by the pink August dawn. A distant blue jay sounds the interceding forest. An albino fox in the cedar verge. Waves on Lake Huron in your sleep they are waves within breathing. The beach intersects distant momentums. Surges linger in a phantasmic waveform. Embro Foldens her children the lake claims by dreaming lay waste the armoured spinal cord. A delirious rush of invertebrate orgasms in the implacable recall of the ocean. I do not consider the waves empty in your sense(s). Free-fall under the swells a pulsing spinal thrill. Diving to the source of neural conductivity. Ammonites a copper mist gleaming dully through the shallow water. Peripheral glimpse of trilobites scuttling into murky water at the edge of the Ausable. Hungry Hollow Hills, memory vapour. Her lissome arms & legs trailing in the tepid summer water as the small boat rounds the bend into the canyon.

Deafening cicadas.

Fierce array of the summer foliage.

Re-group at the air-lock. Her spine ends in four extra vertebrae, prehensile as a finger she shoves it up your ass as you come. Her parents obviously intrigued by the sexual options in the genetic engineering catalogue. She has slight webs between her fingers. The limestone heaves up & dissolves in an awesome rumbling giving up all the time trapped in its layers. Legions of extinct creatures crawl up through the rubble, transparent with age. The planets converge & hover just beyond the atmosphere in the evening sky, barely opaque in the haze. The electromagnetic fields generate huge scarab beetles. Iridescent elytra & fabulous horns. Cascade of night & night wind coming in the livingroom window drugged & cool. Full moon. Only the brightest stars glowing in the soft blue summer night. I have learned to love the noctuids.

Cumulonimbus clouds towering with their bases just below the horizon. Pink in the gasoline haze & slanting rays of the setting sun. Billowing like the convoluted foreheads of brooding foetuses, their water-brains filled with grotesque electric thought impulses & thunder. Theiyr silence raining onto the land.

Pier Giorgio Di Cicco

CANZONE

I can't get over tulips this month, they mouth
the sides of fences, taking a wrist-hold on
a clump of sun, and sing it out in my veins, those
beautiful little critters, rose-lipped, those
darlings that hem my life.

And when the world comes apart at the seams,
not the prettiest sight, I pretend a dance
that's made by loosening the heart from the head,
a fancy gesture, not at all becoming,
made to make death a little old with running off
at the mouth.

I do not want to believe for a moment the
way life takes pot-shots at the running children,
sinking their feet into the earth-well of the grave;
head first, the poor babies scream right through
the years until they land, small ghosts of pining,
on an average bed, on an average morning, eating
the breakfast of your lies.

I am done with it. This song tastes of dust,
the lake can never wash it through. My mouth
sings and it is all the same, whether in this
room or in that temple; it is the sound of the
lungs clapping to make up a hope; a way of breathing

the eyes back into god, a way of touching the rose
in the lover's hand, without telling him the hairs
of that peachy
world, his heart, are burning.

THE HEAD IS A PALTRY MATTER

The head is a paltry matter; feed it crumbs, it goes
on singing just the same.
Much too much is made of it; it goggles over a bit of
fresh wind, is perfectly astonished at the touch of love,
doesn't know what to make of itself but crosses, bearing
its own dull weight along paths it imagines have to do
with the heart.
No more of it. I'm giving it nothing to feed on.
Old lump, let it do its crossword of a grave.
You and I have better things to do, namely wrapping arms
around each other tonight, while it hangs around, poor sot,
childlike, finding a little of what it is
that lovers do, the dark between them like a clock
and their lips set to ignite one future after another.

THE MAN CALLED BEPPINO

When a man loses his barbershop during the war
as well as an only son, and his wife and
daughter sing the blues of starvation, the man

believes in the great white hope, now the red white
and blue. The man ventures overseas, and lands finally

in Baltimore, Maryland, USA – destined to be the
finest barber at eastpoint shopping plaza.

The man works for nothing, because his english is
less than fine; the customers like him,
and the man is easily duped, he believes in the
honest dollar, and is offered peanuts in return.

This while the general manager runs to Las Vegas
to take porno pictures of himself between
tall whores.

The man who lost his barbershop during the war
loves great white roses at the back of a house beside
a highway. The roses dream with him,
of being understood in clear english, or of a large
Italian sun, or of walking forever on a
Sunday afternoon.

Never mind the new son, the family. It is this man, whose
hospital cheques are being spent in Las Vegas,
it is this man whose hair will shine like
olive leaves at noon; it is this man who will sit
on his front lawn, after the fifth hemorrhage, having
his last picture taken,
because he drank too much.

It is this man who will sit under his mimosa
by the highway, fifty pounds underweight, with no
hospital, and look

there are great white roses in his eyes.

REMEMBERING BALTIMORE, AREZZO

The night begins slowly at first, large slow flakes
descending out of the sky's one fist.
And the bed waiting, and friends perched on
their solitudinous thrones wherever the heart
has brought them.
It seems that spring is still out of season,
the white trucks go in and out through the
darkness, the lake has the same reach night after night
a little bored with its old speech of seagulls frozen
in the dank air. There is a house not far from here, though
you would think it many miles, a house of roses, with an
old man on the front lawn, twirling his moustache,
having his last picture taken. It is my father,
before the dream blew up, of America, of uncles, older
    brothers,
of streets of gold, of Aunt Margaret and the open steel
mills kissing the harbour. It is the dream of America,
ages ago, that I run from, hiding my head in the snow,
pretending it never was, and saying yes, it should have
    started
again here, without a father's grave, with my mother
dancing lightly through the rooms of kitchen smells,
and I am nothing but a last outpost, a huge construct of
    blood
with roses that conjure houses, homes, a decent happiness.
I am not alone, I have never been alone. Ghosts are barking
in my eyes, their soft tears washing us down to
Baltimore, out the Chesapeake, round the Atlantic, round
    the world,
back where we started from, a small town in the
shade of cypress, with nowhere to go but be still again.
It is a way of saying twenty-five years

and some German bombs have made for roses in a
   backyard that
we cry over, like some film which is too maudlin to pity
and yet is the best we have to feel human about.

WILLING

That black apple the sun is dead,
mouthfuls of it taken, by poets,
lovers, the inebria of scuttlefish,
joe blow; all lamenting the sun, all a praise of
the sperm-god sun; all a wishful May-dance
around that rooter of lilies, the sun; oh world

plum of an afternoon, unhinge from it, sail yourself
through dark; open the way you do in my head, say
at 3 AM; you do not need a sun; you need
the cartilage of my need to make you hang well.
Where would you be without me? I have done with praising
the exterior villains of a rutabaga world; that sharp fist
your heart is hung right through to a dream I had
of children, their moth eyes filling the gardens with
delight, the warheads emptied from their hands.
It is the same dream I propose to you: love this boy,
blue-eyed and fair, do homage to his excellent exercise
of keeping you fit for a lifetime.

THE JUMP ON DEATH

I'm going to charge this one up, the old machine, the stop
and start thing, the heart;
christ it's taken it this long to make the music,
it's taken this long for the castle, the air,
the music in the throat, the lump washed out
that is a summer in disguise.

I've got words to make this map out, following the breath
down every channel, the blood down every artery,
the words down every teardrop. The words have it.

I say them on a monday afternoon, or on lonely nights,
under the arch of trees, the moon dimpling its way
across the mouth of a star – I say them, hey loser,

hey son of man, stalling out another
terror, you've everything to make up for, you are the
no-stakes winner, the need to make good in a house of bone,

the thankless operation of making the heart stand on its
   head.

FLYING DEEPER INTO THE CENTURY

Flying deeper into the century
is exhilarating, the faces of loved ones eaten out
slowly, the panhandles of flesh warding off
the air, the smiling plots. We are lucky to be mature,
in our prime, seeing more treaties, watching
TV get computerized. Death has no dominion.
It lives off the land. The glow over the hill, from

the test sites, at night, the whole block of neighbours
dying of cancer over the next thirty years. We are
suing the government for a drop of blood; flying deeper
into the century, love,
the lies are old lies with more imagination;
the future is a canoe. The three bears are ravenous, not
   content
with porridge. Flying deeper into the century,
my hands are prayers, hooks, streamers.
I cannot love grass, cameos or lungs.
The end of the century is a bedspread up to the eyes.
I want to be there, making ends meet.
I will not love you, with such malice at large.
Flying deeper into the century is beautiful, like
coming up for the third time, life flashing before us.
The major publishing event is the last poem of
all time. I am a lonely bastard. My brothers and sisters have
had sexual relations, and I am left with their mongrel sons
writing memoirs about the dead in Cambodia.
Flying deeper, I do not remember what I cared for, out
of respect. Oh *Time*, oh *Newsweek*, oh *Ladies' Home*
   Journal,
oh the last frontier, I am deeply touched.
The sun, an ignoramus, comes up.
I have this conversation with it. Glumly, glumly, deeper
I fly into the century, every feather of each wing
absolution, if only I were less than human, not angry
like a beaten thing.

MALE RAGE POEM

Feminism, baby, feminism.
This is the anti-feminist poem.
It will get called the anti-

86

feminist poem. Like it or not.
Dedicated to all my friends who
can't get it up in the night,
accused of having male rage during the
day. This is for the poor buggers.
This is for me and the incredible boredom
of arguing about feminism, the right
arguments, the wrong arguments, the
circular argument, the arguments that stem
from one bad affair, from one
bad job, no job – whatever; fill in the
blanks _____ _____ , fill in the ways
in which you have been hurt. Then I'll
fill in the blanks, and we'll send rosters
of hurt to each other, mail them, stock
them for the record, to say: *Giorgio Di Cicco*
has been hurt in this way x many times.
We will stock closets of Sarah's hurt,
Barbara's hurt, my hurt, Bobby's hurt.
This is where the poem peters out . . . oops! – that's
penis mentality, that's patriarchal bullshit,
sexist diction and *these line lengths are*
male oriented.
            Where did he get so much male rage?
From standing out like a man for a bunch of
years, and being called the dirty word.
"When you are 21 you will become a Man."
Christ! Doomed to enslave women ipso
facto, without even the right training for it.
Shouldn't have wasted ten years playing
baseball; should have practised
whipping, should have practised tying up the
girl next door, giving her cigarette burns . . .
oops! Male rage again! MALE RAGE – the words ring out –
worse than RING AROUND THE COLLAR, worse than
    KISSED
THE GIRLS AND MADE THEM CRY, jeesus, male rage

in kindergarten. MALE RAGE. You've got
male rage; I look inside myself and scrounge
for all this male rage. Must be there
somewhere. Must be repressing it. I write poems
faster and faster, therapeutically, to make sure
I get most of the rage out. But someone's
always there to say Male Rage – more Male Rage;
I don't leave the house, working on my male rage.

Things may lighten up. My friends may meet
fine women at a party someday and know
what to say to them, like: "I'm not a Man and
you're not a Woman, but let's have dinner
anyway, let's fuck with our eyes closed and
swap roles for an hour."

I'm tired of being a man.
Of having better opportunities,
better job offers,
too much money.
I'm tired of going to the YMCA and
talking jock in the locker room.
I'm tired of all the poems where
I used the word "whore" inadvertently.
I'm tired of having secretaries type out
all my poems for me.
I'm tired of being a man.
I'm tired of being a sexist.
I'm afraid of male rage.
I'm afraid of *my* male rage,
this growing thing, this buddy, this
shadow, this new self, this stranger.
It's there. It's there! How could it have
happened? I ate the right things, said

yes to my mother, thought the good
thoughts.
        Doc – give it to me straight.
How long do I have before this male rage
takes over completely?
                The rest of your life.
Take it like a man.

RELATIONSHIPS

Everywhere they are talking about
relationships, though they hate the word,
though no one visibly vomits over it, and
everyone sneaks it into the conversation, using
the word for the sake of, you understand, convenience.
Everyone is talking about it. Primary, secondary
relationships, bad relationships, short-term
ones, long-term, relationships that
couldn't work out, unhealthy relationships,
monogamous ones, a relationship lasting two or
three years, two or three minutes, a sexual
relationship, my favourite, phrase that is.
Relationships they work at, comfortable relationships,
the first big relationship, the relationship
I'm into now, the positive relationship, the
negative, a relationship based on understanding,
the relationship that's falling apart, the
strong relationship, the superficial relationship,
the relationship between two people, an honest
relationship, the mature relationship, the dead
relationship, the new relationship – though no
one likes the word, everyone uses it, all on
related ships, on ships with some

relations, relative ships, relating, shipping
some off to relatives, relishing tips on how
to have better relations.
                                    Everywhere
they are talking relationships
and not having them, having them and not
liking them. Everywhere they are using
the dirty word. Relation ships us all off
to lonely places. In love – no one is in love;
they're working at the thing, committing, cementing,
forming attachments – it's all a bunch of
brickwork, constructing a sound relationship,
ironing out problems, breaking down barriers,
making a firm foundation, picking up the pieces
from a relationship. We are all frustrated masons.
Let's all build a good relationship and
crawl into it, let's all drag in ex-lovers
and bore each other to death, discussing it.
Let's discuss it and not do it, let's not and
say we did – let's be really careful about it so
a brick doesn't fall on our heads.

Let's look at a whole bunch of empty
rooms and discuss it;
let's get really old waiting
for a relationship that's right; let's
write more articles on relationships and
feel liberal, bohemian, enlightened.
Let's become the ministry of relationships,
the high priests of it, let's really get
down on our knees and bark at the moon,
meaning love, meaning the oval, heavy syllable
spilling out of our mouths and onto the
grass; let's wonder why sixteen-year-olds
are wary, conservative, going into law
instead of english. Let's wonder how long
before we're out there, pushing buttons,

not knowing other ways to say I love you,
wrapping up the foetus of fireballs.
When did we start discussing? What's this relationship –
this one-night stand with the earth?

BRAIN LITANY

The brain is a network of connections of cells
It is not a connection of cells
It is a connection of information
It is not a connection of information
It is a connection of blue vases
with red flowers in them
It is not a connection of vases
It is a connection of living memories

". . . when we think of coconuts and pigs, there are no
   coconuts or pigs in the brain."   *–Gregory Bateson*

where are they
where are the coconuts
where are the pigs

The brain is a network of behavioural potentialities
The brain is the mind
The brain is the central integrative role in human
   performance

where are the pigs
where are the coconuts

The brain is a compendium of holographic mechanisms
Help me find the coconuts Help me find the pigs
The brain is a neuro-physiological metaphor

The brain is an illusionist's exercise in Euclidean geometry
The brain is a vibrational amplifier for ambient field
    quanta
Find me the goddamned coconuts the pigs
The brain is a cybernetic miracle with a three ring
triune brain circus at its centre
The brain is an enchanted loom where millions of flashing
shuttles weave a dissolving pattern
I know I saw the coconuts
I know I saw the pigs
The brain is an evolutionary archaeological site
Show me those pigs one more time

The brain is a dance among three interconnected bio-
    logical
computers
I saw the pigs
I saw the coconuts

The brain is a bi-cameral structure for playing
epistemological handball.
I know you have the coconuts

The brain is a reality structurer with lacrimal glands
The brain is an international casino for quantum
    indeterminacy
The pigs
The pigs
The pigs

When we think of brains, there are no brains in the brain.

The coconuts
The pigs
The brain is a psycho-biological tar pit give me
the fucking coconuts in an emotional jungle you bastard

or the brain is a macro-evolutional myth for the
 maintenance of
I'll bash the brain is an omni-directional time machine
clogged with death consciousness

I could cry

Show me those pigs
Show me those coconuts

THE ABRIDGED CARTESIAN VERSION

I think, therefore I am.

When we think of the "I", there is no one in the brain.

Where am I?
Where am I?   etc.

LETTER TO DING AN SICH

Dear Ding an sich.
I miss you.
I have looked through all the drawers,
found what maps I could find and they were
stamped Where is beloved Ding an sich?
Physicalists mourn and search
in long cathedrals, dimensionally twisting
for the lateral apparitions of Ding an sich,
the old boy we'd hob-nob with in the schoolyard.
We try to be ourselves, to emulate like handing
down a story. It's the most we can convey of that
era. You should have been there, is the

common retort. You are like much
of a shadow, an adumbration of thought, like
a sense of old citizenry before a migration
to a land where the natives see height in terms
of width, and our new membranes, squint as
we may, retain a fore-image of something we
sometimes call platonic, but is too much
like the tang of a sunday sauce, lingering
on an equally platonic palate. It is like being
in water, and the textures oscillating before
you grab them. Of course the fish are elusive.
They're not dumb, though we ascribe talents to them
in terms of extra bio-systemic dimensions. It fools
no one. Sleep is similarly bombastic. We pretend to
be scared of the ogres and precipices, and this is
a way of learning how to wake in the new land.
All in all, it was better with you. The delights are
various. Don't misunderstand! The logic, slow
as molasses from the charmed trees; it's like you'd
want to de-evolve into a fat white caterpillar, when
the air won't sustain wings. And now you'd have to
jump. That's part of the rules. You can't use
the convenient paraphernalia you thought would come in
handy for the trip.

    Mother would have liked it here. There are things
we kept secret, you and I. And no one is ever going to
come and get us. Remember how we used to pine
for that luxury? It was a game, just to keep us
from boredom. We thought they'd never find us in the
boiler room. They sure as hell won't . . . . It will
get lonely until the cataracts grow in.

David Donnell

LAKES

I

People who want to live beside the ocean are funda-
  mentalists.
The juxtaposition of land and sea makes a natural dyad.
Jane has a cottage at Musselman's Lake and Karen has a
  house
on Parkside Drive, bay-windowed, with a recording studio
  in the renovated basement.
I visit Jane on Sundays, pushing the Ford van up Yonge
  Street
and turning east into the small townships that occur before
the land spreads steadily north, ploughed field after field
of what was unlimited and natural in the 19th-century
Scottish/English push from lake-front into the dry mouth
  of colder weather.
The trees are yellow and orange and green the fields dark
brown with the last corn in crisp waves under the breeze.
This is the country I grew up in, a short region to the west,
St. Marys, Hamilton, Galt, small towns surrounded by
  fields,
and still remember as tangibly as a natural pattern.

We sit on two old lawn chairs on her front porch drinking
warm water and scotch while the sun falls slowly over the
  lake
and a fine line of sweat snails down our shoulders.
Brahms. Brahms.
Our knees bump like bass fiddles until we go inside for
  coffee.

She undoes the clumsy buttons on the plaid shirt after I kiss
her and stands quietly in front of me naked from the waist
in the dark light, her smile Dutch somehow, one hand busy
with the air, balancing it,

>   playing, then I am lost in her

our bodies fitting together like the lake and the rough
   stubble
along its edge. The clock ticks. Dogs bark outside.
Her underwear lying on top of my corduroy pants looks like
a surreal image of my connection to the country I grew up in
   and left foolishly
to waste my time in violence museum city,

of history, John Galt, Goldie's eventual millions, my
   grandfather
walking from Ayr to Galt once a month with a sack of flour,
of Jefferson and the separation of powers, of the lakes,
of Edison with a black tie, of silt drifting downstream
   in the clouded Potomac.

   2

But naturally I go back to my apartment in the city
with its general disorder, papers, books, junk, the day turns,
the nights are huge dark highways full of train wrecks
literature, love, sex, daily news, Dewar's, hangovers
   and scrambled eggs.
I go out with Karen and feel at home in the city.
Karen is like a corn field with a bush of blueberries
at the heart, rehearsing a new performance piece in the
   middle
of her livingroom, morning sun leaf-strewn wild blonde hair,
plants, books, brass, a picture age 17 at highschool in
   Des Moines.
We make love on the green livingroom carpet and it almost
feels like the country. Who makes love out of doors
   anyway?

We get dressed and have a plain supper of bean sprouts,
yogurt, asparagus soup, apple betty, tuborg; we drink some
   scotch and I think
I am every adolescent boy in every novel from Sacramento
to Whitehorse and down again by train or imagination
continually choosing between different women
not even sure sometimes why I love them
as if they represent my ravished grandfather Duncan,
my lost aunts and uncles,
six-foot Hugh who parlayed a sack of flour into
   executiveship,
my dead father's medals and the clear steady hazel of
   his eyes
that burned out at you like the sun falling on slow poplars,
my mother's mother's great house in Washington where
   the boys
bet five-dollar gold pieces on which way the sun would
   shine,
or my father's wild mother lost in San Francisco with
   her bags
and her canvas bundle of brushes, burnt sienna, raw ochre,
   chromium yellow.
The pain of history is summarized by the way that simple
   geography
separates the powers of love and nostalgia, fern and brass,
past and present, until the general disorder of random city
requires more explanation, my disordered rooms, socks,
the dark elegant bar at the 22, my books, notes, the squared
calendar, wheat germ, eggs, the sermons of John Donne
   with the bark
of the tough brown flea and the Puritan uprising behind
   them.

   3

I am the red and yellow and blue in that bundle of
   paints
against my will or otherwise

and lost in a history to which I am willing to be lost,
a farm boy intoxicated with a sense of distant events,
I understand this is a love of process not dissimilar
to the love of land that moves farmers in the early morning
to finish their coffee and walk to the barn still half asleep,
cows, chickens, pigs, bits of harness, plough points, wire.
I want to break backwards into my family history
and emerge with something more North American than flags
    or bunting,
the Wilson brothers muttering in the steamy 5 A.M. barn,
the city turned around to face the Americas instead of the
    North,
some chicken feathers and tar for the fat mayor,
I want to put the different parts of our lives together,
the farms and the cities, the highways and the trains.
The dichotomies of North America confuse me.
Something happens to me with women that confuses me.
Ideas are simple.
Work is simple.
I associate Jane with the country and simplicity.
Karen with the city.
My desire for synthesis gets caught between highways.
Sometimes I think women are my connection with history.
My mother was my childhood geographer
and the men in my family were intellectuals and pragmatists.
Myself part both.
The city hums with all its different parts.
I walk west on Queen Street late at night
thinking about Galt and St. Marys and San Francisco.
The offices south of Queen are bright against the dark sky.
I turn up University walking slowly in the quiet
slight mist of the city after 12
two horse-drawn caleches for tourists
the city not completely asphalt
all these elements of the country still present
flickering in our consciousness like the flare of a gasoline
    match.

David Donnell

THE CANADIAN PRAIRIES VIEW OF LITERATURE

First of all it has to be anecdotal; ideas don't exist;
themes struggle dimly out of accrued material like the
   shadow
of a slow caterpillar struggling out of a large cocoon;
even this image itself is somewhat urban and suggests
the tree-bordered streets of small southern Ontario towns.
Ontario towns are eastern; French towns are European;
the action should take place on a farm between April and
   cool October;
nature is quiet during winter, it snows and there's a lot of it,
the poem blazes in the schoolteacher's head like an image
of being somewhere else like Rome or Costa Rica;
the novel shifts in the articulate reporter's head
and surveys the relationships between different farms.
Sometimes the action happens in the beverage rooms and
   cheap
hotels area of a small town that has boomed into a new city;
Indians and Métis appear in the novel wearing the marks
of their alienation like a sullen confusion of the weather;
a woman gets married and another woman has a child;
the child is not old enough to plough a field and therefore
does not become a focus of interest except as another
   mouth.
They sit around with corn shucks in their head and wonder
who they should vote for, the question puzzles them,
vote for the one with the cracked shoes, he's a good boy,
or the one who jumped over six barrels at a local dance;
their regionalism is like a nationalism of the land;
the small farmers struggle against equipment dealers;
their wives struggle against patriarchal cowshit;
their intellectuals dislike the east which gives them form
allowing their musings and discontents to flower into
   rancour.

Afternoon light, aged 12, I walk down the small side
streets of Galt, past South Water, musing and rancorous,
   adrift,
not quite like Rimbaud leaving Charleville for Paris,
my hands in my windbreaker pockets like white stones,
and promise myself once again that when I get to the city
everything will happen, I will learn all of its history
and become the best writer they have ever dreamed of.
I'll make them laugh and sometimes make them cry,
I'll drink their whisky and make love to all their wives,
the words tumbling out of my mouth as articulate as
   the young Hector,
the corn under my shirt awkward a little rough light
   brown dry
and making me itch at times.

TRUE LOVE ISN'T HARD TO FIND

One of the most beautiful things that can happen
between a man and a woman lying naked in a large
   white bed
her tawny hair falling over one shoulder   lamplight
the man erect, an intent satyr, kneeling in front of her
one of the most beautiful things that can happen
between this idyllic couple   is a mortadella sandwich
piled thick with tomato and sweet pepper on caraway rye
the sandwich split in half and eaten between them
the way she pushes her hair out of her eyes and takes
a first bite   blushing slightly and laughing as she swallows
not using the back of her hand as he does but the tips
   of her fingers

he eats faster than she does and is finished first
rubbing the muscle in his left shoulder and gazing idly

at the tent of white sheet around her knee
a small piece of red pepper has fallen on his cock
she bends over gracefully holding her hair back with one
    hand
and picks it off with her raspberry pink tongue
a train whistles somewhere in the night sliding west to
    Regina
the man stretches out with one leg over her left knee
and begins to read a book on the history of Canadian
    railways
the woman rumples his hair   picks up several more crumbs
and sits with her arms around her knees   listening
    to the sound
of the crickets dark and manic in the white snow outside

ABATTOIR

A wooden mallet hits me over the head as the chain hook
    lifts me
above a cement runway flooded with water and blood.
I call out as loudly as possible
"Don't do this to me, you're crazy, I'm a man . . . you
    assholes,"
but nothing happens in the liver-coloured dream
except a muffled squealing sound
going 'eeee eeee eeee'
while the overhead chain-winch hauls me above the block.
The wooden block hurts my stomach.
I flail at the air with my powerful male hands
but all I can see in front of me
is my small trotters beating against the chipped wood.
The bearded kosher butcher turns his head away.
A young blond midwestern guy in a blue apron walks up
carrying a 12-inch knife as sharp as a razor.

He drives the knife into my stomach above the groin
and rips me open up to my pulsing throat.
Circles break in the dark water like photo-electronic flowers.
I can feel blood swirling in gutters as I break to the surface.
"David," she says to me, stroking one of my cold trotters
the way shoppers feel up a tomato
"darling, the way you grab me by the ass sometimes,"
my hand is on her thigh or at least I think it's her thigh
"I wouldn't want anyone like my mother to notice,
but hey, darling, boychuk, I love it,
it makes me feel so wanted
I could nibble and kiss you all over,"
and she plants a giant-size crimson lipstick kiss
smack on my left pink porcine jowl.
I stand and hold her smiling,
my great sides heaving like a wake,
my squat bone trotters around her waist like handcuffs.
No honest   I didn't want to disrupt anyone's evening
not me   the son of a famous local historian
a beautiful boy
a champion high-jumper   a basketball fan
a baseball cards collector
a man with ideals and a vision of America.
We embrace like dancing partners,
Maisie and the giant pig,
looking out the picture windows at the dark Toronto night
the tall columns of cubed light blinking in the distant south;
her skirt comes off
she brings her adroit knee around me like a forward,
I thrust my huge schlong between her thighs
thinking of sea-birds over the grey Atlantic where
my death and Maisie's are plankton in the sea lions' snorted
    breath.
I squeal with light.

David Donnell

EMILY DICKINSON'S HORSES

All the horses she owned in her field of poems are black
tall graceful part Arab horses from Essex
geldings or colts is never clear
the question not raised let alone resolved
these are horses of life but also horses of death
carriage horses that pull phaetons
saddle horses that dance at the edge of meadows
at the edge of her mind before the poem begins
at the edge of her mind where her mind paused
   and put in flowers
these are silent horses but they scream roses
2-year-olds is unlikely
2-year-olds are green
3-year-olds are larger but ambivalent
these are 4-year-olds with a knowledge of life

these are the male horses of her imagination
and even these are only mentioned from time to time
tall graceful part Arab horses from Andalusia
colts that masturbate against the fence of their stall
broad-shouldered percherons that pull carts wagons
   or heavy ploughs
rose rose rose   symbol of life of the mouth of female
sex the pink lips petal on petal but as durable
as shoulder or hand
these are silent horses more stately than visiting princes
but they kick down fences stall walls dig up wooden floors
frustrated with anger or confinement masturbate com-
   pulsively
distrust other (male) horses but make friends with goats
   or rambunctious sheep dogs
emily emily emily my sister retiring upstairs with a plate
of celery and cold sliced potato
wet under your stiff white dress stolen from nuns

dark hair coiffed back in a neat roll your teeth gleaming
the face of a young boy stoned on Seville brandy
you rose in a white dress you green colt with small breasts
english professors with dandruff on their tweed jackets
glyph through the milk-white gypsum notebooks of your life
but never meet you standing at the top of a stair
with the light from a small landing window striking across
   your huge dark eyes
and your tongue moving suddenly in your pink mouth
as you sense one of these horses starting up in the green
meadow outside your house and outside these poems
where you trapped death like a piece of mica
fragment of black obsidian
and tossed him under the hooves of these horses
these 4-year-olds restrained by carriage traces
released from box stalls
let loose on dirt roads
these wild-eyed responders with a single rose between
   their teeth

LOUIS ARMSTRONG'S HANDKERCHIEF

Louis Satchmo Armstrong used to have a trick when he was
a young man & starting to make a splash in the clubs
the locked-door speakeasies & the black after-hours spots;
he used to put a handkerchief over his right hand while
he played some of his most original melodic solos,
& explained himself after the band took a break
by saying, "I don't want those other musicians
to steal my stuff." His stuff was important. His
originality. His breaking down of the English hymn
& popular song structure into bourbon jazz. He didn't
   want
the other musicians like Bix to take away or pick up on

his particular work, heart, his heart, of which he had a lot,
beating in his own 2/2 time & wanting to sign its name.
Another way of saying you can share the meal I'm eating
but don't fool around with my head. Louis was a poor boy
as are we all & wanted to make it in the big cities of New
York & Paris. Men are like this about women sometimes.
About imagined infidelities or lapses that are not that much
more important than imagined infidelities anyway.
They're afraid the lapses will interrupt the pleasure of being
reassured by somebody who acts like a partner. An ego
partner. A body partner. A partner in quiet drinks after
evening love-making when there is no one else but the two
people & the bed still warm & rumpled from the moving
    around
& the cold sharp rich drinks (whoever invented ice-cubes
was also some kind of genius, a Norwegian perhaps sitting
around in the back room of a small factory & drawing
    diagrams
of freezer coils on sheets of brown wrapping paper),
some clothes on the back of a chair & some books open
on a table & the large window with some distant traffic
& the moon. A body partner. A social partner. John down
the street didn't mind his friend Allan not paying back
the 500 dollars for 6 months but went red blind with rage
when he walked into the kitchen & found Allan kissing
his wife in the middle of the half-lit kitchen floor. Men
are like that or at least the historians or history say we are.
Women are also perhaps but less given to screaming &
    outraged
vocal expression. Women are more socially constructive
    anyway.
More tuned to children. Pick him up before he gets into
    those
tools you've left on the floor. This is simple & not a
limitation. But Louis Satchmo Splendiferous became
    mellower
as he got older. He became mellower as he made records

that were distributed through stores & played on large
   Victrola gramophones.
The solos were recorded & dated & filed in their neat
   envelope covers. Louis Ambitiousdellamostus became a bit
mellower. He had gone into the clubs & come out with his
   hands
full of yellow flowers. He could drink a little now & think
about Paris & Amsterdam. Men are often like this about
   women
but women are different. The body partner. The social
   partner.
Tawny & blue. This is someone you can't play solos with
every night of the week.

HOUND

Hound is liver-coloured and smooth after his evening run
laps up the bowl of water in the half-lit kitchen and sits
licking his lips as the shirtsleeves man drinks coffee.
The maples outside are yellow and most of the flowers are
   down.
He stretches like a sleek single muscle under the table
and points his long head at the ceiling lights the doorways
opening into the cool air and whiter light of other rooms.
This is the quiet moment at the slow close of every evening
looking out over the city hazing south and west
the big neon signs turned on for the night and the rough
   country
stretching green and brown to the north past tractors and
   groundhogs.

When he hurls himself against the door he makes the catch
rattle in the lock and the garage in the gauze curtain tilt
  sideways.

People who don't know anything about animals say that
  dogs are reflexive and can't experience a contemplation
  of what they see.
Dogs have no names or causal index for things.
A factory is a series of dark rooms and smells of grease.
Dogs do a lot of the same things people do   eat run sleep
fall in love fart take an active interest in the world.
People eat work sleep get married and drink too much.
What fascinates me when he sits staring out over the yard
is the way that chicken gravel car tree announce themselves
without index cards and more fluidly than they come to me.
Calm is as calm as the wind rustling through trees in a poem
but the desperation in the eye of dog is more human than
  salesman.
The shape of a tree in his mind is large and green and wet.
He knows my feet shoes I wear baths and the way I walk
more thoroughly than a friend or the men and women at
  work.
My hands have no secrets from him my pockets are shadows
where hands disappear from time to time and come out
  naked
smudged sweaty grains of tobacco empty since water and
  food
especially giblets liver the ends of a roast are kept in
  kitchens.

He follows me sometimes at a distance sniffing the wind
  ground
air and wherever I go is a definite point on a four-
  dimensional

map that has no words or tags or exploded diagrams.
The shape of a fire is enormous but contains images that
are discrete and pass on to meadows rivers gravel driveways.
He know my thick voice when I have a cold or a cigarette.
Dog is a museum of perfect objects banked in chemical
    reflexes.
My body is my body.
I am lonely without him and the yellow air of the kitchen
    goes dull
until I hurl myself at the door and go out on the back porch
to gulp the air put the garage right side up wet tree on cheek.
He sits intent crooning tail wagging head quick as traffic
wants to run down chickens and thinks this behaviour on
my part is as shadowy
as my pockets and not sensible like dark or light.

Brian Fawcett

LAMENT

The uniquely human impulse to *speak*
as opposed to yapping or whining about the bosses

is the brain of beauty,
but not the way beauty has come to mean

those quirks that, born of leisure
thrive as style or ignorance,

an iridescence as the real world slips beneath them,
power moving silently to power. Rather

trees at dusk, the stars blinking out
as a full moon rises.

This may be the last century
in which poets make speech of such things,

these the last years in which poetry
will be written and read aloud

as if the mind of beauty
could be brought into the world. Ah

drive that old car of yours into the nearest sewage lagoon,
get blind drunk, observe the stately elegance

of the overhead buzzing transmission lines. *So
be it.* But with reluctance,

slow and careful as the silence
that precedes all eternal songs.

The trees and stars will make their way
without our help,

are worth the effort speech will cost us
before whatever silence the night holds

after our song ends
clangs down around us forever.

THE HAND

Trees,
and the wind,
the moon rising out of the southwest
over the calm lagoon

like a Joseph Conrad story,
nightbirds and all that,
the traditional things of poetry
at hand.

But the pleasure of it
trickles through my hands,
the old sense of beauty
feels perverse, and slipping through
the mossy pickets of the old delight
a stench now carries on the wind.

Conrad's tropic palms here
are common firs in shadow, both
are rooted in a dark

that whispers, like beauty does,
because the things we live with every day and take for
   granted
are rooted in the degradation of this planet
and the misery of countless human beings.

In the mostly private tangle poetry has fallen to,
I want to force the appearance of these shadows
to slime the Beautiful with facts
like those of the systematic murder in the Congo
of as many as twenty-five million people
between 1890 and 1910:

facts not secondary to
nor separate from
the leisure to write poems
or even watch the moonrise on a summer's evening.

I'm thinking of the battered amber wings
of a butterfly my son rescued from a tangle of weeds
just this afternoon, proudly cupped to show me
in his two small hands.

For him if nothing else
I want to evoke these factual disturbances
in the act of thinking and writing
until what I've learned as beauty
becomes accountable to
the terrifying facts of the world

or if those facts are to be partitioned
from the concerns of Art
then Art must be recognized
and condemned
as an accomplice
in maintaining the conditions
was you and me

that make misery and violence
the dominant experience of most human lives.

I want to learn
to turn my hand against mere beauty
until such facts are a bad memory
unthinkable in the acts of living men and women.

I told my son to let the butterfly go
that it has a message to deliver
in the several days of life it has

that nothing beautiful
should be made a captive.

He smiled, then opened up his hands to let it go:
it spilled out, fell into the weeds once more
but then it flitted, it took flight. See?

I've let the butterfly exist
no longer an event of isolated poesy
removed from the twenty-five million Africans
murdered in the economic service of what was set up
    by the European powers and the u.s.
as a "free state"
under the sadistic governance of Leopold II of Belgium
who used the proceeds of the rubber trade
to buy the finest art of Europe
repatriating the Flemish Masters
and filling the museums
any number of us
have wandered through in awe.

As the shadows descend across the lagoon
the news on television shows us
footage of another war in Africa,

seems puzzled at the African's hatred
of everything we are and do.

Our best writers casually estimate the Congo death toll
between ten and forty million human beings
uninterested in a variance of thirty million lives
more interested, as poets too often are,
in catchy metaphors
about a once-dark continent on fire

as if an artful phrase explains away
the unburied bones piled up in every Congo village,
explains administrative massacres:
the documented practice
of making the Congo constabulary account for bullets used
with severed human hands,
meaning should a soldier go hunting for food
or fire his rifle at some passing phantom
say six times –

six right hands
usually of women and children
a few of whom survived to be photographed.

And now those photographs stand
alongside the beautiful reproductions
of Renoir's rosy-cheeked children
or the works of the Flemish Masters
that crowd the walls of Brussels' galleries.

And in this splendid northern new world dusk
longshoremen unload wine and fruit
from South Africa and Chile,
and in this peaceful place
the moon will peak too soon,
as if it doesn't want to crown this sky with light.

And there are whistles in the dark, too many things
so easy to believe or conjure up
or fall before in worship or in fear.

What matter that butterflies drift
across the path of the descending moon?
What songs do the nightbirds sing for us?
Do we hear what they really have to tell us?

Who captains this craft
across the nightmare beauty hides?

What should I do
with these hands?

THE CITY

How not to give in to
the magnificence of cities, shining spires
in the morning mists, wet birch trees
in quiet streets and the first traffic
at 6 A.M., lights flickering on
in kitchens, people moving softly
not to wake

The systems drift out of dream, awaken
further systems, cross
uncross, the human mind
unloved and lost within them
must not give in to, must
waken to them, once again
must find suspension outside dream
beyond this traffic

that betrays the world with cities
nothing more than motion

        This awful tension
of living in one kind of world
and imagining another (this city
changed, people coming and going
among spires, magnificence
they have sense of
and responsibility for

driving their cars or whatever else
is common practice, isn't poetry
but might amount to
decency and knowledge.

I want poetry to become more
than a system of polished images
shining dreams of wealth

not possible
to give in to
the city of

from *Tristram's Book*

25

It's been so long I can't remember why
sleeping with you was so great

I would spurn all else alert and alive
for the touch of your sleeping hand.

Brian Fawcett

Love, what was it?
It's been nearly a week.

The green crystal light
is a blue fog,

Diana Ross on the FM
sounds like another world.

Maybe I fought all those dragons for you
for nothing, maybe

it was all just heat
inside my helmet. Maybe

there were no dragons, no castles,
not even a windmill to attack. Just

women and men, men and women
and infant dreams

of purest crystal.

42

How many times I've wanted
to forget you, forget

the things you told me in the dark
sweet scents of your body,

forget the perfume that intoxicated
the hours we knew together, all

elusive and shortlived, overpowered
by the empty habits

that kept our life
from flowering. Yet

each time I've tried to forget you,
foul with ruined sleep or too much drink,

I remember wildflowers,
and the faintest rueful scent of you

blossoms in the dusty air.

43

Now you have gone
and memory fails me, turns to anger

and spreads in this dark, takes
from the world its form,

all light and colour. I know nothing
now, even pleasure is forgotten.

I am trying
to remember you

your hands, your arms
your neck, your shoulders

your breasts your stomach the hair
on your stomach, your buttocks

your labia   your thighs
your calves   your ankles the

soles of your feet
on my shoulders your

cries your whimpers your shudders your
scent your mouth your eyes your forehead your

hair your perfume your darkness
your love your

absence.

50

Enchantment that lasts a lifetime
is a wonder, turns the world
into a single blessed
excruciating obsession.

But if it lasts only two years, three
the hangover is unbearable,
the lovers turn into saints and maniacs
in tales told by old men and women
with broken bodies and bitter hearts.

So you tell me it's over,
the enchantment a memory only half pain,
the other half walks on the beach
enjoying your solitary thoughts
about how sweet it was. Nothing

to be done with the tyrant king, duty
calls to you like the braying of donkeys,
Vogue magazines lie open on the table
between phonecalls from friends and clients,
trips to the islands with new lovers.

I can't shake off the hangover,
nor the pride that demanded a life-long enchantment
when all of it

in an opaque world where magic never works for long,
drunk with smelling and touching
one another and the fabulous beasts
of an unending story

where human paradise and possibility
are a forest, a city, a drinking in

of the other

against the countless dragons
of everything else.

Paulette Jiles

WATERLOO EXPRESS

The Waterloo Express is big and important with its
glass eye, the eye of a fanatic. Sometimes they are

so important they pass you by, headed for a great
destination and bending the rails into a pure musical phrase.

Snatched loose from my baggage and address, goodbyes
   falling
away in flakes of dead skin, you'd say I was a high

pariah, sleepless and nowhere to go. Who do you think
I am? I bet you think I'm running away from home or

a man who never done me wrong. I bet you think
I'm twenty, with the fragile soul of a wild fawn.

Well, I used to think so too, but the job didn't pay much
and anyhow I never liked the taste of wages.

I like it here in the middle element where this
express is ripping up the dawn like an old ticket

whose engine is blowing the towns away
and even I am barely holding on.

There they go – a toe, a finger, my coat – honey,
you'd hardly recognize me, pared down to one white eye.

It has the cynical glint of a dynamite salesman.

THE TIN WOODSMAN

This is Hill 49, an arena for bad dreams.
The wind is flaying this ridge to the bone,
peeling up membrane after membrane
of snow from the rocks.
A prismatic ring in the sky
wears the moon like a monocle.

I wonder what it's like under
that mild counterpane
where the low degrees that signify
      NO HEAT
would agree with my metal lips and cheeks
that clang together
and betray me when I speak?

I am not a tone or note;
I harmonize nowhere.
The creaks, the shrieks of alloys upon alloys
are my joints of knees and pelvis
moving in groups
the stiff, sequential troops of rivets.
I'm held up by an armature of nerves,
for which I take pills.
Mechanics come along and tender to my ills
with oilcans and greaseguns.
My eyes are red and full of thumbs.
This is sleep falling on me; snow –
it constitutes a resolution.

And now, Dorothy, they are coming up the hill.
If, like a shotgun, I blew my brains out,
how many could we kill?
Tough luck for you, you pink thing,
all full of corpuscles and organs.

The shotgun hollers in a big balloon of sound
goodbye, goodbye.
Rusting is painless.
I will settle
in the shadow of this dry rock
and be metal.

CONVERSATION

Honey, you know when you talk like that
you're the only man I'll ever love.
Just keep talking.
That's what you're good for.
Over your voice my mind
snaps taut as a sheet in a high wind.
Here you have my history
written in the text of my left hand.

I am on my feet for another year
and the next one after that.
Just keep talking.
That's what you're good for.
I am quiet, quiet,
listening for a step at the door,
the approach of morning.

FAR AND SCATTERED ARE THE TRIBES THAT
INDUSTRIALIZATION HAS LEFT BEHIND

Things never go out the way they came in yesterday.
          Years fold up;
they collapse like promises, like balloons, infinitely
          repeatable.
Our bodies change under us, they do not want to
          lift up and go away
anymore, but sit on the ground. Our bodies are part of
          something else.
Their allegiance is elsewhere. The air they once
          contained is a gaseous
concoction, we are full of it.

And now the sand banks in. It is too early for this;
          the valleys fill up
like tanks. I wonder if this substance, crackling
          like a bad transmission,
has anything to say to me or if what I hear is
          rumour and repetition.
It is an equator we will run around again, we will never
          get off.
I don't know whether I met you last year or the year before.

The earth now seems to be a balloon. Whose string it hangs
          on I can't tell,
but I can see the beginning of its curve there on the horizon
          of the sea.
Around it satellites ring like cowbells, the core shifts,
          iron-bone ball
of the centre.

Women walk upon it in neat packages. I used to think I was
part of them, that I knew them. I used to want to package
          myself in the

same way. Now I know they are an old tribe,
       they are disappearing
one by one from the neck down. I am tired of this
       heaven of beautiful
women. It is an afterlife already here, with a god and
       everything.

I have been living for too long with a one-eyed thing
       in the shape of a
lighthouse; the lighthouse has lost its beam and
       the beam flown loose
down the coast, a bookmark between the mountains
       and a reminder.

Far and scattered are the tribes that industrialization
       has left behind.
Let us make supper together, shyly, like newly married
       savages;
let us eat it as if it were a beautiful woman.

BODY

I want to desert you;
you have been terrible to me,
disregarding me, making me jealous.
If only you could be punished
and left on a highway somewhere;
you would be so ashamed of yourself
with nowhere to go,
No one would speak to you,
no one would take you in.

PAUL REVERE

I

We are coming up the highway at
top speed, we have a message
to deliver; the message is this:

everything is out of control
cars tear past
    my mare has gone through the bit and
can't be stopped or turned
    at the top of this hill we will
meet a logging truck, it
will be a surprise, the driver
    will say O
        no
so will I. The horse says nothing,
they never do.
    I remember now,
it was to be memorized and not
    written
down in case the enemy.
You can let go now.

2

Later I can lie on a hospital bed
    and think about
things.
I have a stunning concussion.
We are small, small I tell you,
    among all these animals.
We can be thrown great distances,

we bounce when we hit.
    You stand several miles away at
the bedside and grip my hand.

We will come to this final
    parting too, it will be
similar, the same charge and wind
and fear of dying, a separation,
    the slow wheel in mid-air, maybe
we can fly after all,
    the same (O

no) impact and pain arriving
like sirens.
Afterwards we lie like a thrown rag.
I almost feel happy.
You can let go now.

WIND POWER

The power of the mind
is greater than that of a toaster, for instance,
it is not greater than the wind, or of
spruce roots which halve boulders of granite.
We have been assigned these
bodies and we live
on this planet
among the winds, and ships, office
towers, other people,
the sheet-metal voice of the frog.

Psychics sit on windy headlands
seeking power over wind, they

levitate and cast shadows
with their astral bodies. They claim
Atlantis clashed with gold and magic.

The power we have over one another is
power enough.
People are tortured in blank rooms to no purpose
(nobody wants their pointless information, their
confessions, they want the begging
and the teeth),
eyes are pierced, small
children are brained with stove-lids
in drunken fights.
This is a greater power than levitation.
Not so great as the wind, perhaps, but
it is power enough.

NIGHT FLIGHT TO ATTIWAPISKAT

We are flying directly into darkness, the
dim polestar rides on the starboard wing, Orion
and his blue gems freeze in the southwest.

Our rare and singular lives are in the hands of the
pilot; after him the radar and one engine. There were
two engines when we started out but the other one
died. We watch

the starboard propeller feather in slow, coarse
revolutions. The pilot says we will make Attiwap-
iskat or
some place.
                    Icarus, our pilot and our downfall.

Two thousand feet below dim lakes pour past as if
on their way to a laundromat. How could we have
sunk so low?
At times like this I consider life after death
as if it were a binary system, there are
no half-lives. We track cautiously down
the Milky Way, home of nebulae and Cygnus.

We are footloose in the corridors of the aurora.

The long stream of my life is flying out behind
this airplane like skywriting on the subarctic
night, fluttering, whipped with urgency. Each
episode was always cut off from the last, I used
to find myself a series of hostile strangers, startled
in doorways. Now they

gather themselves up, the wives, daughters, friends,
victims, perpetrators, the one with the pen and the
other carrying a blank mask, another at present
at the cleaners.

They catch up and slam together like
a deck of cards, packed into the present
moment. Is there a soul in there, a queen?
I draw one out; it's the ace of airplanes.
The radar repeats a fixed,

green idea. The pilot feels for the radio touch
of Thunder Bay.

At a thousand feet we make quick decisions
about our loyalties, the other engine might fail,
the suitcases of our hearts might be opened with
all that contraband, the jewels and screams, we
might have things to declare;

the observable universe is my native country
poetry is my mother tongue
the ideas I have purchased on this side of the
border don't amount to more than a hundred dollars.
What comes after this?

What do you mean, what comes after this?
This is it.
Attiwapiskat approaches, a Cree village
on a cold salt coast, flying patchwork quilts in
several more colours than are found in nature,
shining with blue-white runway lights.

We will sleep in the guesthouse tonight, that
refuge of displaced persons. The pilot will
go down and repair the valve and say nothing happened.
(We flew into darkness at the rim of the world,
where distant lights broke through and something
failed us. Then at the edge when we were stamped
and ready to go through we were turned back.) We
can unload and forget it. But I will remember
and then go back and forget again.
This is Attiwapiskat, everything is as it should be.
We slide down to the airstrip through salt fogs
from Hudson Bay that slip through the night like
airborne bedsheets.
We get off, still life with sleeping bags.
Approaching us is an earthman,
speaking Cree.

WINTER NIGHT ON THE RIVER

The cabin is dipped in darkness, tie-dyed.
Only the red from the woodstove grate and reflections

on tin plates escape. Sirius picks at the window. Diapers
   wave
at half-mast, desperately clean. The children watch

the insides of their eyes. Things will be revealed in dreams
to them, economy-sized revelations, tiny ideas.

The body shuts down. Hot pine ticks in the stove.
We sleep because we have to dream, as when

we are awake we must speak. Speech and dreams;
behind the banner of these old imperatives we

have marched for two million years, to what
(unspeakable) end? On the banks of the Severn

River and the subarctic night; and now one of the
children calls out sharply, ambushed by dreams.

FOURTH DIMENSION

There is another world, close to here
where people do not stand on the edges.
They live in the middle. Every morning birds with
rust-coloured wings untuck and shake off
   the stars that have grown on them. The sun

rises holding screens of pine
in front and the water stirs;
    once: twice.

Everything takes a deep breath.
This is before the bread is baked.
    No one hopes for anything,
these people are ghosts of what went on
before. They have lived through some
blast and were burnt away, they are
without fingerprints, they are like dough.

    They bake themselves brown every morning,
and the sun floats at noon over the single
    street, crisping the tops of their hair.
Only in the night with the rhythmic bark of
a dog does their news reach us,
their smiles, their press releases. That life is
without hope of any kind, that life is
    one day after another, always the same day.
    Expect nothing,
not even the sun.

Robert Kroetsch

STONE HAMMER POEM

1

This stone
become a hammer
of stone, this maul

is the colour
of bone (no,
bone is the colour
of this stone maul).

The rawhide loops
are gone, the
hand is gone, the
buffalo's skull
is gone;

the stone is
shaped like the skull
of a child.

2

This paperweight on my desk

where I begin
this poem   was

found in a wheatfield
lost (this hammer,
this poem).

Cut to a function,
this stone was
(the hand is   gone –

    3

Grey, two-headed,
the pemmican maul

fell from the travois or
a boy playing   lost it in
the prairie wool or
a squaw   left it in
the brain of a buffalo or

It is a million
years older than
the hand that
chipped stone or
raised slough
water (or blood) or

    4

This stone maul
was found.

In the field
my grandfather
thought
was his

my father
thought was his

5

It is a stone
old as the last
Ice Age, the
retreating/the
recreating ice,
the retreating
buffalo, the
retreating Indians

(the saskatoons bloom
white (infrequently
the chokecherries the
highbush cranberries the
pincherries bloom
white along the barbed
wire fence (the
pemmican   winter

6

This stone maul
stopped a plow
long enough for one
Gott im Himmel.

The Blackfoot (the
Cree?) not

finding the maul
cursed.

?did he curse
?did he try to
go back
?what happened

I have to/I want
to know (not know)
?WHAT HAPPENED

7

The poem
is the stone
chipped and hammered
until it is shaped
like the stone
hammer, the maul.

8

Now the field is
mine because
I gave it
(for a price)

to a young man
(with a growing son)
who did not

notice that the land
did not belong

to the Indian who
gave it to the Queen
(for a price) who
gave it to the CPR
(for a price) which
gave it to my grandfather
(for a price) who .
gave it to my father
(50 bucks an acre
Gott im Himmel I cut

down all the trees I
picked up all the stones) who

gave it to his son
(who sold it)

9

This won't
surprise you.

My grandfather
lost the stone maul.

10

My father (retired)
grew raspberries.
He dug in his potato patch.
He drank one glass of wine
each morning.
He was lonesome
for death.

He was lonesome for the
hot wind on his face, the smell
of horses, the distant
hum of a threshing machine,
the oilcan he carried, the weight
of a crescent wrench in his hind pocket.

He was lonesome for his absent
son and his daughters,
for his wife, for his own
brothers and sisters and
his own mother and father.

He found the stone maul
on a rockpile in the
north-west corner of what
he thought of
as his wheatfield.

He kept it (the
stone maul) on the railing
of the back porch in
a raspberry basket.

II

I keep it
on my desk
(the stone).

Sometimes I use it
in the (hot) wind
(to hold down paper)

smelling a little of cut
grass or maybe even of
ripening wheat or of
buffalo blood hot
in the dying sun.

Sometimes I write
my poems for that

stone hammer.

Robert Kroetsch

HOW I JOINED THE SEAL HERD

I swear it was not   the hearing
itself   I first refused
it was   the sight of my ears

in the mirror: the sight
of my ears   was the first
clue: my head did not please me

the seals so loud   I could hardly
accept the message: she wanted
no other going/than to be gone   the

neat bed itself   strange in the
mirror, she   kneeling across the bed
to close the window: maybe

I have this wrong: but only then
I saw   my ears/the difference
she wanted to go   I heard

a loud snort   a throaty grunt:
it was the breeding season   the tide
low, the wind still: they'd be wary

I knew, the seals   lying together
in the hot sun   maybe 300 seals
I counted   slipping off my shoes

the effect was immediate   I learned
to let my body give   it was not I
who controlled the rocks   I learned

curling my stockinged toes   to the
granite cracks and edges: maybe
I have this wrong   but I knew

in the first instant   of my courage
I must undo my very standing/crawl
on the wet rocks, the sand   not

standing   ease down on my belly:
it was strange at first   looking up
at the world: but I arched my back

I turned my head and paused   what
was I doing there on the beach/   wait
the luminous eyes of a young   seal cow:

I, the lone bull seal   bravely
guarding the rookery   alone
holding together a going world/   but

frankly, I wanted to get laid   she was
maybe five feet tall (long)   the cow:
I could see   she didn't like my clothes/

moving carefully   avoiding any fuss
I unbuttoned, I unzipped   squirmed
out of my shorts, my socks   it was, yes

quite frankly   love at first sight/
flicking, with my left hand   some sand
over my back   for an instant

I thought of my wallet   my driver's
license, my credit cards: she had dark
fur on her belly   a delicate nose:

she went towards the water   looking
back over her shoulder/   the water
looking iceberg cold   I wasn't quite ready

she was rushing me: men in their forties
I shouted after her   are awfully good
in bed (on a sandbank   I corrected myself)

alone   I lay in the sand, I lay
watching   the slow coming of each wave
to the merciful shore   I humped

down to the water's curl   I, yes
without thinking,   *without thinking,* I
dove   my ears shrank

back   to my badly designed skull: under
the water: opening my eyes   I saw
the school of herring   SNAP

I had one in my teeth   I surfaced
hungry   I let myself float head up
on the lifting waves   I hauled out

I lolled: the cow that nudged me
awake: she might have been just plain
curious   my ear-flaps, my exterior testicles/

that crossed my mind   or slightly perverse
but the sun had warmed me again   we were both
well   I was still a man, I had to talk:

my nights are all bloody   I whispered
god, I am lonely   as a lover/my
naked body swims   in the leak of light

death has a breath too   it smells
of bedclothes   it smells of locked
windows   my nights are all drenched/

my body/I   saw she had no idea
well/that was nicer, even   than the
moist hunger   in her eyes

I brushed   at my grey beard/
my flipper   trying to make the hairs
look like   vibrissae (I believe is the word)

I wasn't quite ready when   the bull hit me
I whirled   caught his neck
in my teeth   roared at the sonofabitch

slammed my head   against his nose:
he was gone/   the cow had noticed
everything   I could tell/she would

dance now/first   dance, slapping
the rising tide   to a quick froth:
she/I   rolling the waves themselves

back to the sea   I dared beyond the
last limit   of whatever I thought
I was   where, exactly, I asked, is –

my only question   and when she gave
herself/took   me out of the seen land
this, for the gone world   I sang:

America was a good lay   she nearly
fucked me to death, wow   but this
I'm a new man   (mammal, I corrected

myself) here   and yet I was going
too far   too far past everything
dispersed past   everything here/gone

dear, I whispered   (words again,
words)   I wanted to say/I am
writing   this poem   with my life

I whispered,   I hope (the rising
tide had lifted my socks   had swum
them to where   I might reach)

dear, I whispered   I hope my children
(ours, I corrected myself)   their ears perfect
will look   exactly like both of us.

SKETCHES OF A LEMON

I

A lemon is almost round
some lemons are almost round.
A lemon is not round.

So much for that.

How can one argue that a lemon
is truly a lemon,
if the question can be argued?

So much for that.

I said to Smaro
(I was working on this poem),
Smaro, I called, is there
(she was in the kitchen)
a lemon in the fridge?
No, she said.

So much for that.

2

As my father used to say,
well I'll be cow-kicked
by a mule.

He was especially fond of
lemon meringue pie.

3

I went and looked at Francis Ponge's poem
on blackberries. If blackberries can be
blackberries, I reasoned, by a kind of analogy,
lemons can, I suppose, be lemons.

Such was not the case.

4

Sketches, I reminded myself,
not of a pear,
nor of an apple,
nor of a peach,
nor of a banana

(though the colour
raises questions),
nor of a nectarine,
nor, for that matter,
of a pomegranate,
nor of three cherries,
their stems joined,
nor of a plum,
nor of an apricot,
nor of the usual
bunch of grapes,
fresh from the vine,
just harvested,
glistening with dew –

Smaro, I called,
I'm hungry.

5

What about oranges?
At least an orange
looks like an orange.
In fact, most oranges
bear a remarkable resemblance
to oranges.

6

Smaro is rolling a lemon on the breadboard.
The breadboard, flat, horizontal, is motionless.
The lemon rolls back and forth on the motionless
surface.
Smaro's hand moves horizontally, back and forth,
over the rolling lemon.

One could draw a diagram of the three related objects,
deduce therefrom a number of mechanical principles.

7

I had a very strong desire
to kiss a lemon.
No one was watching.
I kissed a lemon.

So much for that.

8

I bought a second-hand car –
Okay, okay.

9

If someone asked me,
how is a lemon shaped?

            (the salmon
            (the oven
            (the lemon

I'd say, a lemon is shaped
exactly like an hour.

(Now we're getting somewhere.)

10

The lemon cure.
In each glass

mix: 1 stick cinnamon
         1 teaspoon honey
         2 cloves
         2 jiggers rum
         half slice lemon
         hot water to taste

Repeat as necessary.

11

poem for a child who has just bit into
a halved lemon that has just been squeezed:

see, what did I tell you, see,
what did I tell you, see, what
did I tell you, see, what did
I tell you, see, what did I
tell you, see, what did I tell
you, see, what did I tell you,
see, what did I tell you, see,
what did I tell you, see, what
did I tell you, see, what did
I tell you, see, what did I
tell you, see, what did I tell
you, see, what did I tell you

One could, of course, go on.

12

This hour is shaped like
a lemon.　　　We taste its light

on the baked salmon.
The tree itself is elsewhere.

We make faces, liking the
sour surprise. Our teeth melt.

Don McKay

ALIAS ROCK DOVE, ALIAS HOLY GHOST

How come you don't see more dead pigeons?
Because when they die their bodies turn to lost gloves
and get swept up by the city sweepers. Even so
their soft inconsequence can sabotage a jumbo jet
the way a flock of empty details
devastates a marriage.

Someone down the hall is working on an epic cough.
Another makes it to the bathroom
yet again, groping past my door. All night
the senile plumbing interviews itself: some war or other.
The faint sweet smell of must.

Along the ledges of the parking garage they flutter
wanly as the grey blue residue of nightmares.
Softness of bruises, of sponges
sopping up exhaust.

City poets try to read their tracks along the windowsill
    for some
announcement. Such as our concrete palaces
have the consistency of cake. Such as
Metropolis of Crumbs. Such as
Save us, Christ, the poor sons of bitches.

THE GREAT BLUE HERON

What I remember
about the Great Blue Heron that rose
like its name over the marsh
is touching and holding that small
manyveined
wrist
upon the gunwale, to signal silently –

                                    look

The Great Blue Heron
(the birdboned wrist).

A BARBED WIRE FENCE MEDITATES UPON THE GOLDFINCH

More than the shortest distance
between points, we are
the Stradivarius of work.
We make the meadow meadow, make it
mean, make it yours, but till the last
insurance policy is cashed in we will
never be immune to this
exquisite cruelty:
                    that the knots in all our posts remember limbs
they nested and were busy in and danced *per-*
chic-o-ree their loops between,
that the fury of their playfulness persists
in amputated roots.
Remember us
next time the little yellow bastards lilt
across your windshield. No one
no one is above the law.

Don McKay

ADAGIO FOR A FALLEN SPARROW

In the bleak midwinter
frosty wind made moan
earth was hard as iron
water like a stone

Sparrows burning
                bright bright bright against the wind
resemble this item, this frozen
lump on the floor of my garage, as fire
resembles ash:
              not much.
A body to dispose of,
probably one I've fed all winter, now
a sort of weightless fact,
an effortless repudiation of the whole shebang.
I'd like to toss it in the garbage can but can't let go
so easily. I'd bury it
but ground is steel
and hard to find. Cremation?
Much too big a deal, too rich and bardic
too much like an ode. Why not simply splurge
and get it stuffed, perch it proudly on the shelf
with Keats and Shelley and *The Birds of Canada*?

But when at last
I bury it beneath three feet of snow
there is nothing to be said.
It's very cold.
The air
has turned its edge
against us.
My bones
are an antenna picking up
arthritis, wordless keening of the dead.

So, sparrow, before drifting snow
reclaims this place for placelessness, I mark your grave
with four sticks broken from the walnut tree:

one for your fierce heart

one for your bright eye

one for the shit you shat upon my windshield
while exercising squatters' rights in my garage

and one to tell the turkey vultures where your thawing
   body lies
when they return next spring to gather you
into the circling ferment of themselves.

And my last wish: that they do
before the cat discovers you and eats you, throwing up,
as usual, beside the wicker basket in the upstairs hall.

FIELD MARKS (2):

Distinguished from the twerp,
which he resembles, by his off-speed
concentration: *shh:*
                    bursting with sneakiness
he will tiptoe through our early morning drowse
like the villain in an old cartoon, pick up
binoculars, bird book, dog,
orange, letting the fridge lips close behind him with a kiss.
Everything,
even the station-wagon, will be
delicate with dew –
bindweed, spiderweb, sumac,

Don McKay

Queen Anne's lace: he slides
among them as a wish, attempting to become
a dog's nose of receptiveness.

Later on he'll come back as the well-known bore
and read his list (Song sparrows: 5
                  Brown thrashers: 2
                  Black-throated green warblers: 1)   omitting
all the secret data hatching on the far side of his mind:

        that birds have sinuses throughout their bodies,
        and that their bones are flutes
        that soaring turkey vultures can detect
                    depression and careless driving
        that every feather is a pen, but living,

        flying

TO SING AND FEED

among the spruce: Bach
would put this evening on the cello
and chew it.
You would feel the long strokes
bite and sweep, everything
curve away, arching back
against the bow.
You would know the end before the end
would understand the Red-winged blackbirds calling
konkeree konkeree the sexual
buzz the silver
falling whistle hanging from the top spines of the spruce

like tinsel.
You would dwell in imminence.
You would arrive home empty

covered with burrs

ready

TAKING YOUR BABY TO THE JUNIOR HOCKEY GAME

Watch for it to happen out there on the ice:
this music they fight for.
You can feel her beside you as though poised in front of
                                                    a net
circling
circling.

Christ, you'll say,
baby if you were a forty-three-year-old Montreal potato
    merchant
I'd be your five-iron.
I would never dissolve, in the middle of a rush, passes
coming snap snap crossing the blue line barely on-side, never
dissolve into adolescence fumbling
for control.
I would cleave
I would be your hawk
I would be silence.
Forests.
And baby, you'll say, if you conducted the Bach Society
            Choir in town

Don McKay

I'd be a dentist's wife
straining among sturdy contraltos after your unheard
    perfection
longing with them to devour your wrists, your boyish wit.
I would finish your every mad flight through the defence
with deft flicks to the lower-left and upper-right-hand
    corners,
inevitable, the momentary angel,
your right wing.

I SCREAM YOU SCREAM

Waking JESUS sudden riding a scream like a
train braking metal on metal on
metal teeth receiving signals from a dying star sparking
off involuntarily in terror in all directions in the
abstract incognito in my
maidenform bra in an expanding universe in a where's
my syntax thrashing
loose like a grab that like a
look out like a
live wire in a hurricane until

until I finally tie it down:
it is a pig scream
a pig scream from the farm across the road
that tears this throat of noise into the otherwise anonymous
    dark,
a noise not oink or grunt
but a passage blasted through constricted pipes, perhaps
a preview of the pig's last noise.

Don McKay

Gathering again toward sleep I sense
earth's claim on the pig.
Pig grew, polyped out of the earth like a boil
and broke away.
            But earth
heals all flesh back beginning with her pig,
filling his throat with silt and sending
subtle fingers for him like the meshing fibres in a wound
like roots
like grass growing on a grave like a snooze
in the sun like furlined boots that seize
the feet like his *nostalgie de la boue* like
having another glass of booze like a necktie like a
velvet noose like a nurse

like sleep.

NOTES TOWARD A MAJOR STUDY OF THE NOSE

First, introduce some animal,
your own dog for instance, and describe its
"sense of smell" pointing out the brute
inhales whole Mahler symphonies.
Contrast yourself. Explain how ancient humans
nearly lost their noses with their tails
from sheer neglect, how face campaigned
to have them designated edifices
of aesthetic and historical significance.
Establishing the basic terms, the septum
architrave, chiasmus, intercostal
vaulting, and the styles evolved
by race and class, proceed

to demonstrate the role of blowing nose
in the histories of music and the martial arts. Then,
a detailed study of the nose-for-nose-sake movement,
    separate
chapters on De Bergerac, Disraeli, Parker
and De Gaulle.
                    And all this
but preamble to the major phase:
your discourse on nasality itself.
Emphasize the key
polarities of thrust and introversion,
arrogance and sniffling.
Dramatize them with the myth
of Mentholatum and the Fair Vibrissa, drawing out
the themes of metamorphosis and psychosexual
intrigue.
Consider how her shrine,
seen from the south, presents
twin portals in a simple rounded arch
where fair vibrissae, nearly
invisible, nearly
resistless, comb the air as seaweed sadly
fingering the tide. (Idea: print this doubly as
remorseless mirrors,
rectos reflecting versos and vice versa.)
Pause.

Now to remove
the training-wheels of logic while you warn the reader,
gently, of the treacheries to come.
Of head's deep coils and echoes utter
nothing. Let the rumours
murmur in the writing as a rumble
gathers in a mosque or in the marbled
washrooms of Toronto's Union Station.
Recollect that Boom Boom
Geoffrion would stay behind to practise

hours on the little rink, creating thunder while the
twilight crispens and the membranes
meditate like monkish
worms, the very air
is crawling with the past, curls and
recoils seductively as celtic script or hair in shampoo ads
    you've
lingered over somewhat longer than
was necessary, and from which

it will be hard to extricate yourselves.
If nothing else undoes the spell, a brisk snort
will create a localized tornado that should
blow you back to Kansas, Dorothy and Toto
in reverse.
                    Of course
you should conclude with thoughts on eschatology.
Why not ask,
bluntly, if a skeleton
is nosed?
Let this sink in for an empty paragraph.
The Archduke was, it seems,
a temporary tent across a manhole, into which
the reader stares
appalled. At this point, casually
vanish. This will be tasteless,
odourless, and quite without the echoes
of enchantment.
                    Unlike ordinary scholarship,
this work will impoverish the understanding,
performing for us all the satisfying, sharp
katharsis of a sneeze.

Don McKay

VICKY

For centuries we've been sitting in the sand, your words
are blubbing as a one-holed can
of juice.

Your thoughts
are blotches in the air, useless placentae.
The landscape is as smeared, daubed as the walls
of a cave.

Vicky, you've lived in that squirrel skull nine years eating
and excreting your own mind –

    your ripped red dress your clairol mother oh
    Henry bar father your unmade bed a dish falling
    off a ripped red grin your unmade mother oh
    Henry bar bed your falling off father his ripped
    red dish her clairol bed your falling off grin his
    unmade dish her oh Henry dress your clairol
    falling off unmade oh Henry ripped red –

             purée
you return to with such multiplied disgust.

No wonder you take a vacation.
No wonder you detach – beautiful, a White-throated
 sparrow –
from your bunched self in the sand.
I sit holding your body, your bad dreams until you come
 back for them
while your pain slinks away to its own unknown arroyos.

HOAR FROST

Who says the dead have no imagination?
The outdoors
holds its pose. In roles
of this and that appear
their ghosts, furred and still
as harp seal pups in photographs.

Breath grows mossy, visible
cliché. My car
also wishes it were dead, repeats
were dead, were dead
before it kicks and runs.

By ten they are slipping
softly off their wires and branches,
tender panties dropped
for no one in particular.

May my last words be so apt,
so accidental.

TERRITORIALITY

So he built her a prick of steel
                    The Airman's Song

        I

Along the creek bank and among the scrub
by railway cuts and in the marshlands moistening with spring
they are sewing their imagined patterns
vertex to vertex perching on the spruce tips

and the frayed cigars of last year's cattails
singing konkeree konkeree
flashing epaulets of red with yellow fringes
hunching forward
signalling the outlines of their small and shifting kingdoms
to the others who are signalling
the outlines of their small and shifting kingdoms back.

And if we imagine the creek bank as a living map
each kingdom is a pulse, shrinking and expanding
in concert with its neighbours as their patterns intersect
and overlap, a jigsaw puzzle
with each piece beating like a heart.

And if we listened for an evening we would learn to hear
        konkeree   konkeree
the liquid whistles breaking into buzz
like new life catching hold, brave against the wind
as Louis Armstrong's trumpet, rich with chance
and with the thought of females flying north
not black not red of wing but
soft mottled browns surround the song
as eggs surround their yolks along
the creek bank and among the scrub
by railway cuts and in the marshlands moistening with
   spring.

2

With others it is different.
They dig inverted silos in their land
and stock them with extinction, sheathed
hair-triggered negative
erections, aimed at their enemies who dig
inverted silos in their land

and stock them with extinction, sheathed
hair-triggered negative
erections, aimed at their enemies who dig –

       nobody
       backs down.
       All crave release
       which is unthinkable.

Their music is the locker room and mess hall song
about the airman with the wife he couldn't satisfy
the prick of steel he built for her
the sexual machine he couldn't stop
the mutilation of the wife.
But it is not a sad song and they sing it with gusto
laughing hard and smashing their glasses.

   3

Suppose we induce schizophrenia in mother,
carefully of course, and run
her suicidal frenzy through a dynamo:
       this generates sufficient energy
       to move Manhattan Island to the Caribbean.

Or suppose we find the secret
sacred place where each thing speaks itself
then split that word:
       the shriek
       will flatten Leningrad (formerly
       St. Petersburg)
       four times.

Lastly, consider all the waste
kinetic energy of pain. Suppose
we channel all its currents –

forepangs, fibrillations, Beethoven rages, grey
weights and lustful tongues, its
eddies, arcs, *accelerandos* – all
through an enormous generator
to be situated in the region of ground zero:
>   this will function as the afterburner of ourselves
>   a billion-watt flashbulb photographing nothing
>   but registered as a definite
>   twitch, a quick wink in the long doze of the gods.

Erin Mouré

CARDIAC GRIZZLIES

At Banff this summer, the river lunged steeply at us,
ungainly beings picking our bodies across the rocks,
balanced incredibly on the cliff above.
Or alone
the three of us hulked over coffee in the Praha
working our way thru the mood
of each other, the speeches.

Sooner or later the rain falls out of its cupboards
& cries.
Ratty wet sparrows in their summer clothes
pick the earth up in their beaks;
when they shake it out
their heads tremble wildy among the cars.
We sit on the furniture in the rented rooms, three
cardiac grizzlies with our huge heads,
the hair painstakingly combed,
the human   well-learned, tho
our talk sounds like leaves that talk
to leaves, on the dark side of the tree.

Our own wildness by the river, outpouring our own
    banks too,
the feeling of this tangled getting-together
twice a year, not enough
by a long shot but

better than staying alone, in the rough den of our cardiac
    lives
on two sides of the Rockies.
It's us,   the crazy silent pawing ones, the ones
that crash thru underbrush to keep myths alive,   capable of
finding each other when we need to,
in uncertain territory.
Capable of sustenance & love

LENORE

Here is the woman hurt all her life
by money, walking away
from it walking away from her, leaving the children behind
with her in the house she bought from Rose
in 1958,
how she took in ironing 8 hours a day & fought
for the pay from that.
Next week, next week, was all she heard.
She pegs the air with her cigarette & tells of
borrowing 5 dollars from Mike at the Legion
just to feed her girls.
& the house not paid off yet, 22 years later.
Still she thinks everyone has money but her.
Rose has money, Bob has money, this & that one
fade into the haze of happy strangers,
alive with money, she thinks.

She sees her future self in her mother at Edson,
75 years old & still cleaning hotel-rooms,
getting up at 4am to heat water
for her laundry,

wondering "Is it clean?"
This is Lenore with no money, the future eaten out of her
& the past aching,
a woman once *so elegant*
tethered to house payments & the girls, now grown,
& the aunts who accused her of drinking.

Today her friends anger her; the toughness she's made of
breaks down slowly, & she cries about
money & Rose & her washed-out loneliness
unconquered in more than 20 years, even by the men she
   held
to relieve the quiet urge of her body.
Never thinking of the love she'd need,
never dreaming this far forward,
to her daughters gone from her unpaid dwelling,
to this Legion & the breakdown of caring;
where her fears gentle her & she drinks her Scotch,
lost with us in the cold
heart of her family.

HAPPINESS

Happiness
isn't my strong suit.
As the afternoon climbs past each of us, separate,
like a grey
beetle on the rusty porch, I watch
my brother playing with the rain, younger than me & not
   listening,
cutting his boots thru the wide
rails of water.
In the back rooms or hallway

Erin Mouré

my mother is calling; the storm is passing
by her at great speed.

She is finished vacuuming or she wants to lie down -
She wants to be a heroine in the afternoon
movie, or
to think about the cardiac therapy -

My brother is not listening, he is turning
the seam of wet lawn into a blanket,
a hairpiece, pegged trousers.
Could it be this one
that my mother calls?

Or is it me, from my place on the low verandah, listening;
when she calls again
I know she wants to lie down, she wants me
to enter the hallway &
lift her sore feet upon the pillows
in her room among the papers, musty closet, my father's
    clothes;
so she can ask me
not to be lonely; &
to call my brother, bring him in,
& we watch him then from the window, separate or alive,
    gazing out
as he carries
the finery of the rain, muddy, exalted,
his heart-beat skipped, not hearing
anyone

TRICKS

for Trix, a dog

This is a life in which
a case of whisky is one drink.
In it, a dog goes totally blind & no one knows
if it remembers its young doghood,
the smell of wild mountains carried in storm
from the high passes.

I feel I am in the world & there is no god in it with me.
These days my husband gets up & sits
on the edge of our bed & says
a case of whisky is one drink.
He says there are glasses as big as women filled with rye &
    he wants
to marry one.
This is what I listen to, no wonder
I can't sleep.
Faintly
I hear the heart-tick of my old dog in Calgary, 800 miles
    away.
She sleeps on the porch, & shies away when the footsteps
come, crying gently.
When there are no footfalls, she rests & waits to die.

I want to leave my husband & let him marry
all the bottles in Vancouver,
while I go to Calgary to sit beside the blind dog of the
    family,
her eyes muddy with cataract,
& tell her of her old/young doghood, of hikes to the ice-
    caves
with a black pup in '71, who was herself
splay-legged on the fireroad.
I want to tell her she is a dog who loved the mountains,

& she should be proud even in blindness
that she saw them & climbed their hard trails,
& camped there with the humans
like a god.
Now she is only afraid, of being stepped on.
She knows our voices, even mine that she hears so seldom.
She speaks back in her small voice
& snuffles nearer.
I wish she would remember & be proud, but she lives
only the present in her dogged blind way,
fighting the back stairs.

Without her memories I am alone in the world, the god gone
    out of it.
My husband murmurs over, *the root is still there,*
in the whole world there is only whisky for one drink.
No wonder I can't sleep.
No wonder to look at the world is to go blind in it

TONIGHT MY BODY

Tonight my body
won't come home to me, it won't
hug me at all
It huddles naked three blocks away,
on the roof of the stone Chinese church
by a belltower
How its lungs howl out its anger,
its heart fizzes in the dark
rain!

Tonight I am faithless & wayward, I am
my cousin & my aunt
sitting on the shoulders of my body three blocks away,

both of them howling
fit to burst my ears, & me stupefied & cold.
My insides are smeared with warm sperm,
don't talk to me!
Tonight it's my body, I'm stuck with it, don't
talk to me, I'm finally out of the woods
& off the ferry-slip

over the Lion's Gate &
into Vancouver,
my skin lonely as a sail,
I've climbed up the wall of the Chinese church
& left my body angry there
When I cringe
it shudders three blocks away, I can't
comfort it, or coax it out
from under its relatives, to come nearer
to home,
& hear me, who cries for it -

WHITE RABBIT

From the third storey window, you hung
your rabbit from a long chain.
He's there tonight, quiet & strangled,
bobbing a few feet off the lawn.
His fur shows
which way the wind is blowing, or
which way I am driving, up the roadway
of gravel & weeds, if I could drive/

Instead I am standing three weeks from now
below your window, in the empty lot
where they tore down the house beside yours

last week, I guess.
Don't ask me where the neighbours went,
or if they saw the rabbit hanging
& left, because of it.
I don't know, & you
have three weeks to figure it/

Stop saying you let him down to feed him & there wasn't
enough chain!
Your story doesn't wash & I'm sick of it.
For three weeks your rabbit has been hanging from that
   window
without saying a word, or even touching grass,
let alone eating it.

I'm going away myself
in a few minutes, never mind where.
Three weeks from now you'll see me turn
from your window & walk off across the darkened lot,
I probably don't even have busfare.
You can watch me as long as you like.
It doesn't matter.
Even when I don't see your window, I see
the blasted rabbit, his face is dry & black
& he's started singing a bit, some silly tune/

FUSILLADE

You who claim to pretend nothing
in your neediness.
Your ruse only works for awhile, then ends.
To pretend the heart
a palpable organ, for donation or transplant:
for months, when we walked or drank beer as friends,

or spoke of the fine glow of oranges,
took baths in sunlight, coffee, soft brown bread

I wore your heart in my chest
stubbornly,
pumped my own blood thru it into the air,
my chest delicate, touchy, angered
by the least sentiment.
My chest ate & ate to keep your heart alive,
the famished convert.

The heart is yours, I'll shovel it out of me.
I'd rather depend on my own.
You can't climb in & out of my chest, like a cupboard.
To you, a bowl of saliva!
A lettuce with flames!
No more!

Your heart is not Shakespeare.
I've thrown it out of me.
It's not a grenade!

CERTAIN WORDS, A GARDEN

I am a terrorist in my life,
each morning arrives again to me
holding the accident of birth, a blanket, my mother's
deep sighing.
To get up, cherished, & not cry out to anything,
neither wet doors, the shorn corridor,
odour of cabbages caught against the stair.
Refusing to trust in the talk
of pistols, its grimness deafens a whole garden,
breeds sentinels on the roofs of buildings, feigned

relaxation, dedication, fear.
Instead to dress quietly in the old coat & my usual
   shoulders,
empty of ancestors,
rejecting the innocence of age, the white step
of the fou with his crumpled ass
& nightgown.

After all night throwing knives against
the kitchen table,
against the lampshade that spoke your name,
you catch yourself, ticking, certain words.
You touch the holy palms
brought by your accidental brothers, given to you,
hold them free of the
ceremonies.
In the morning, now, the neighbours
hear you laughing

because the law is a gone story
awaiting apprehension, because it is not enough
to sell your furniture;
your life alone has reached you, captive, stubborn:
in its arms at last
your terror rises
with red wings & a lonely heartbeat, & your voice
opens up a whole garden

PARADISICAL VALLEJO

He died of the war before it came,
his eye too hurt by pardons,
the talk of armed men brave before dying

Sometimes I am only a small wound,
a small hole in the skull
thru which brilliant light leaks,
a flaw betraying paradise.
The paradise in me that I mistake for loneliness
& tramp around it, hunched over like bears.
For spite!

What gamble he played, his hair combed freely
to the point of a flame,
his boots studded with worship,
he stood in the noise of red earth furrowed
until he died of growing

He was a poet that paradise leaked thru,
that shone thru his skull's plate
before I was born,
before any Franco, any penalties, or cure

& paradise leaked out of both of us
in the boom of a million guns, in sonar, in
blips or ack-ack, in tin mines, in Cruise
& won't come back ever.
Yet waits in us like bears
so faithful: his photograph bowed at the road-side,
this hard poem

Susan Musgrave

FISHING ON A SNOWY EVENING

How close you come
to being alone.
How close you come
to needing no one.

River is silent, silver
over stone. You are a link
between air and water.

You are alive.
You cast your line out
into the cool shallows;
river rises into shadow
secret and heavy.

A fish jumps.
River ripples and bends –
how close you come
to your own reflection.
Your body surfaces and breaks –
how close you come
to perfection.

Snow falls from the cold
sky, snow covers your closed
eyes. It drifts into your
deep tracks, over the way you
came, over the way back.

How close you come
to innocence at this moment,
how close you come to emptiness.

Snow falls down
out of the cold sky.
It fills your narrowing hours.

NIGHT AND FOG

These are the black woods,
my first asylum. Down at the
river's edge, in my own way
given to the monstrous.

Voices I called to
out of the blind fog
drew me that way.
Into the wet woods
calling them: they do not
answer and I am
possessed again.

> *Stay with me – you who are*
> *other to all*
> *I am – you whose darkness is the*
> *shadow of my birth.*

I could not escape it –
they were everything.
Moss grew over their
faces, seaweed was
their hair. Theirs

was the way the
wet sounds as
everything condenses.
Theirs were the still fires,
the moon's frail worth.

> *Stay beside me – you I have*
> *returned to*
> *more times ever than*
> *anyone; you I have returned to*
> *other than anyone,*
> *other to myself.*

I shiver. It edges
the unfamiliar; it
lessens me. Dark with the secret
I am hunted under,
theirs are the wounds
beneath the scars.

Voices out of the night
and the fog, voices of the womb
conceiving me. I believe in
creation, in flesh that binds
and is mine without knowledge.

I have forgotten more: I have
lost more than remembrance.
While I slept the voices were
dying – they are dead now and
do not answer.

> *Stay with me. I need your*
> *comfort now. One wish is that*
> *you would return and*
> *all would be warm again.*

Stay with me. Out on the
trailing edges of darkness
I scatter their last bones before me
to my will.

RIGHT THROUGH THE HEART

and out the other side,
pumping like a bitch in heat,
beast with two backs, the
left and right ventricles.

It has to be love
when it goes straight through;
no bone can stop it,
no barb impede its journey.

When it happens you have to bleed,
you want to kiss and hold on

despite all the messy blood
you want to embrace it.

You want it to last forever,
you want to own it.
You want to take love's tiny life
in your hands

and crush it to death before it dies.

BOOGEYING WITH THE QUEEN

down along the old canal
wearing an ankle-length overcoat
in spite of the heat

sucking sweets By Appointment
To Her Majesty –
the old girl got a good kick
out of that one.

You should have seen her
doing a gang-scuffle outside the
dancehall

or perfuming her body in one of the
lavatories:

she was perfect.

She dressed for the occasion,
a crowbar up her skirt and a
quantity of quicklime.
Hard luck to the whore found dead
in a weedbed

she was queen of the quick throw,
queen of alley ways.

She was beautiful and we
loved her

pock-marked with a pistol
she danced naked over our faces

queen of the underground

it felt good, good, good
to be lying beneath her.

They all loved her,
the tarts and muggers on the
commercial road.
She had a full heart for a
hatchet-man, a kiss for a killer.

You should have seen her
teetering on spikes

a grudge-bearing scullion she was
obvious royalty.

When she danced we came alive,
when she danced she was really living.

There was no dance she couldn't do,
hard and fast in a small lifetime.

I TOOK A WIRE CAGE INTO THE WOODS

I took a wire cage into the woods
in which to sit and watch the animals.
They gathered round me as I'd hoped they would
and sat, expressionless, with closed eyes,
warming themselves in the sun.

Their bodies were beautiful, unlike mine;
their bodies were solitary, never lonely.
They must have sat for hours in one place
as if to reassure me all was understood.

Their patience was exhausting. All night
I watched till dark and light were
blotted out and whole seasons passed.
I did not leave that cage again but lay
under the cool influence of the stars,
awake and dreaming.

My dreams were always the same.
Always in my own image those animals rose
out of the dust, animals with human faces
whose eyes were open, sorrowful.

Their bodies were broken.
No longer content to sit and stare
at one such as this, confined by choice
within the shadows of a spectral cage,
they paced as those condemned, and wept,
while I, the guilty one, was saved.

"EXILE IS IN OUR TIME LIKE BLOOD"

You are beautiful: it hurts me.
All knowledge of you is pain
and after that knowledge is nothing.

I know you.
You take me and I change.
I break from your body
make with our lonely bodies one flesh, love,
and that enough alone.

I fill up my days with you
my nights are filled up.

Something I am grows emptier
something I am holds on and will not let go.

Time passes, only just.
You are more and more beautiful: it hurts.
Each time I reach for you something is lost;
something is born again
over and over.

MY BOOTS DRIVE OFF IN A CADILLAC

Always when I am dreaming
my boots, with my socks inside them,
drive off in a Cadillac
and I have to go barefoot
looking for nightlife.

The car has California plates –
I'll never forget it.
I'll never forget those boots, either.
They were handtooled in Italy.

They were always too big for me,
they slipped off easily.
I never did think they were meant for me.
They were made for someone who was
far less flighty.

The socks had a special significance,
they were given to me by a sailor.
They were a size too small but he
wanted me to wear them.
He wasn't what you'd call a sophisticated
person.

I don't know what it symbolizes,
this dream where nothing fits properly.
It's almost as if I were going around naked
or, worse, with no body at all
to make the old men wet their lips and ogle.

The men think they can buy me.
Up and down the strip I walk with a
hard line for takers – I'm no bargain.
I'm looking for a good time, a change
won't do it.
I'm dreaming of something more than a change
when my boots drive off in a Cadillac.

SIR LIONEL LUCKHOO, LISTED IN THE GUINNESS
BOOK OF RECORDS AS THE WORLD'S MOST SUCCESSFUL
ADVOCATE WITH 228 SUCCESSIVE MURDER ACQUITTALS
HUMBLY LAYS HIS ALL AT THE FEET OF JESUS

There I stood in the rain
black skirt hitched up high and a
hint of lace at the neckline when someone,
Jesus it seems, smiled down on me,
opened his large good arms and
offered me his deckchair under the tarpaulin.

I walked up to that deckchair
with little faith in anything,
quite ready to turn my back on life completely
but fearing the inexorable conclusion.

I admit I was impressed by his
impeccable manners, old heart-throb he
with teeth flashing.

Like daggers of bone, that smile hit home –
he was a shark feeding on cool wedges of
sunset and dark eyes flashing under the jacaranda.

I admit I was feeling divided –
the fish of my flesh could easily have fed a
multitude – when Sir Lionel arrived in his
chauffeur-driven Mazda.
Jesus skipped the reception line to mix with the
common people while I sat there watching,
confused by a spectacle that others seemed
to be taking for granted – the crippled rising up
and dancing, the blind unbandaging the injured.

Wine flowed like blood from the throats of the
flowers while birds sang from the trees.
The sun and the moon shone at once in the
same sky, and all the stars became butterflies,
frail and dazzling.

Sir Lionel looked amazed; he quickly adjusted
his cufflinks.
When his voice was raised his words were barely
audible; for the first time in his life he had to
compete for an audience.

But when the dust had settled over all the
bright dancers, and the stars were only stars
again in a sky that loomed over us as if in
final judgment, Sir Lionel led the crowd
in prayer, and left shortly afterwards
with Jesus in the Mazda.

The crowd followed.
So much for me, all sudsy heart and soul –
I was left sitting there.
I had to make my own way home:
the way was clear and I went alone.

REMY IN THE THE BENTLEY

The corpse was dressed in the
back seat of the car and
I couldn't resist – I kissed him.
Right away he sat up; I could
feel his heart quicken through the
hot silk of his shirt.

My husband was asleep in the
front seat at the wheel. He is a
holy man given to easy women.
I am quite easy myself these days,
giving myself freely and for
no good reason.

This isn't a confession.
The sun was coming up and the
corpse too, for light and air,
for another shot of cognac, and,
if I'm honest, a closer look
at my cleavage.

It was the 5:30 ferry and we
were the only passengers. My
husband was reading the scriptures;
my scruples, you might say, were
about to be compromised.

The corpse was unbuttoning and
I was inclined to watch, when off
Beaver Point a fleet of blackfish
surfaced. They swam towards us like
undertakers out of the mist and
surrounding the boat they shouldered it.

Like a coffin we were carried
out beyond the islands. My husband
prayed – a calm man in a storm – while
the corpse got dressed again and
I grew increasingly silent.

For the whales, I heard them,
were singing – of their past lives.
or our lives brief in passing –
I'll never know which for there
they left us stranded.

My husband prayed for wind while
the corpse and I resumed foreplay,
less earnestly than before with
an empty bottle between us.

When back into the mist, as
things will, the whales went,
black sails growing slack and
finally invisible.

I remember afterwards that the
sea stayed calm, blood calm for days
and the kelp gulls cried over us.
But always late at night we could
hear that ghostly song.
The words floated back to us like
wreaths over the gulf.

Sharon Thesen

LOOSE WOMAN POEM

for Victoria Walker & Penny Kemp

A landscape
full of holes.
Women.
Pierced
ears voices piercing
the ceiling, a little choir
stung by wine:
I Fall to Pieces, and
Please Release Me.
After which I put on my old wedding band
& go to the party.
Next day 222's
& the moon falls out
of my fingernail.
The house smells like oysters
& a moon is on the loose
a woman in the bathtub   another
talking on the phone, their presence
shimmers, I'm fed up
with the wages of sin
put on some Mingus
& hepcat around

how come
it's always a question
of loss, being sick of self
displaced & frantic, chopped out
of the World of Discourse

waylaid
on the Bridge of Sighs, a net
work of connections coming down
to getting laid
or not getting laid & by whom.
Except getting laid
is not the way she thinks of it,
more like
something that her moons
can waylay waylay waylay
in the dark.

PO-IT-TREE

It live under the stars.

It be handsome man.

It gather the bay leaf
for a crown

It dance at the wedding party
up & down.

It love licorice ice cream cone

It hang out at the Roller Dome

It ask the book for an answer

It feel all alone.

It feel everything It be alive

It dream under the covers &
in the car

It laugh at the Polish joke

It sing along
with the singalong.

It map the heavens

It be handsome man

It gather the bay leaf
for a crown

It dance at the wedding party
up & down.

DEDICATION

To "honeybunch," you stupid fucker, you never thought I'd
do it did ya, you slimy hogstool, I hope you rot in hell you
no good bum with your big mouth and your endless threats
about breaking both my thumbs. What a joke, it was just a
lousy way of shutting me up and you knew it. Well you can
take your finger out of your ass and shove it up your nose
for all I care, because it's no goddamn thanks to you, hiding
my typewriter and always wanting fancy dinners all the time,
well why don't you get one of your girlfriends to make your
dinner eh? and now we'll just see who's going to incapacitate
who from now on. So eat your heart out shitface, and just
for the old icing on the cake, you remember how I told

you that big black guy was "just a friend"? Well, he was considerably more than a friend and furthermore has a whang the size of a Coke bottle. So go wipe out on a freeway, creep, cause I'm not taking anymore of your CRAP.

EVOCATION

Among the many
& many things
there is a place
for you & you & you.
Among the many melodies
the dustcloth plays upon
piano keys there is
Heart of My Heart.
The sound each has
is light or dark, the light
darker than dark.
For every human misery
there is a Centre,
likewise for every rose,
every small wheel churning.
Among the newness
of spring, sunbeams
discover the spiralling dust.
The man on the dump
awaits the bright moon.
Our breathings thicken
the windowpanes. The
painful yellow tulips
open & open & open.
A fly buzzes, removes
the room, swallows the yawn

of the man in the moon.
This pulsing thought
that thinks of things,
how yellow petals of the sun
are metonymy for roses
the bees devour.
In three-four time.
Any one delightful
deliberate waltz
a tapestry a populace
a scene of dancing things.
Upon curve upon curve
of the sky-smacking earth.

SPIRITUAL

City streets full of silver imports:
the rainiest May yet shifts
into a rainy June & the impatience
wears, oh it wears

black toreador pants burgundy hair
crosses on a yellow light
the silver imports stop for,
wipers wagging, oh they wag away

the rain
has a grey rinse in it,
is not water but a special
substance, yes it is

soapy & benign, leaves a foam
against the curb
where the silver imports sleep

the night away, oh they sleep
that bad old night away.

PRAXIS

Unable to imagine a future,
imagine a future better
than now, us creatures
weeping *in the abattoir*
only make noise & do
not transform a single fact.
So stop crying. Get up. Go out. Leap
the mossy garden wall
the steel fence or whatever
the case may be & crash
through painted arcadias,
fragments of bliss & roses
decorating your fists.

'TIL THEN

On the edge of tears
brought here by an hour's
immersion in my own
adolescence & the first snow
of the season falling –

the things, in a cardboard box –

souvenirs of summer
holidays at the lake,

the autograph book (Yours
till I.D.K.)
colored picture of Jesus
rescuing a stranded lamb,
silly porcelain ornaments
sent by prairie aunts at Xmas,
the typical teenager scrapbook
I'd felt obliged to fill
with greeting cards & bad snapshots

Whatever has brought me
to this, what ridiculous ornaments
still lurk in the background
as I hold the little baby
& smile for the Polaroid,
my own son nearly as strong
as me & grey hairs discerned
in the bathroom light –

  "When you get married
  & have a divorce
  You can come to my barn
  & marry my horse,
  Yours till the kitchen sinks"

and the darkness falls
into the blanked-out
snowy world
& the little lost lamb
& the horse smiling slapstick.

FROM "LONG DISTANCE: AN OCTAVE"

2

The enchanted
body sings.

At the centre
of the garden

a sculpted angel
from many angles

seems to dance:
material, loving.

4

No love poem
this, but even so
the morning sunlight
catches at the throat
like desire & my voice
in the echoing wires
sounds false & afraid.

Because it is, & yet
I report the catalpa
blossoms strewn like
an epithalamion over
the tenderness of everything
jostled in the breezes
of, God help me, life.

Nowhere else is this
sound coming from,
breathing off some satellite

in the dark, catching voices
caught in the throat
by desire, the wind's presence
trembling the blue
hydrangeas, scattering like ashes
the casual blossoms
of ghostly witnesses

& I am carried away
by images of loss
though I speak to you
nothing of this.

6

Dreamboats and mercy
all over the place. Roses
made of pink kleenex
blue departures
broken things

& sweet unforgettable
Prince Charming
advancing up the sidewalk
in a panoply of mirrors.
He lifts his face
to the sun & dreams,
sidestepping blossoms.

There are words
that would introduce me,
could be advanced
like flowers
held out with both hands.

I wind & unwind
the telephone cord

coiling fingers
one by one
saying yes, yes, yes
& watching the sweet Prince
be himself.

8

Old Europe endureth
parsed
by structuralists.

Damp volumes of Petrarch
Rilke, Catullus –

one for every bird
that eats
out of an old man's
hands,

one for every
speechless lover

going home.

from *Confabulations: Poems for Malcolm Lowry*

2

At the bottom of the garden
the hidden bottle. He makes
a rectitudinous beeline
for it, plain as day

his casualness an effort.
The heat spreading
everywhere, his mind
up to tricks his face
won't believe.
His stiff walk,
bones poisoned.
How he loves it all,
the amorous snake
in the amorous grass,
the disgusted neighbour
watering fruit trees
is his best friend.
The distant tequila the key
to the day, the beauty
of all things burning
through whitened glass,
his open heart
a surgical instrument.

7

The five little garter-snakes
assemble for the concert.
He's found their tastes
run to the gloomy.
His ukulele twanging out
hymn tunes
in diminished sevenths.
The pink grass swaying.
The clouds farting thunder.
The butterfly caught
in the jaws of the cat,
pulsing wings
frantic emerald curtains.

21

To be rescued from hell
you have to be in hell
so they put me
in some laboratory of it
& sit outside taking notes
every time I scream
nightmare & vomit.
Unlimited supply of gin
interrupted by injections
of apomorphine, a red lightbulb
burning constantly *to increase
the horror effect,* he tells us
over his clipboard.
I was locked in.
Got so damn thirsty
I drank my own piss,
went so crazy there's no words
for it except I saw angels
on fire & so vile
they were laughing at me.
It wasn't so bad.
Outlasted the guy before me
by five days the first time,
sixteen the next. Told them –
the stupid bastards –
I'd had the best time of my life.

22

The poets' lake country
the final cure,
sheep in pastures grazing
& Wordsworth's daffodils
exactly the host

he said they were – oh bleak
bleak days of separation
from self & catastrophic
state of mind.
He writes with a brave face
to the old fisherman in Dollarton
birthday wishes & fondest love.
They have found a lovely cottage
in the quiet village of Ripe
& listen to music on the radio
& walk and talk with the neighbours
sometimes,
go to The Lamb for a pint
or two or twenty –
it makes no difference.
Alone in the garden
after a violent night
he kisses the bright pink faces
of peonies along the fence
tasting bees & the hereafter.

24

A lot of rain falling
& wasted days
but a few gins
& I can still get off
a decent letter.
My personality comes & goes
like the mailman, however
& I can honestly admit
(at my age, how embarrassing)
that I have no idea
who I am. Was always
good at sea, though.
Without a storm

I'm useless.
Other than those
literary parties in New York
where they loved me,
they loved me not
there's one thing
keeps coming back:
we're on our way
to the ferry terminal,
black hangover & arguing
inlet to the left beating off
the morning stars & Margerie
suddenly quiet
puts her hands over her face
& starts to laugh. And somehow
it all seems so comical.

Colleen Thibaudeau

POEM

I do not want only
The shy child with the shock of slippery wheatlike hair
Standing alone after her first communion
By the white picket fence,
She is light and airy
She is for once still and stilled her shrill voice,
She is like a beefy window curtain
Or a lacy Breughel
And must be trained in the right way
Lest she twist and turn like a very poem.
I want the others too.
I want the baby in –
He who sits under the hollyhocks
His behind the exact same shade as the Purple King
    hollyhock at the very top.
I want too the neighbour looking over with a leer
At the big sister got up to look like Rita Hayworth
White as white as in a restaurant.
I want the young Socialist on the corner with his cough.
I want the mother
Though they tell me she lies in the churchyard
That is halfway up Montreal Mountain.
I want the man who sits on the steps of the Mayfair
    Washing Machine Co.
This morning and every morning
Wearing a dirty hockey sweater and holding his head in
    his hands.

And I too
After adjusting the focus

I shall go just as natural among them all;
Why must the lover and the sufferer be out?
I do not want the shy child only
Aloof for the one minute of her life;
I want it to be like a lacy Breughel.

THE GREEN FAMILY

I will begin to delineate the green family.
Under the shade of the mother sat the father
small weedy and seedy
wearing his light hair daubed on his forehead;
he was a salvation army man, weekdays
he moved ashcans for the city.

His children were all mouths diligent with love of honey.
They could have spelled down anybody's child.
Sitting in the front row at the library hour
they let their darned black legs hang down,
all of them thin as water spiders, and the gold
dream of his trumpet kept them whole.

Summer sand could have held them
like five smooth stones. Off to one side
was the mother being a flowering-bush in her housedress.
They consulted about the special ride; at twilight
he took the three biggest ones aboard
that marvel of a varnished speedboat and went off in
    a wave.

He could not walk on water. When the shock came
he was a gallant giving his arm
in perfect faith to his three small daughters,
told them the longest story they had ever heard;

going along that hollow wooden walk by the lake
they came to the all-gold sugar bush of the tale.

The airforce dragged
him up pale as a weed-draped Shiva;
one of the other mothers told that she was knitting
a wee red jacket for her Rita that would have been
more mere red flesh though and no sort of preserver.
Henry had been an angel.

I cannot bring my heart to mourn
his unreturn,
nor can the remnant that remember him
remembering he looked last into the sun
that was a golden gabriel and sang him home.

MY GRANDDAUGHTERS ARE COMBING OUT
THEIR LONG HAIR

my granddaughters are combing out their long hair sitting at
    night
on the rocks in Venezuela   they have watched their babes
falling like white birds from the last of the treetop cradles
they have buried them in their hearts where they will never
    forget
to keep on singing them the old songs

brought down to earth they use twigs, flint scrapers acadian
their laughter underground makes the thyme flower in
    darkness

my granddaughters are thin as fishbones & hornfooted   but
    they are

always beautiful under the stars: like little asian paperthings
they seem to open outward into their own waterbowl

mornings they waken to Light's chink ricocheting
off an old Black's Harbour sardinecan.

Reduce them the last evangelines make them part of the
     stars.

my granddaughters are coming out by night combing their
     burr
coloured hair by the rocks and streamtrickle in Venezuela
they are burnt out as falling stars but they laugh
and keep on singing them the old songs.

THE BROWN FAMILY

All round the Browns stretched forty acres of potatoes.
They lived like squatters in my father's little chicken-house
That grew to lean-tos and then to a whole shack-town
     where married Browns
Slept God-knows-how hilled in the darkness all night long,
Mornings how rolled out to breakfast on the lawn
Sitting in crumbs and clover, their eyes still glozed over
With dufferish sleep, and all stuffing away like Eskimos.

Brown boys had greasy jeans and oilcloth school-bags made
     at home
And sneakers for quick escapes through orchard gates,
Tom had two left thumbs while Ted was tough and dumb,
     but there was much
Of army sadness to the way all their heads got furry as
     muskrats by March.

Well after meagre spells Fall was their full season when they
    dropped
Partridge, pheasant and squirrel – shooting as if they would
    never stop
As later they crazily shot up even the apple-trees at Caen.

Their sisters inevitably called Nellie or Lily were deliberately
    pale,
Silly incestuous little flirts whose frilly skirts were dirty
From every ditch in the county. On lonely country roads
    under the moon
Their sadness lit like incense their sweet ten-cent perfume.
But at hint of insult their cheeks took on fiery tints those
    summers
When they hired-out to cook. And their eyes often had that
    strange blue look
Of the blue willow plates round a rich farmer's plate-rail.

"What I can touch and take up in these two hands," said
    Mrs. Brown,
"Is what I trust!" Accordingly on the bashed piano and on
    the floor, dust
And rich potato-coloured light everywhere mingled: scraps,
    fronds, gourds,
Teazle, fossils, hazel wands, turkey feathers and furs...
    goods
All lovingly hers tangled. And all could be taken up,
    stroked, cajoled
In the same manner as her Old Man: for Mr Brown's heart
    was pure glossy gold
By tender handling, of all that's drossy, slowly, suvendibly,
    rendered down.

But as alike as Anna Pauker's brood so that it tears the heart
    to see

Was that last lot and will all Browns ever be,
Picking and pecking at life, scratching where something is
  cached.
What are they looking for? Not lots to eat or wear. Not lots
  in town.
Strangely, that same thing *we* want would satisfy a Brown –
Something of the sort God gives us every day
Something we can take up in our two hands and bear away.

I HAD THE WINDOW OPEN

I had
the window open, giving
my Matisse
a good shaking,

when, suddenly (from the l.h. corner
near the frame) a golden gourd
throstled into a yellow bird
and was nabbed by my cat.

I was aghast
lest there be a space,
but my smallest child's smallest hand
fitted the place;

and now I have this golden girl
under a canopy of mandolins
and bottle shapes, seriously
playing out her very shady role.

WALK 3

Hand in hand we walked all round
   The world at the Equator:
Very little we saw, he
Was too busy watching out for me
And I was too busy watching the way –
   Silly because you can't go astray
   Simply following the Equator.

            •

And who did we meet, walking all round
   The world at the Equator?
Some rather recognizable faces
Tho' connected with other times, other places,
   We nodded but made a moue of doubt –
   It seemed the whole world was out
   All walking round the Equator.

            •

We grew old, of course we grew old,
But all of it has been told and retold:
All the Problems solved – how to count the many
Steps in a day, how to walk over any
Sea, how to get back to the start-
   ing point with a whole heart,
   Just how to walk round the Equator.

            •

No wonder we were often weary of walking round
   The world at the Equator.
   But it was something to do.

We thought, someday when it's all through
And people ask, we can say:
   Well, it's the well-travelled any-old way
   Following round the Equator.

LETTER EIGHT

Place was that piece of ground between house and swing,
yielding to the foot,
covered with reddened strawberry leaves
and that small vine that isn't wintergreen.

Among the cedars, some of them struggling still like old
   limbo dancers,

covered with a lighter green lichen,

there on the day that William Faulkner died I came and
   stood
and even if I had not willed it so, down my head would have
   gone down,

thinking definitely about something:
God, how I love this little part of ground.

LULLABY OF THE CHILD FOR THE MOTHER

The child who never lived was the real child
whose lovely eyes were seas
and little limbs were lullabies
and lovely seas

He said, my mother is a street
where strangers pass
her hair winds like the wind
round wooden poles

Her lovely eyes are seas
Her hair is wind that shakes the elder tree

He said, my mother is a stair
where strangers pass
and when night rocks me round
then I am sure

Her hair is wind that shakes the elder tree
her eyes are seas

SPRING POEM

HEARING: hearing: hearing:
The Engine warming up: warming
And the Earthworm going zupzupzup through the brown
    ground
Chased by that same hot crank.
Through the tunnelled air trundle the marvellous merry
    birds:
All carrying rich pokes, wearing super stoles
And showing off the fine detail of freckles on their tails; just
    as clearly
As the big block: the elephant block: the big E
Of my mammoth city shows its grim windows and dopey
    blinds.

O the Engine: the Elevator: of me and mind:
It goes down its stretchy rubber cables:
Capable or incapable:
But going zupzupzup.

THIS ELASTIC MOMENT

Yes we are that too: we are everything who feel it.
Everything that has meaning has the same meaning as
    angels: these
hoverers and whirrers: occupied with us.
Men may be in the parkgrass sleeping: or be he who sits
    in his
shirtsleeves every blessed Sunday: rasping away at his
    child who
is catching some sunshine: from the sticky cloud hanging
    over the
Laura Secord factory: and teetering on the pales of the green
iron fence: higher up than the briary bushes.
I pass and make no sound: but the silver and whirr of my
    bicycle
going round: but must see them who don't see: get their fit,
    man
and child: let this elastic moment stretch out in me: till that
point where they are inside and invisible.
It is not to afterward eat a candy: picket that factory: nor to
go by again and see that rickety child on the fence.
When the band of the moment breaks there will come
    angelic recurrence.

Colleen Thibaudeau

MY GRANDMOTHER'S SUGAR SHELL, ONTARIO BAROQUE

My grandmother's sugar shell (spoon), Ontario Baroque, has
   just fallen
out of the uncleaned silver bag.
What does it mean, I wonder.
One day only I saw her stop work.
We lay out on the grass by the highway under the big maple
and two cars went by toward Owen Sound. When she heard
their car coming for dinner, she got up, a big woman
with Scottish shoulders, built too heavy on the top like
all the Stewarts, her leg-bones stilt-like in proportion
to the square rest of her.
                   And she rose all of a piece,
I remember that she rose up somehow straight and not
hinging her knees, nor using her hands, nor her elbows,
nor leaning her head forward. So that
she was the reverse of a tree falling before a quick gust.
That is, she rose on a slant as if pulleys were attached
to her everywhere   or as if
the kitchen woodstove were a magnet that suddenly
drew her inside.   One minute she was
all green and gold lying there dappled. The next
she was half-way up the lawn and in motion over the steps.
The door opened magically and she disappeared. She would
never wonder about anything, just say, "That spoon needs
   cleaning."
And yet I think it means she needs remembering.

INTO THE TREES

"dear woods I know them all...
                         the day
when I have to leave them my heart
will be very heavy." Ah yes, Claudine.
Above my head the porcupines steadily munching chips,
on the edge of Grogan's old clearing a deer
poised leaf and silent in the glades
as sound of paper (pencil on)
pages,   leaves falling,
through the grey-brown shapes of sound
& the imperceptible drawing back of the bow.

Peter van Toorn

THE CATTLE

In the hairy grass, or in bench shapes under trees
even on roads, just crossing

for	outstaring even the hypnotic oxeyed daisies	no peers
for	finding their legs in one million kilowatt thunder	no peers
for	fluking a shotput of steaming Tudor turd	no peers
for	capsizing neatly like stacked wood	no peers
for	mooing into hundred gallon green unchanged	no peers
for	rising like yeast in the ovendoor evening sun	no peers
for	stomping through the refrigerated ferns	no peers
for	souring the milk on the run	no peers
for	coming into view like crowds at bus stops	no peers
for	plastering the nubile grass with ten-ton drool	no peers
for	eating falling asleep and falling asleep eating	no peers
for	standing the simmer of flies in standstill sun	no peers
for	crowding in with clueless beerfuzz eyes	no peers
for	lowering their horns like wet apple branches	no peers
for	shaking a head full of moo at the rain	no peers
for	breathing steamy up at the cold steerhorned moon	no peers

in the hairy grass, or in bench shapes under trees
even on roads, just crossing

the cattle   the cattle   the cattle

ELEGY ON WAR: INVENTION OF THE SWORD

Who was he, this first butcher and weaponmaker
who simplified dying and growing up for a boy?
He must have been old and grisly, this first soldier
(poured in the same mould as his pig-iron sword),
forgetting to patent the world's most patented toy.
Old fool, probably forged it for hacking up wood
or butchering bears; and no one understood –
till there was a market for it. All the same,
his armlong blade was soon tooled into a cold
killing machine. I suppose brains are to blame –
or this Age of Iron with its manic drive for gold.
For long ago there were no wars; and no weapon-
makers. Our food was served up in beechwood bowls.
Those days even a herdsman could safely bed down
among his slugcoloured flocks and claim a day's work
without reporting to ramparts, forts and foxholes.
Imagine living then – even as herdsman: no hand
in this racket of arms, bivouac and command.
And this insanity – for years on end; stuck
far from home, only one song in your head:
your life made lousy by bum gear, piles, pot luck
and the endless bungling of bureaucrats – the sweat
pouring down at the sound of each bugle call.
Like the one that's blasting us out for a roll call
right now. Just think of it: some energetic jerk
on the other side's probably polishing blades.
Maybe just for the sake of doing some work.
Chances are one of them is going to stay
behind and rust away in my guts one of these days.

from Tibullus

Peter van Toorn

MOUNTAIN TAMBOURINE

A crew took part of the big tree away
on my street. A poplar, it was throwing
its ashes, its dirty pillow stuffing,
around too much. So they said. Anyway,
people were tired of it. It was too grey.
It might drop a tired branch and hit something,
a power or phone line. What's still standing
they'll come for tomorrow and chop away.
It doesn't make much poplar talk now. The big
clatter's gone out of it. On the older
side of the street, the last tree stands, tall, big,
full, leafy – a fine shade and rain holder.
It leans to one side at a warm angle,
like Annie, whose door it covered last fall.

SHAKE'N'BAKE BALLAD

In 100% surefire arsenic
in snowwhite lye
in lepers' bathwater
in strychnine buttered with lead
in scrapemash off soldiers' bootsoles
in 7 cities' drainmalt
in snot pastry
in wolverine toad and turkey gall
    and in viler things
shake'n'bake their envy-schooled tongues.

In pencilpaint and braspy mulepiss
in rabid dogdrool
in long peels of oven grease

in wormpie and roachpaste
in cigarettesog of tavern urinals
in rats' sewer water
in coffinslag and maggotmatting
in plasters of runover skunk
   and in viler things
shake'n'bake their envy-schooled tongues.

In battery acid and engine goo
in egglacquered ragrot
in soapfoam and mosquito spray
in flubbery diaperslop
in stiff dishwater
in surgical mustard (morgue scraps)
in cat toad snail and tire wipe
in dead fish and ulcer ooze
   and in viler things
shake'n'bake their envy-schooled tongues.

Prince
push all these into a crush
and if you haven't got a strainer handy
use the back of your pants.
And make sure there's enough batter –
roll on pig manure – before you
shake'n'bake their envy-schooled tongues.

from Villon

MOUNTAIN MAPLE

I can't help it if you're under my leaves
when they start skipping around in the breeze
and some wetness on them shakes down on you.

Listen, there's enough wind on this mountain
to send us all skipping, and fire and rain
to blow our noses clean and steam our tears.
Is it my fault you like to lie around
with your head in my lap? I'm too busy
to be looking out for you all the time.
I don't know what I'll be doing this time
tomorrow. Maybe I'll stand here, shifting
from side to side, soaking up dew. Maybe
I'll stand here counting the cracks in my crown,
or sail off, roots and all, in a typhoon.
It all depends on what you think I'll do.
If you think I might drop a fist of keys
on your head, go ahead, and I just might.
You can stay here, or you can go away;
but before you do, try to remember
what you used to do on a scorching day
for some shade. And how did you go about
for a salad without a spot of green?
Oh, yes, let me know, if you ever come
this way again, how you treat your water:
how much you dish out to air in the sun
for the mineral sparkle in the dew,
and how much of it you store up in each root
to go under ground on all winter long
and still come up with syrup in the spring.
And talking about the talking of trees,
what are the birds going to touch down in?
At least my roots pose a problem for you,
so you think twice about axing me down.
I am one of a kind that carry fruit,
feed stoves by the boxful all winter long,
cover the tables with bloom in the spring,
and change with the splash of spring in the fall.
I'm grease on your gums, I'm sweat on your skin;
where my branches are, there are antlers too.
And who is going to do the dancing

that I do – be all arms and legs moving
but standing still, cradlewood for the moon?
On me you scratch and blot your bitter ink.
I make the matches, handles, and boxes
you burn me, cut me, and bury me with.
I am a cross between man and grass, and
grow in the thought of him from the ground up.
Is it for cutting me down for no use,
for letting too many of us go, till
everything's up to the nostrils in snow,
that you sing and cry and write down this thing?

MOUNTAIN MIRROR

I've rubbed noses with the earth's kitchen smells,
and danced to the world's cosy supper bells.
Whatever you can have a ball about
while going strong, I've had a ball about.
Had coffee and cake by the cup and plate,
and been lucky in love and stayed out late.
Worn silk vests, the finest hats, and jackets
that rhymed with the money in their pockets.
I had it made. I rode a steppy horse,
lived near tennis courts, swimming pools, golf course,
slept in fields where the flowers thought out loud,
and found silver linings in every cloud.
Laurel twigs were tucked into my hat band.
I had as many dreams as I owned land.
Life was just one long rosy month of May.
It was peaches and cream; it was child's play.
I was tickled pink. I thought death had died.
Pheasants flew right into my mouth, deep fried,
and friends used to tap on my window pane

for mountain picnics and allnight champagne.
Oh, I had visions all right! But you're right.
They were bubbles that went *pop!* overnight.
There I was, stretched out in a one-room shack,
with stroke, fever, and this arthritic back.
My skin had as many holes as sweat pores;
what the bed bugs didn't touch went to bed sores.
As for running after my heart's desire,
I wrote it off, shivering near the fire.
Then my ink froze and I had to borrow,
put on a show, and live for tomorrow.
But let's just skip this part of the story.
I wasn't choking for air. And don't worry –
all I want now is my clowning around
should take a breather, six feet under ground.
So long. Time to go now. Bye, bye. Have fun.
Maybe catch you later, back in heaven.

from Heine

MOUNTAIN STORM

*The bitter and the sweet come from outside, the hard
from within.*
>   *Einstein*

Maybe a walk out in this kind of weather
can straighten you out,
even grow on you,
but you have other things to listen to.
So when the growling out there
swings your door open,
and knocks a pan off the stove,
unless elves skip in to mop up for you,
or the fire smeared over the floor is of bronze,

forget it.
It's another kind of weather
makes you feel
up to it –
taking a walk,
opening your coat at the throat,
chewing on a milky nib of grass,
or,
stretched out,
dialling the clouds with your big toe.
And even though an out and out storm out there,
breathing down your neck
and skimming the fat from your hair,
can make you feel like spitting your teeth out
as far as some stars,
and do it,
easily,
true,
as a chainsaw rips a century of rock maple in two,
it's no weather
to open a moody maple like a rare old book,
finger its fresh Indian feathers,
talk a tune out of it,
or take it for a pencil behind an ear of the moon.
So if some rage
(coming over you out of the blue)
makes you feel like bending your head down,
like ducking deep inside the heart side of your coat,
deep as the storm's strong,
and plucking a flame from a match
to get a glow going –
incense, tobacco, candlewax: stick, bowl, or wick –
don't let it eat your heart out,
or throw you off.
It's another kind of weather altogether
bobs the world back up under the balls of your feet,
fresh,

with some of the planets,
and nearly all of the spheres –
juicy pinks, reds, golds, blacks, browns, ivories, and blues –
singing
to your ears,
in, or out of, the weather
still banging into the mountains to tune the trees.

MOUNTAIN HERON

Still fishing the lake,
same spot – after all that rain! –
but with shorter legs!

from Basho

MOUNTAIN BOOGIE

In art, content is very tiny, content.
          de Kooning

O   peppermint moon behind the loud running clouds!
O   aspirin violets!
O   the cue to look up splickering out there in the U-sphere!
O   aspirin ivories!
O   nick nock of madder smoosh!
O   the sparks when she peels her sweater in the dark!
O   sepia blush!
O   pink pink: the fingers' rinks winking with quick!
O   no go zipper zinc!
O   comet locked up in the shed by mistake!
O   the worm in the wick of the fire!

O that sienna stays!
O baby's milkteeth loose in a hailstorm!
O bright-assed baboon who sat on the peacock's glory!
O blue pencils of rain on the rooftiles!
O leapfrog green!
O mouse on the telephone: dunk your biscuit static!
O tapioca from Oka tango!
O chrome shimmy of blackfly blood!
O dill to pistachio!
O trout with a rainbow up, lungs two feet deep in sharp air!
O tobacco nutmegs!
O angel hairs tuned in a cigarbox: *voilà! le clavecin!*
O tiny chrome haypiles of the stars!
O calico cat with the spaghetti whiskers!
O blizzard whites!
O piano crates unloading: thunder over Chinatown!
O old plum tree with the joker of jade up your sleeves!
O peonies! the flutes of spice!
O spinach wrinkles!
O fire chopping a log to stips of ash!
O yoghurt thwop!
O clam-shell tulip-cheeks!
O pink-spoggled eggs on umber craterboard!
O saffron velleity!
O opal winter lightning through the onyx glass!
O bamboo arpeggio!
O magnolia stalled like creamy brookwater!
O icicle pearls!
O for some steamy silvers to kick the goop out of flamingo
    balls!
O mustard glush!
O coffee, khaki, cookie, banana!
O peachy rhum goo!
O sunladder yellow!
O amber hoofclick!
O cowlick of cobalt left in for the last failing argument!
O ozone manure!

O lake red with gold-ishings in it!
O bronze leaf hopping a highway of mint & toffee
    headlights!
O cigarette paper rolled by fog tongue!
O crumpled copper onionwrap!
O perfume of the stars around the moon!
O barnstraw blond!
O lollipop lick of streaming tangerine air!

Bronwen Wallace

THE WOMAN IN THIS POEM

The woman in this poem
lives in the suburbs
with her husband and two children
each day she waits for the mail and
once a week receives
a letter from her lover
who lives in another city
writes of roses   warm patches
of sunlight on his bed
Come to me he pleads
I need you and the woman
reaches for the phone
to dial the airport
she will leave this afternoon
her suitcase packed
with a few light clothes

But as she is dialing
the woman in this poem
remembers the pot-roast
and the fact that it is Thursday
she thinks of how her husband's face
will look when he reads her note
his body curling sadly toward
the empty side of the bed

She stops dialing and begins
to chop onions for the pot-roast

but behind her back the phone
shapes itself insistently
the number for airline reservations
chants in her head
in an hour her children will be
home from school and after that
her husband will arrive
to kiss the back of her neck
while she thickens the gravy
and she knows that
all through dinner
her mouth will laugh and chatter
while she walks with her lover
on a beach somewhere

She puts the onions in the pot
and turns toward the phone
but even as she reaches
she is thinking of
her daughter's piano lessons
her son's dental appointment

Her arms fall to her side
and as she stands there
in the middle of her spotless kitchen
we can see her growing
old like this
and wish for something anything
to happen   we could have her go
mad perhaps and lock herself
in the closet   crouch there
for days her dresses withering
around her like cast-off skins
or maybe she could take
to cruising the streets at night
in her husband's car
picking up teenage boys

and fucking them in the back seat
we can even imagine
finding her body
dumped in a ditch somewhere
on the edge of town

The woman in this poem offends us
with her useless phone and the persistent
smell of onions   we regard her as we do
the poorly calculated overdose
who lies in a bed somewhere
not knowing how her life drips
through her drop by measured drop

we want to think of death
as something sudden
stroke or the leap
that carries us over the railing
of the bridge in one determined arc
the pistol aimed precisely
at the right part of the brain
we want to hate this woman

but mostly we hate knowing
that for us too it is
moments like this
our thoughts   stiff fingers
tear at again and again
when we stop in the middle
of an ordinary day and
like the woman in this poem
begin to feel
our own deaths
rising slow within us

COMMON MAGIC

Your best friend falls in love
and her brain turns to water.
You can watch her lips move,
making the customary sounds,
but you can see they're merely
words, flimsy as bubbles rising
from some golden sea where she
swims sleek and exotic as a mermaid.

It's always like that.
You stop for lunch in a crowded
restaurant and the waitress floats
toward you.   You can tell she doesn't care
whether you have the baked or french fried
and you wonder if your voice comes
in bubbles too.

It's not just women either.   Or love
for that matter.   The old man
across from you on the bus holds
a young child on his knee; he is singing
to her and his voice is a small boy
turning somersaults in the green
country of his blood.
It's only when the driver calls his stop
that he emerges into this puzzle
of brick and tidy hedges.   Only then
you notice his shaking hands, his need
of the child to guide him home.

All over the city
you move in your own seasons
through the seasons of others: old women, faces

clawed by weather you can't feel
clack dry tongues at passersby
while adolescents seethe
in their glassy atmospheres of anger.

In parks, the children
are alien life-forms, rooted
in the galaxies they've grown through
to get here.   Their games weave
the interface and their laughter
tickles that part of your brain where smells
are hidden and the nuzzling textures of things.

It's a wonder anything gets done
at all: a mechanic flails
at the muffler of your car
through whatever storm he's trapped inside
and the mailman stares at numbers
from the haze of a distant summer.

Yet somehow letters arrive and buses
remember their routes.   Banks balance.
Mangoes ripen on the supermarket shelves.
Everyone manages.   You gulp the thin air
of this planet as if it were the only
one you knew.   Even the earth you're
standing on seems solid enough.
It's always the chance word, unthinking
gesture that unlocks the face before you.
Reveals the intricate countries
deep within the eyes.   The hidden
lives, like sudden miracles,
that breathe there.

REMINDER

In a crowded theatre lobby, the perfume
in a strange woman's hair nudges a jealousy
I thought I'd put down years ago.
Unlocks that stubborn convolution of my brain
where it rears and spits.
Even my fingers turn to claws.

Smells like fists.
One whiff of feta cheese and olives
numbs my solar plexus with the blow of a first love,
while fresias are a falling into something deeper,
a loss I haven't even named yet.

I'm told that smell is centred
in our first brain. Primitive,
lizard part of us still cautiously sniffing
its way through colours and mysteries.
The world as it is before we discover
how to shape it into names,
learn to use language like a hope
for the future. Something that could save us
if we use it carefully, put enough words
between ourselves and the past.

A man and a woman sit in an all night
restaurant. She's smoking cigarettes,
he's drinking cup after cup
of black coffee, double sugar.
They're in one of those conversations
you don't need words to follow,
though they're using enough of them, their mouths
so rigid with choosing that the lips

have thinned to that whiteness you find
outside pain, if you tighten your muscles hard enough.

And maybe it's only because I can't hear
what they're saying that I imagine
this other sound, somewhere between a feeling
and a voice. An ache in the bone that sings
of an old wound.   Something you can't put
your finger on.   Right now, it's cautionary,
like a growl, though already their bodies
cringe at it and their hands ride
the waves of its swelling.

Sooner or later it will
rise and she'll start screaming;
he'll retreat into that baffled
silence men sometimes use for tears.

This isn't a lesson in body language.
It's more like a warning, though there's not
much we can do.   We can't go back
to nuzzling and grunting at each other,
trying to sniff out anger or love.
And there's no such thing
as a simpler time, anyway.

You might call it
a reminder, like the dinosaur
bone in the museum,
the one we can touch,
the one worn smooth
with our need.

Meanwhile, the man and woman go on
talking and I can imagine how their mouths
must ache for a word that's as explicit
as the click of her lighter,

his definitive way of measuring
the two teaspoonsful of sugar.
Words are their hope for the future.
They've cherished them like children.
And now their faces have the puzzled,
fragile look of parents
who have taken great care
and are always surprised
to see the past they thought
they'd freed their children from
assert itself. In their way of walking,
in their laughter,
in their sullen, indifferent eyes.

MELONS/AT THE SPEED OF LIGHT

for Carolyn Smart

"Child," said the lion, *"I am telling you your story, not hers. No one is told any story but their own."*
        C.S. Lewis, A Horse and His Boy

I keep having this dream
where the women I love swell up like melons, night after
    night.
It's not surprising, really.
They've reached that age
where a woman must decide once and for all,
and this summer, most of them are pregnant.
Already, their eyes have changed.
Like those pools you discover once-in-a-while,
so deep with themselves
you can't imagine anything else swimming in them.
The eyes of pregnant women. The women I love

fallen into themselves, somehow, far beyond calling,
as if whatever swims in their bellies
were pulling them deeper and deeper.

I think that women's lives
are like our bodies.
Always at the mercy, you might say.
A woman turns thirty-two and her body lets her know
it's time to decide.
Or maybe she just loses her job and can't find another
so she figures she might as well have the babies now as later.
The days become all mouth then
and everything smells of milk.
Her body goes a little vague at the edges
like it felt that time at summer camp
when she was learning how to hang in the water without
    moving.
"Drown proofing" they called it.
Said it could hold you up for hours.
These are the days that slow
to the pace of glass,
the world outside a silent, lazy smudge
on the horizon somewhere.
"After my son was born," a friend told me,
"in those first few months, whenever he was asleep,
I'd spend hours putting on makeup,
just so I could touch my own face again,
just so I knew I was there."

In the dreams they are green and determined,
growing larger by the minute and there's something
I need to warn them about before it's too late,
but they go on ripening without me.
So far, I always find myself awake
before anything else happens,

hands in the dry night, exploring the bed
for a mess of pulp and seeds.

Meanwhile, my son turns ten this summer.
Every morning, he plays baseball in the park next door,
leaving me quiet for coffee and the paper.
But it never works. It's his voice, rising
through the noise of the game that shapes me still,
the way, years earlier, his turning knotted my belly,
the kick under my ribs, aimed at the heart.
When I take my coffee to the bleachers, he ignores me.
He's the smallest boy on his team, but he's got a good arm.
The coach gives him third base, usually, or short stop.
Right field is a demotion. I can tell he feels it
by his walk, though his face shows nothing.
It's like the sadness in his wrists when he's up to bat,
knowing he'll manage a good base hit, probably, but
    never a home run.
He's the kind of player every coach needs on the team
and watching him stretch for a fly ball, I can see
how I'm the one who needs to grow up.
I carried him like the future, unmarked, malleable,
but what I gave birth to isn't like that at all,
isn't a life I can decide for anymore.
This is what my son knows already;
he just wants to get on with it.

What I get on with is this dream
where women swell up like melons,
ready to ripen or burst.
I want to believe I am dreaming for my friends,
for all the things I'd tell them if I could.
How they are bound by this birth forever
to the lives of other women, to a love
that roots itself as deeply
as our need for the earth.

I want to tell them this
is an old, old story,
but of course they can't listen.
They are ripening into their own versions of it
as if it had never happened to anyone else before.
These women I love so much.
Their recklessness. Like that fly ball
at the speed of light
stinging into my son's glove.

COMING THROUGH

It's the time of day you like the best: that hour
just before dark, when the colours
and shapes of things seem to forget
their daylit boundaries, so that the sound
of someone whistling in the street is the last pink
light on the horizon, fading through other sounds
of traffic and laughter into lilac, into blue-grey.

Nothing is solid now. Against the sky the trees
are so still they vibrate with the effort
of holding themselves in and the walls of the houses
hesitate as if they might dissolve,
revealing the lives behind them, intricate
and enchanted as the lives of dolls.

You had a friend who opened
secrets for you like that
and when you think of her now
it's mostly on evenings like this one,
when the last of that light
which is itself a kind of silence

gives to the room a mirror-like quality,
translucent as memory.

You can almost smell the coffee you'd make for her
    then,
see the steam rising from the blue cup, her fingers
curled around it, warming themselves.
You can still see the way her hands moved
when she talked, creating a second language,
drawing you in
to the very centre of her words
where the real stories lived.
And her eyes, following your sentences
wherever they led,
until it seemed those nights
you entered each other's lives
as if they were countries,
not the superficial ones that maps create,
or ordinary conversation, but the kind
that twist and plummet underneath a day's events
like the labyrinths you followed as a child
or the new-made world that opened
for you alone when you discovered lying.

You lived within each other then
and each of those nights was a place
you inhabited together, a place
you thought you could return to always.

The headlights from a passing car outside
startle the bright ghosts that gather
in the corners of the room. It makes you remember
the bedroom you had as a child
and how you huddled under the covers like a snail,
watching the goblins who lived in the dresser drawers
glide across the mirror and over the ceiling

into your bed. It was the smell of your teddy bear
that saved you then and the satin edge of the blanket
at your cheek as smooth as sleep.
It was the voices of your parents in the kitchen,
far away as growing up and as safe. Even by day
your parents filled their lives
with such a confidence,
you believed they had been born into adulthood
or arrived there, years ago, before
there were any history books or maps, and made it
their very own sort of place. Not like you.
Stubbing your toes on the furniture that changed
overnight, your arms suddenly appearing
from the sleeves of your favourite jacket
like a scarecrow's
like somebody else.

You can laugh at it now, although
it's only lately you've begun to realize
how much of your time you've spent like that:
almost a guest in your own life,
wandering around waiting for someone
or something to explain things to you.

It was always late when she left
and you'd stand in the doorway, waiting
till she'd started the car, then
sit in the dark yourself
for the twenty minutes or so it took her
to drive home. As you locked up, checked the kids
you could imagine her doing the same thing,
so that on those nights sleep was just another opening,
another entry you made together.

She's been dead for a long time now.
You'd thought that would make a difference

but it hasn't. And though you feel angry
at your need for an explanation
it's still there. As if she owed it to you, somehow.
As if somebody did.

Oh, you've learned the accepted wisdom of it.
Can even feel yourself healing these days, almost
strong enough now to re-enter the places
you inhabited together. And you know
you'll never figure it all out anyway;
any more than you can understand your neighbours
from what you see in their lighted windows
framed, like public advertisements.

And yet.

A part of you resists all that.
Resists it with the pure, unthinking stubbornness
you lived in as a child,
that harder wisdom
you are re-discovering now.
Some people are a country
and their deaths displace you.
Everything you shared with them
reminds you of it: part of you in exile
for the rest of your life.

Tom Wayman

Mad gnome of an assistant editor
Wayman gloats in Colorado
before the mass of manuscripts now his,
his to edit.

Wayman remembers the mounds of his own mail back
marked: "Are you kidding?"
"What is this grunt?" and
"Do us a favor and stick this up your ass?"

Now the tide is turned: all literary America
lies at Wayman's feet; America, with a poet
under every rock. Revenge, revenge,
the very word is like a Bedlam gong
to ring him deeper into rage . . .
"And that's a literary reference,"
Wayman shrieks, slashing someone's poem to
shreddies as he writes rejections
—the same for all: Miss Elsa Eddington Brewster,
editor Riley of the *South-west Pawnee County Quarterly,*
former associates with their cringing, oily letters.
Only the editor-in-chief's friends
give him pause. Wayman weighs
the first-name-basis missives carefully.
Who is putting him on? Who really studied

under Yvor with the boss? Who knew him when?
Who now? Is everybody faking?

Feverish in the cool Colorado evening
Wayman is hammering away at rejecting
faster and faster. The earth heaves,
the business manager elopes,
the editor is arrested in Utah with the funds,
still Wayman is scribbling: "No."   "No."
Imperceptibly the word spreads outward
to those in Portland, Oregon and Portland, Maine
stuffing their packages of poems
into the 10 p.m. mailbox slots:
"Wayman," the news has it,
"Wayman's editing in Colorado.
All we can do is submit."

THE INTERIOR

[*from "The Chilean Elegies"*]

The smell of potatoes just taken out of the earth.
The problem every carpenter faces, where the wood
nearly fits. The man who secretly wants to leave his wife
and only his fantasies keep his sexual life alive.

These things no government can alter or solve.

The lineup in the small bank branch on East Twenty-ninth
after work on Friday: old boots and the shapeless trousers,
short windbreakers whose sleeves end in hands that clutch

the paper that means life. Other lines
that have worried their way into the faces above the eyes.

These mean an ache for money that lasts an entire lifetime
from busfare each morning through to the tiny pension.
These mean it is luck that rules: the wisps of lotteries,
 horses,
or entering the pool each payday for the best poker hand
that can be gathered from the company's number on your
 cheque.

Also, applying when they're hiring: no government
has been able to touch that.

The small towns of the Interior. The railroad towns deep in
 the forest.
What has the government to do with them?
The struggles of the young teacher
who has arrived to work in the school
mainly of Indians. All the arguing
with the principal, and with the old librarian,
the enthusiasm carried into the desperate classroom.
And the Indians themselves. Their new hall
they built themselves at Lytton, which had to be boarded up
after a month because of the damage. The summer camp
they built twenty miles away in the mountains
where a young boy drowned the second week it was open.
It too is abandoned again to the silence.
Potato chips and Coke the staple food of so many.
And television, television, television . . .

On the Thompson River, or in Parral
the government is not the government of the Indians,

not of the young teacher, not of the townspeople,
not of the lover, the carpenter, the man who digs potatoes in
   his yard.

But where a government takes the remotest of steps
to return home to the ground, and when even this small
   gesture
is embargoed, denounced, plotted against
and at last some incredibly expensive aviation gasoline
is pumped into certain jet fighters donated by another
   government
existing thousands of miles away
there is a loss that goes deeper than the blood,
deeper than the bodies put into the ground,
that descends to the roots of the mountains
and travels that far down in the crust of the planet
along the continental chains
until all over the world another sorrow is confirmed
in the lives of the poor. Once again
we are made less. There are men and women
who in the cells of the fibres of their being
do not believe the Indians are dying fast enough
do not believe the poor are dying fast enough
do not believe that sickness and hunger,
automobile crashes, industrial disasters
and the daily suicides of alcohol and despair
are ridding the earth of us with sufficient speed.
So they call for the only institution
maintained at the highest possible level of efficiency:
the men with guns and capbadges, willing or conscripted,
whole armies and the tireless police. These are the men
who have made of this planet throughout my life
a vast geography of blood.

So many shot for subversion in Temuco. So many arrested
for drunkenness in Lytton.

And there is not a government in the world that wants to
  abolish the factory.

THE DEATH OF THE FAMILY

"You married, Tom?"
                        No, but the girl I'm going with is.
To someone else. Ha-ha. You see...

But they aren't listening.
                        "Tom, I was going with a woman
for two years. A few weeks ago she asked if I was going to
  marry her.
I told her I might someday, but, hell,
I was married all those years
and once I got my divorce I'm not in any hurry to do it again.
I didn't say I wouldn't ever marry her.
I just said I didn't want to right now.

"She says to me: 'Dave, if you don't want to marry me
I'm wasting my time.' And that was it.
I tried to call her up a couple of times
but she said if I didn't hang up she would hang up on me.
Bang. Just like that she stopped seeing me.
I think she's crazy. I know she hasn't been seeing anyone else
but she'd rather sit at home and see nobody
than go around with me anymore if I won't marry her.
I just want someone to visit after work, to go dancing with.
And there's something else: she once told me

if we got married, she would come first.
She meant, before my kids. I have two, and there's her three
but she says she has to come first.
There's no way: my kids come first with me.
Who else is there to look after them?"

                                    And young Bob
over from Cab Build for the morning, to help out when
   we're behind:

"My Mom walked out on us twice.
After the first time, when she wanted to return
my Dad he took her back and it was okay for a while.
Then she left again. And you should see the guy she went
   off with:
a drunk and everything."

                         Then through his mouth
the voice of his father: "We treated her like a queen
but it wasn't enough for her."

All over the plant, through the long hours.
Up to Test to replace a grille's side shell, I hear Jim Pope's
   steady voice:
"When my first wife left me, I phoned in to take the day off.
I had the locks changed by ten o'clock, and was down to the
   bank
to make sure she didn't get a cent.
Then I went to check about the car registration.
You have to move fast when it happens..."

Someone in the small group of coveralls
is receiving advice.

HIGHWAY 16/5 ILLUMINATION

South-east of Edmonton, on the road that leads
to Vermilion, Lloydminster, and the Saskatchewan border
I feel coming into me again like
a song about a man born in the country
the joy of the highway: the long road

that reaches ahead through these wooded rises, the farms
that spread their fields out around themselves
flat to the sun, the odor of hay filling the cabin of the car

mile by mile, border after border, horizon
to horizon. The highway stretches away
in all directions, linking and connecting
across an entire continent

and anywhere I point the front wheels
I can go.

KITCHEN POEM

I put the bacon into the pan.
It lies there, lank and perfectly relaxed.
After a few minutes, though, a marvellous transformation
starts: the bacon begins to whisper, then hiss,
sinks down, becomes transparent, bubbles and snaps
and babbles to itself, turning crinkled and brown and stiff.

Meantime, I cut up some mushrooms.
The knife blade enters the soft puffy white flesh.
What is a mushroom: a fruit? A vegetable?
Inside the cap, as half the mushroom falls away

gills and a tiny breathing space are revealed –
a secret maritime connection: earth-fish, land-anemone
alive in the ocean of the mossy forest floor.
As the mushroom slices are added to the intense heat of
    the pan
each one dries out and appears as a miniature kippered
    herring.

Now I drop in the eggs. Two circular wonders.
The clear fluid becomes white and solid
as the yoke builds its own bright dome in the snow.
Personally, I like to put a lid on it all
so the white covers the yoke entirely.

Food is where everything starts. A thin slice of cheese
melting on my tongue. And I *have* to
talk about salads. Water
fleshed into green crisp ragged wafers:
lettuce leaves torn up and put in a wooden bowl.
With sliced celery stalks: one piece crunching
between my teeth as I work. Tangy radish:
a red warning sign of a coat, and below that
an apparently-calm, deceptive interior. Not like the tomato
which is honestly red and juicy all the way through.
Green peppers are even more deceiving:
really you just eat the rind because that's all there is.
To me, peppers seem a little embarrassed when they are
    cut open.
They have spent so much time attempting to look like an
    apple
that once they are exposed
they try to vanish underneath everything else in the salad.

Avocados. Warm green California memories
shipped all this way for me: a fruit
with a pudding inside, sweet, bland and mushy,
the absolute opposite of carrots

which are delicious edible wood,
staunch and starchy, each carrot disk
slipping off the knife. I pick one out to munch on:
aaaahh.

Then I put my wooden fork and spoon in
and stir the whole pile up. I pour
an oily and vinegary dressing on, slippery and
pungent with spices. Out of the water
and the ground it all comes, to my plate and my fork
and into my mouth.

I eat. Taking the planet as a whole
not very many can do that. Luck
has brought me this food, though something harsher than
    luck
keeps the others away from the table.
I eat, and go on talking.
Others who can't eat, or who can't eat so much,
meanwhile are thinking of something else to say.

But still I love to eat, as a person should.
This is how I know there is something wrong
with those who keep food from the poor.
I think if the vegetables controlled the world
there would be enough for all, since even a vegetable
knows its duty is to feed the earth. Something lower than
    that
must have its hands on things: some sickness
that decrees some people will eat and not others.

Yet food has its own revenge.
Hugo Blanco says that in Chile, under the generals,
when every form of resistance was mercilessly stopped,
the men with the guns had to allow
people to buy food and cook together
since conditions under military rule made this necessary

if many people were going to eat at all.
Now for this activity you need some sort of organization
Blanco says, and you can't stop people talking to each other
while they're stirring up the soup. And they don't
Blanco says, always talk about food.
See how sneaky eating is? I think if you want to control
human beings, you really have to keep every bit of
   nourishment
away from them. For if someone once opens his mouth
   to eat,
who knows? instead of rice going in
a word might come out.

Myself, I go on eating, as I go on breathing.
But I hope these two acts are all that ties me in this life
to those men and women who for now decide who starves.

WAYMAN IN LOVE

At last Wayman gets the girl into bed.
He is locked in one of those embraces
so passionate his left arm is asleep
when suddenly he is bumped in the back.
"Excuse me," a voice mutters, thick with German.
Wayman and the girl sit up astounded
as a furry gentleman in boots and a frock coat
climbs in under the covers.

"My name is Doktor Marx," the intruder announces
settling his neck comfortably on the pillow.
"I'm here to consider for you the cost of a kiss."
He pulls out a notepad. "Let's see now,

we have the price of the mattress, this room must be rented,
your time off work, groceries for two,
medical fees in case of accidents. . . ."

"Look," Wayman says,
"couldn't we do this later?"
The philosopher sighs, and continues: "You are affected too,
    Miss.
If you are not working, you are going to resent
your dependent position. This will influence
I assure you, your most intimate moments. . . ."

"Doctor, please," Wayman says. "All we want
is to be left alone."
But another beard, more nattily dressed,
is also getting into the bed.
There is a shifting and heaving of bodies
as everyone wriggles out room for themselves.
"I want you to meet a friend from Vienna,"
Marx says. "This is Doktor Freud."

The newcomer straightens his glasses,
peers at Wayman and the girl.
"I can see," he begins,
"that you two have problems. . . ."

A CURSING POEM

[*from "The UIC Poems"*]

This poem curses the Unemployment Insurance Commission.
This poem curses it.
This poem curses it in the centre
and on the left hand and on the right.
It curses each clerk and official

every benefit control officer
who does not flare up like a fire in the night
and cry down the masters of the Commission
and drag them out, the mad animals who have turned them
into the policemen of lives.
Let them tear off their own shirts
and cry in the streets for pity
for the nation they have built
out of anger and black despair.
Where do they think a man goes
when they turn him away?
Where does a woman go
on two-thirds of a salary already not enough?
They turn into a country of hatred and fear.

Then let them cry this out.
Let them cry for forgiveness
for it is they who have fashioned a nation of clear wind
into a pit of tar.
Let them leave quickly now
so the wickets stand empty, the tills ajar
no one standing behind the counters.
Let them move to the rear of the line-ups facing themselves.
Otherwise the curse of this poem will strike them.

A small red maple leaf
will appear in both of their eyes.
Everyone will see that they are *Canadian*.
Each one knows what a *Canadian*
does to his countrymen.

That is the curse of the centre.
And Welfare is on the left hand, where you go
when there is no money.
This poem curses it.
That one person should hand another so tiny a sum

and ask him to live out his days on it
in this country
cannot be forgiven.

Though they pretend this woman will drink away the money
they cannot be forgiven for what they do to a single life.
Though they complain that this one is retarded
they cannot be forgiven
for what they do to a single life.
Though they say this one could get a job
if he really wanted to
no one sees them leaving their own odious work
to get the other job they could find if they really wanted to.
They believe that the poor are the same as themselves
but have fallen from grace. For this
there is no forgiveness.
I cannot forgive them. Jesus cannot forgive them.
In the eyes of every man and woman they meet
is their curse: they will burn with shame
through their lives on the ground.

And on the right hand is Manpower.
Manpower is a slime, it is a room of fools.
They exist to dispense jobs that do not exist.
They are a palace of lies: upgrading courses
that do not lead anywhere; faked statistics
based upon work paying less than a loaf
promoted by men who have already stuffed themselves
    this day.

The poem curses it.
It names it a mouth, of useless advice:
"The yellow pages are full of jobs. Begin with the A's."
But it is a mouth with teeth, the teeth of rats:
"If you do not co-operate with us

your unemployment benefits will be withdrawn."
So it is a sink of oil
all the arrogance of those with jobs
talking to those without:
"Do you know how to conduct yourself at an interview?"

This poem curses it, stupidity grown so fine
it appears as thin as paper.
It is the curse on everyone who lies:
none of them shall escape. They will dig a hole
in the weary sand. Presently they will be told
to fill it in. Soon
they will be directed to dig it out once more.

Dale Zieroth

THE HUNTERS OF THE DEER

The ten men will dress in white
to match the snow and leave the last
farmhouse and the last woman, going
north into the country of the deer. It
is from there, and from past there, that
the wind begins that can shake
every window in the house and leaves
the woman wishing she had moved away
five years and five children ago.

During the day the father of her children
will kill from a distance. With the others
he will track and drive each bush
and at least once he will kill before
they stop and come together for
coffee in scratched quart jars. And
sometimes the November sun will glint
on the rifles propped together in the snow.

In the evening, as they skin and gut,
they talk about the one that ran three
miles on a broken leg and the bitch wolf
they should have shot and how John
the bachelor likes eating more than

hunting and they pass the whiskey
around to keep warm. In the house
the woman makes a meal from pork.

These men are hunters and later,
standing in bright electrically lighted
rooms they are embarrassed with the
blood on their clothes and although the
woman nods and seems to understand,
she grows restless with their talk.
She has not heard another woman in fourteen days.

And when they leave, the man sleeps
and his children sleep while the woman
waits and listens for the howling of
wolves. To the north, the grey
she-wolf smells the red snow and howls.
She also is a hunter of the deer.
Tonight, while other hunters sleep, she
drinks at the throat.

FATHER

Twice he took me in his hands and shook
me like a sheaf of wheat, the way a dog shakes
a snake, as if he meant to knock out my tongue
and grind it under his heel right there
on the kitchen floor. I never remembered
what he said or the warnings he gave; she
always told me afterwards, when he
had left and I had stopped my crying. I
was eleven that year and for seven more years
I watched his friends laughing and him
with his great hands rising and falling

with every laugh, smashing down on his knees
and making the noise of a tree when it cracks
in winter. Together they drank chokecherry
wine and talked of the dead friends and the
old times when they were young, and because
I never thought of getting old, their
youth was the first I knew of dying.

Sunday before church he would trim
his fingernails with the hunting knife
his East German cousins had sent, the same
knife he used for castrating pigs and
skinning deer: things that had nothing
to do with Sunday. Communion once
a month, a shave every third day, a
good chew of snuff, these were the things
that helped a man to stand in the sun for
eight hours a day, to sweat through each
cold hail storm without a word, to freeze
fingers and feet to cut wood in winter, to do
the work that bent his back a little more
each day down toward the ground.

Last Christmas, for the first time, he
gave presents, unwrapped and bought
with pension money. He drinks mostly coffee
now, sleeping late and shaving every day.
Even the hands have changed: white, soft,
unused hands. Still he seems content
to be this old, to be sleeping in the middle
of the afternoon with his mouth open as if there
is no further need for secrets, as if he is
no longer afraid to call his children fools
for finding different answers, different lives.

BEAUTIFUL WOMAN

I

Beautiful woman, you crown the hours
and we grow wonderful, we grow secret
in the assumption of our life. How easily
the electric night warms us. Fish
swim past the edges of our bed, oceans
in their mouths. The morning will never come
and break down this fever to be mad in each other's
warm white skin. We go down
like children, we go down into a great moaning
with silence forgotten and floating through the ceiling
like balloons. See me, see me dancing
to your terrible music, woman. The room
is filling with candles, the sun
is inches away: it smells
of your hair and lies writhing in your palm.
See again the sun and the bed wet with warm rain.
Wave after wave it comes, wave
after wave stones
break open at our touch, small bones break free and drift
out of you into me. And the skin
becomes water and salt shuddering
out past fingers – bloodfilled and animal –
towards the centre
of a thick and velvet earth where the sun
burns a hole in the sky.

2

Yet even from this bed
the anger rises day by day
and digs trenches to fortify its seed. So we
swear, accuse, sometimes punch flat-handed

the stubborn skin. You tell me
what it means to wait and work afternoons
with dishes and floors. You tell me
my friends who pace and strut ignore you, or notice
only your sex. How you hate them!
See your tears fly out at them like diamond-headed
spikes. See that it's me you've hit.
Let that sound surround our bed, let it
fill up the room as high as the windows.
Put your hungriest cats to prowl inside my skin.
Let nothing escape: the mouth
will stretch and harden into my best smile.
(You know this is not like a movie, you know
this is not in our dream – yet it continues.)
Everywhere muscles are dying. Out of my throat
you will hear me cursing, you will hear me
roaring. When it is my turn
nothing will change. The mirror
will fall, history will vomit at your name.

3

It is morning and the yellow sun falls
through the window like a stone. In the kitchen
the dishes wait and bits of swollen meat
have stuck to the sides of knives. All around us
broken flesh is aching. Tonight
we will go deep into our powerful
bodies again. Or we will do nothing
and survive just the same. Woman,
wake up and hold me, I have
nowhere else to take my anger. Wake up and let
your hands spread like warmth along my back.
Now that the skin is dead. Now
that both the music and the bruises have gone.
And all that remains refuses to begin

Dale Zieroth

without falling, is
caught and held in the light that spills
off the floor and stains the bed
like wine.

BAPTISM

In mid-river we join the ancient force
of mud and leaves moving in their journey
down the face of the continent and after
the first dance of leaving
one element for another, we fall quiet,
waiting for the silence to give us a
glimpse of history. In mid-river, it is
still possible to imagine Thompson's world,
without roads or bridges, rivers that
go back beyond white lives into the rocks
that push and fold, fault and break
as the new world rises from
the old.
          Yet this is still our river.
It does not matter that we are not
the first, what we will find today
has been found a hundred times before: it is
the ancient story of men meeting water,
as if there were a time, or faith,
when all of us were rivers, one
strength sliding out of the sky and into
the sea, one direction in us all.

But the river churns here and beats along the shore.
It picks up speed on the outside curve
cutting past the cottonwoods and under the deadfalls
that sweep across the water like the last arm of the land

and the water takes command.
I bend my paddle in my hand and my friend
digs in but there are branches like dead fingers in our faces
and there can be
no avoidance now, water comes up up and the
snag bends us down until my lungs
are in the water they are stones and I am
grabbing for the tree as if it were
my friend while the current sucks on me and my arms
go heavy as lead, a scream
goes dead in my throat, we do not
belong here, it bubbles and swallows
silt, the taste of ice,
there are blue stars somewhere and all the sounds of water
are alive and they pour in my ears,
into my eyes as if the river is already sure
how deep it will carry me,
what it will do with my skin, how it will dissolve
and burst and thin out the blood and I roll over
in a dream of clouds, willows, catch the edge
of a bank beaver's hole, brown mud like gold on my palm,
my feet still pulling for the ocean and then they find
gravel, the river rock, the river
pushes me away and I am shaking in the air again,
shaking for my friend riding the canoe's bottom
like a drunken pea pod, he grinds on the bank
a hundred yards downstream, his boots sucked off,
his body like a hole in the sand.

I breathe in the sun, take it yellow
into the body that spits grey in the river.
The baptism is over.
We have walked away without the grace of
fish or grebes, and the river is still the same.
I sit and watch the water with the oldest eyes of men:
if I trust the river, I will be
caught in it, rolled backwards into the

simplest race of all, the first, and the river is hard, it is
carnal and twists like an animal going blind in the rain,
but it leaves me pouring water from my shoe and then I see
him stand, wave, we have
first words.
Soon our paddles will bite the water but they will not
break it: our place on earth is rich enough,
the sudden rush of birdsong, our own
mid-river laughter as the warmth begins again.

COYOTE PUP MEETS THE CRAZY PEOPLE
IN KOOTENAY NATIONAL PARK

Brian brought him in
dumped in the back of his warden's truck and we
    watched him
die, a gasp at a time
spaced so far apart we knew he was
gone but suggested this or that anyway,
his breath hooked on a bone in his lungs,
his brown sides heaving for the sky
and we all felt for him in our different ways
which are the differences between men.
And twice Larry said, "Poor little fellow."
And Brian: "I could give him a shot of 'nectine
or a bullet but all I've got
is the .270 and that's
too big." So we hung on
till Ian pushed down on his ribs:
"Not much there." And still we
wanted him to run like the wind for the bush.
"Is that it?" I asked, hearing his
last lunge at the air, which it was, anyone
could tell he was gone,

off in a new direction
heading out somewhere else and leaving all
or nothing behind in those damn yellow eyes
staring out at me, out into a darkening world
where four men shuffled and laughed,
went in for coffee.

Inside with the rest of the crazy people
sitting down for coffee,
making words do all the work, talking shop, talking
park in the jargon of the civil servant man,
we know what chairs to sit in
we listen to the whirl of tongues
and the talk goes wildlife and telex and
choppers   it goes numbers and man-years and
stats it goes nuts for
fifteen minutes
and behind the words sometimes we hear
the anger and sometimes we hear the pettiness
and then the hurt. And someone tries to tell me
what this park really needs
what this park is really like, but I know already
it's like a dead coyote pup
lying out in the back of a warden's truck
waiting for the plastic bag we're
going to stuff him in and then we're going to
shove him in the freezer along with
the lamb that got it from the logging truck
along with a half dozen favourite
birds wiped out by cars, specimens now
and we'll save you that way, fella,
we'll cut off your head and throw it
up on the roof and wait till the bugs
clean you up and someday your skull will be
passed around
hand to human hand
and not one of them will be

afraid of you   not one of them will let himself know
how the last gasp was also like a sigh
how it was the wrong way to die   in the back of
a warden's truck   looking at steel
watched by humans   handled and pitied and
down on your side in the muck
a pup   seven months out of the den.

Coffee's over   we turn from our chairs
notice the blue sky outside
the cold sweet air that comes from the breath
of the animals and we hurry to our places
the crazy people and me, we gotta get back to our
paper work.

THE TRUCK THAT COMMITTED SUICIDE

In one major operation he tore out her
big black heart of an engine and threw in another.
His fingers worked over her,
tightening and touching and leaving
little drops of blood that mixed with the oil and the mud.
He drove her on pavement and gravel and dirt,
on ice and muck and trails that ended like lines in the dust.
He drove her on the road to work,
down the Mile Hill where the deer
come out of the mountains on their way to the river for
    that is
their work, to get across the road, their daily task
looking both ways and taking their chances when the
big trucks come down on them, the loggers and the
cowboys, the tourists and the housewives up early,
the drunks trying hard in the middle of the night
with the booze inside them like a golden plastic fruit,

seeing a pair of golden eyes and sliding
into them, opening them up in the middle of the highway
that is a slab of noise and light, the wind
whips back and forth through their big mule ears, the hair
ruffles and they look like they're asleep,
can't quite get up yet. And later there is a stain
on the asphalt like old red paint where the ravens hop
forward and peer into the eyes as if to ask
one last question, and over near the edge there are
other birds taking their
share of the work as
his truck goes by.

Rolling down the hill into work
and the sight of ravens black as old women started
touching off nerves that went down deep, bringing back
a wave that went through the man and then
over him, a direct hit, leaning forward into something
not quite known and the truck felt it.
The two of them at once
crossed the yellow line, crossed the asphalt on the
other side and touched the guard rail.
There was a humping sound like the sigh of
extinction, a wrenching as the things that fit together
broke apart, doors swung open and she tipped and
    broke and
roared. His head
touched the windshield that broke then
shattered into all the smallest pieces,
some falling out and down to the ground
even before the two of them stopped at the bottom of
the Mile Hill, rolled up
against a tree with their black wheels spinning slowly, a tree
on fire now and burning with them and
adding its odd woody smell to their
oily exploding he/she smell, the smell
that would still cling and hold them together

after the necessary tasks of removal and identification,
after the separation and the final washing
there would still be that one vague and bodiless smell
it would stay the way it had formed in the last moment
out of paint and sweat and dust and blood,
one smell   so strong and rich and different it left other
  men sad
and gagging under nearby trees
retching and hawking and then recognizing once again
the sound of the ravens arriving for work
the smell in their hairless wings.

THE BOAT

I

I go back to the boat, and then
nothing – across the ocean
no peasant in a sheepskin
smiles and offers his calloused hand,
no milk maid teases – Yet
at the lip of a decision
somewhere in Prussia or Poland,
where the borderland shifts
under their bed, two of them
talk across the continental night,
the promise of land tumbling out
with every word – and the fear
never quite laid to rest
by the kiss, the thrust, and always
the promise, his great promise

and her looking up into the unborn night,
Europe crowding around, dark as a cowshed.

I dig up old letters, written
in a wavering hand, all gothic
swirls and I imagine
this is the Atlantic in their veins,
the boat rocking under them night upon night
then pitching them up
on a cold green land – Or so I imagine
when I trace back to the boat
and find no sign of them
stepping off, all the talk
at an end, the tough job beginning,
holding the fear close enough
to smell it – after all that salt sharp
air, still the slightest whiff
of the dung.

2

He goes back to the boat
and the boat is not there, it has
set out again and
all around the world it is
picking up its people, the ragged
ones who can't decide
and in the last moment a man
appears suddenly under the tree
at the end of their street – and they flee
to the water, to the boat
churning up the sea, throwing
up its own citizenship of foam and tears.
These hopefuls reach

into their bundles and pull out icons, crusts,
potions that grandmothers made,
the old women who couldn't come
or wouldn't make it
but who waved and were the end of history
in that place
forgoing the boat for the comfort
forgoing the promise for the familiar fire.
– The boat gets away
just as the old walls fall
and two people are clinging to each other
and to the dream approaching,
unaware that the shore changes
with each new wave,
and sand is what they share
with the solid citizens.

3

So you go back to the boat
– and no foothold,
no blood line swims ashore, no rat
leaps along the anchor line
and makes you home – And what still lives? –
the slow wash against the sand, a lap lap
lapping that says over and over
nothing of you crosses this chasm,
all of you springs up
from this plank, this board
ripped from the ship and planted
here, sprouting into a wave green tree
out of which your father fell,
out of which your mother decided
it was time to come down to earth.

– and they took you
from the water's edge, and sat you down

in the middle of the continent, dusty
and without knowledge, and on the days
of the heavy rain, when the leaves curled down,
you cried
and they could not understand
they would not remember
the old voices you kept hearing
in the rain.

Part Two

Jeni Couzyn

THE RED HEN'S LAST WILL AND TESTAMENT TO
THE LAST COCK ON EARTH

Mr Cockatoo I'm through.
                    You
can take your splendid
reasoning and quick
precision and elegant
vision somewhere
else.

    You can take your
fine red comb and fast
feathered sex and high
concepts somewhere
else.

    Your race can take its
good influence and careful
words and strong wings and
bright eyes some other
place.

    You may be the
last manifestation but
you're not worth it.
                    Now
that there's artificial
insemination since the
evolution of the cock

as a different species
you may as well wither

too.

      Hens need something
else. You make us feel
abandoned. You make us
feel like a place cocks
pop into. We stay in the
place alone.

             We await your
visitation. You pop in and
pop out. When we wake up
in the morning it is
silent.

         All the hens in the
farmyard feel exactly as
I do about you. We have
decided to quit.

            You all
can take off on your
massive Coxes High Powered
Jet Propelled
wings.

        We hens will stay here
laying our eggs in the
warm straw, dreaming of
foxes.

EARTH RESIDENCE

My secret longing is for a friend
from another planet. I've been ready for years
watching the moving lights in the sky.

Now landed
right into my belly from a world I can't even
imagine as a star

bundled up in my flesh
preparing yourself for earth – little budded fish
with tail and cells set aside

for every organ of your future.
My mind wriggles with discomfort, will not hold
the image.

I struggle against instinct strong as breathing
to stay and observe
those pieces of meat, kidneys bowels lung skin

labouring in the dark, keeping faith.
A shaggy fungus with a myriad darting tongues
burrows into the fleshy lining

of the inverted earth. Blood coursing
through spiderthread river tangles.
Embryo, jelly-lump, shadow of a god.

Dreamily I stare at picture books
to make the difficult leap inside my skin.
Little curled animals.

In the second moon now
you have eyes under sealed lids. Like black beads
they shine through milky skin.

Can you hear yet? Are you dreaming?
You begin to wave limbs like gentle sea-flowers
each tiny frond tipped with a nail

and transparent as jellyfish a frail skeleton
sketches itself lightly in.
You're as long as my index finger – impossible

that a person could be so small.
My mind somersaults in alarm – a giant growth
an alien life

inside my body. I touch my belly, sing a lullaby
to make you mine.
Oh oh oh my dear invader, they've given you

a visa for earth.
Now in this one body, this ship
we are sailing to that strange country.

Mary di Michele

AS IN THE BEGINNING

A man has two hands and when one
gets caught on the belt and his fingers
are amputated and then patched
he cannot work. His hands are insured
however so he gets some money
for the work his hands have done before.
If he loses a finger he gets a flat sum
of $250 for each digit &/or $100 for a joint
missing for the rest of his stay on earth,
like an empty stool at a beggar's banquet.
When the hands are my father's hands
it makes me cry although my pen must keep scratching
its head across the page of another night.
To you my father is a stranger
and perhaps you think the insurance paid is enough.

Give me my father's hands when they are not broken
and swollen,
give me my father's hands, young again,
and holding the hands of my mother,
give me my father's hands still brown and uncalloused,
beautiful hands that broke bread for us at table,
hands as smooth as marble and naked as the morning,
give me hands without a number tattooed at the wrist,
without the copper sweat of clinging change,
give me my father's hands as they were in the beginning,
whole,
open,
warm
and without fear.

POEM FOR MY DAUGHTER

Toys, the blue rhinoceros with the spidery lashes,
the monkey coyly seeing no evil,
hands taped over his eyes,
a truth barrier, his long sad tail
like a phallus soft with spent love,
the flower rattle, the pink squeeze-toy
and an Indian doll whose black braid you use
to tug her along,
such are the objects you have so far
to know yourself.

Emily, these baubles that people your world
have no desires of their own
baby woman, what can I tell you to try to be
without being wrong?

Try to live intelligently and be happy
as you are
as your mother read too many books
thinking she could not be pretty.

A single season may strike campfires in a man's blood.
Keep what you feel underground.
Only the lead in your pencil
as you note these things
need poison your reflection
wanting the power that can make an old bone
rise.
Few men may come back from the dead for you.

I can tell you this because I have found a man's duty
a cold bed to sleep in
and his lust a fast train,
because you are not unique,

you who have so soon discovered your hands and feet,
because even Sartre betrayed Simone de Beauvoir
for every half-baked dish in Paris,
I advise you to steel yourself
although there's no escape from pain
you can burnish with it
like an iron in the fire.

FALSE ANALOGIES 2

I know at least one book
arguing men and women
evolved from different species.
Women cry more easily because
they still carry so much
of the sea in their bodies.
It makes them feel incomplete,
lonely for a self that gets harder
and harder to define.
Tears, blood, and amniotic fluid
have the same salt
composition as seawater.

Religion comes more easily to women
because a regular release of hormones
makes their bodies swell as if with tides.
In pregnancy they carry 50% more fluids
in their bloodstream.
So the feeling some theologians
describe as "oceanic"
comes naturally to them.

Only that dark bosc pear of the uterus
can contract and retract

more than any other muscle,
a dwarf star.

Men, those extraterrestrials
angels or devils
made a truck stop here
for mother and home cooking.

Don Domanski

THREE SONGS FROM THE TEMPLE

for Jeannette

I

what are we to do with a heaven
that moves beneath stones
and fallen trees?

a heaven
that keeps good company
with vermin and blackbird
and the far off hills
staggering through?

with a lumbering paradise
that sleeps beside a dog's bowl
until fed?

an ether
that muds its nose
and feet?

2

lounging in this day's elevation
heaven sprawls its unearthly hulk
an inch above the pond
to finger its brainwork of flies
and dream of adorations

to dream it is more
than a toad's placid heart

more than a bullhead's
righteous appetite

something other than the distant
misery of foliage
rising up in prayer
along the horizon.

3

all night heaven dances
brimming with its brutal hugs
and tremblings

twisting its bodiless form
above our beds

uprooting us suddenly
from sleep
to endure the full outcome of love

whose reek of pleasure
hangs in the morning air?

CAMPING OUT

for hours I sat kennelled
beneath the sleeping tarp

listening to a spasm of ferns
push to the pond's edge

to a tongue wag
in the thick neb of the land

to the clarity of stones
mouth the heart.

all night a half moon
and a wind goading
the stain of my small fire

here is the black rent
at the end of memory
here is the starlit anonymity

face down in the world.

A SMALL PRAYER TO HEAVEN

O grimace of star on stone
O stony nightmare
mogging through our vacant hearts

O heartbreak covering the seafoam
covering the subsoil
covering the latitude of open air

do not disappear from our only eyes
do not leave us alone on the impassable earth

O earthlight shimmering in blood
do not forget our heads positioned
in the trees   our guts cushioning the mountains

O mountain kiss us once good-bye.

Paul Dutton

from *So' nets*

ess o en en ee tee ess
o en ee tee ess o en en
ee tee ess o en ee tee ess
o en en ee tee ess o en
ee tee ess o en en ee
tee ess o en ee tee ess o
en en ee tee ess o en ee
tee ess o en en ee tee
ess o en ee tee ess o en
en ee tee ess o en ee
tee ess o en en ee tee
ess o en ee tee   ess o
   ess o en en ee tee ess
   ess o   en ee tee ess

•

s   ss   s   ss   s   ss   s   s
s tonn tonn tonn tonn tonn tonn tonn
s   tt   s   tt   s   tt   s   t
s nonn nonn nonn nonn nonn nonn nonn
t   ee   t   ee   t   ee   t   e
t ness ness ness ness ness ness ness
t   ne   t   ne   t   ne   t   n
t sess sess sess sess sess sess sess
n   st   n   st   n   st   n   s
n sott sott sott sott sott sott sott
n   oo   n   oo   n   oo   n   o
n tott tott tott tott tott tott tott
    s   ss   tonn   tt   nonn   ee   ness
    t   ne   sess   st   sott   oo   tott

•

onset tense no tone to set
no sense to note not one no none
so one soon tosses on to net
tenses notes tones one soon sees one
to ten senses soon one's not too tense
one's not sent to see eons nest
on stone tenets set to sonnet's sense
one senses sonnets not sent to test
sees no noose set no nonsense no
set one-ness one senses entente not
tense tones no sonnet's set to tote so
tense not testes on notes to one's tot
    noon noses onto settee son's set on
    one not seen to toss stone sonnet net on

•

s s s s s s s

o o o o o o o o

n n n n n n n

s s s son n n n

noon noon noon noon noon noon noon noon
noon noon noon noon noon noon noon noon
noon noon noon noon noon noon noon noon
noon noon noon noon noon noon noon noon

s s s s s s s

e e e e e e e e

t t t t t t t

s s s set t t t

   sonset sonset sonset sonset
   sonset sonset sonset sonset

Raymond Filip

THE MIGHTY BUCK, THE IMMIGRANT FUCK, AND
MELTING POT LUCK

Right off the boat, or Boeing,
I admit being tongue-tied.
For I am the language that is lost,
The name that is changed,
The ghost of welcome houses and Saturday schools.
I am men in sheepskin coats from the Old Country;
I am their New Country descendants: women in Persian
lamb.
I am Euro-paeans:
Songs you won't sing and dances you won't dance.
I am hard money.
I am the inalienable right to alienation.
The Horatio Alger Algerian, the Haitian electrician,
The Cuban security guard, the cab driver from Calabria,
The Jewish landlord who lives in Florida,
The Vietnamese orphan, the Romany musician.
I am Hutterite, Mennonite, Wahabite, Bahai, Sikh, and
Alcoholic.
I am the Canadian Mosaic: a melting pot on ice.
I am always the next generation,
The child with which good immigrant fiction ends.
I am that child grown up, writing in English,
Mother tongue in mind, adopted tongue in cheek.
You were Commonwealth, I am common loss.
Like a citizen of the world, in exile,
Or an overseas package returned to sender,
I am nothing left to be but Canadian.

TORCHY WHARF: VERDUN BOARDWALK

for David Fennario

Spot the river, a chaser,
Sousing the sky in its juices.
A poor boy's Walden Pond.
A place of struggle you revisit habitually,
Or else struggle to forget, habitually.
The whole city sees you down this embankment,
This pitch apron, this water, these memories.

As a scapegoaty kid with a rat-hat haircut and rakish smile,
I would escape to its landscape after playing hooky,
Or shoplifting, to hide out of view as perfectly
As the harmonica I had muffed into the murk
Like a diamond into the deep blue sea.
King-sized Queen Anne's lace and clouds: all for me.
I brought bread crumbs for the sandpipers,
And toothpicks for the seagulls.
My Donald Duck imitations scared off the pintails,
Not pollution.
Once I was frightened by a stoned voice,
So horrible in its hardness the words were hailstones
Against my ears as I shot pebbles into
Minnow shadows like laying bricks.
It was a gray, cynical, old man, telling me to scram,
As if I were tossing away what remained of his day.

Fishing here, without patience, or bait,
A patient from the Douglas would pop down
To swish through the wash welter-skeltering the shore,
Trousers rolled up, slippers sopping with weeds.
If you landed a lunker, he would always skip over,
And ask for a touch, politely,

Picking up the catch by its eyes,
Ventriloquizing the voiceless scream,
White water streaming from his lips like Lachine Rapids.

While the boys and girls high above the canal
Hunted for butterflies and buried treasure
In their family garden for the family collection,
We caught rats, at night, with flashlights and landing nets,
Flushing the underbrush and rubble all along the boardwalk.
One evening we ambushed seven, as big as cats,
Delivered to the Recreation Centre Sock Hop,
Unboxing the beauties on bobby sox mopping the floor
The squealing and laughter inseparable:
Sweaty little pussies go-cat-going to Elvis Presley
And the snappy incisors of oversexed rats.

But the best game of all was Nigger Pile:
The shout you let out
Before leaping like a pile driver
Into a mass of asses,
Free to hurt anyone as hard as you wanted,
Or just to endure the pyramiding pain
Without being injured.
If you chickened out,
A backstreet escort of law-and-order anarchists
Would bum rush your breath away boom into the river:
A bobbing target for razor-sharp rocks and broken glass.

This is the place I'll revisit habitually,
More often than the ferry that steamed to a stop here,
And more full of good stories than the good people on it –
To renew old habits beside children
Not knowing what I am up to, and I,
Not knowing what they'll think of me:
An old man, throwing stones.

Judith Fitzgerald

PAST CARDS 21

37 Albermarle Avenue

back in '77 the year we bought the datsun
I paid for and you drove
we were a trio, the gimp, the simp
and I was the imp, understanding
that simp wasn't short for simple
though it could've been, simpler
than it was, safety checks
were the death of us, then the choke
went and the head light
fixed only temporarily
plain gave up and the emergency
brake which brings me to later
when the emergency task force cop said
you gotta get this heap up to keele street
but I'm getting ahead of myself
and the brake was an on-again, off-again
kind of affair and that was much later
much later

a week later, after I'd bought the car
and had cut onto the highway from avenue road
and off again in the east end
with the sun exiting in late spring
exciting to be tooling around
listening to the ballgames and cfgm
playing the greats, playing Jim Reeves
and he'll have to go
but he played in the majors for a time

we went down to ring music
and picked out your Les Paul Custom
a yellow one, in a yellow house
with me kneedeep in Olson
listening to you practise with B.B. King
records and thinking, now
that's music
they should make it mandatory
with the window open
on the stereo

until the midwich cuckoo, the emcee
as I called it but nobody got the message
and then, it was may with me slipping
inside a bottle and wilcox
singing about full-time willie, singing
absolutely high gear songs, full speed
ahead and just flying –
it was may and magically mad, even the miraculous
was mundane to you
though it wasn't and you were playing
all jellyroll and jazzamatazz, developing
a skyhigh style and we were driving on

it was may, the emcee, and music
coming out of our ears
and too many misunderstandings
that you just couldn't understand
understand that I was meeting my father
later that day, afterwards when
at the emcee you disowned me
claimed you'd never known me
you came back from packing up
your yellow Les Paul
banging against your leg
each step you took closer
I was in the middle of explaining

my afterclubhours existence to some god-
damned new waiter who was repeating
after me

you're waiting for the guitar player?

like a parrot

I live with him

and he's gonna take ya home?

he is, he is

you're drunk

I am, I am, but I'm celebrating, I just
met my father for the first time today

that's what they all say

too drunk to see red, hysterical
wishing I wasn't drunk, you looming
towards me with your oh no, not again
fixed forever in your movements
dragging me up the stairs, going black
and blue

we were driving home in the datsun
cruising too fast and me thinking

drunk but deliberate, that this was
it, that I'm either going to jump
or get out of this, quick and succinct
with you occasionally glancing
in the sideview mirror, racing
along gerrard, just missing me

furious, driving furiously, driving
to park and pull on the emergency
brake, turn off the ignition,
lock the doors
back up the stairs of the yellow house

I took my pictures off the wall
clothes, dumped them into boxes
and sprayed the boxes with raid
and prayed the cockroaches stayed
with your heart of many colours
and that's when I decided, later
that night, morning almost
no more gimps, no simps
and no imp
looking onto that street
thinking lucid
you're not going to drive my car anymore

Jon Furberg

INTO GOES IN

[from *Prepositions for Remembrance Day*]

into goes in. "Wake up."
Here comes Dad into the dark,
brings me and Mom out into
the wet grass quickly up
the little rise overlooking
the old orchard stone white
in the moon, and there
are the doe and fawn
tasting the last silver apples

a gateway, a doorway into mist
horses whinnying far off away
wind hums in the fencewire.
come day, swim with the sleek
serpents, chase the mouse,
mole or shrew slips into
the burrow, deep, kneel and peer
into there, here comes a heron
smokey blue into the shallows,
stands still a long time
bends, parts, enters, lifts
a little fish flashing white
slender water, there goes
the sun, you've seen it

Hey, there's a war on! Here
come the soldiers – drums and guns
haroo haroo, flowers, kisses

boots – one leads into the next:
the house, into the path, into
the car, driving into town
slowing as we passed the place
that burned down last night,
smoke still rising and two
little girls gone. Where?
Mom said, "Into the air."

from *Anhaga*

MIDDEN YARD

I don't know for the world
why the soul does not darken
to remember them quick, and how
swiftly they fled– courage and strength
gone over to the far shore,
all mortal kindness sunk in hollow skull.

Eager for glory, we sought battle,
hoarding our fame, wearing our pride
more proudly than armour–
and when it walked it wore
a mask of rust, shield slung
on a bone arm.

In the last hour of light,
no thing stirs and rises, no form
against the sky goes humanly;
trees are lifeless sticks,

the cloud won't budge an inch.
Space takes the rubble in its claw,
things slip and shrink to make
an artless mass of weed and dust;
the sea lies sprawled along the cliff,
one darkness nudging another.

Each day weakens and sinks,
till earth is a tumulus—
mound of relics, dump of bone shards.
Death is the common father of our deeds.
We came and killed,
never learned to weep.

THE WALL

Where friends once walked
stands a wondrous high wall
laced with serpent shapes,
as if their words were graved
in every crack:

"Power of weapons hungry for flesh
has swept us away. This is our glory."

Storms flail the stonecliffs,
thick snow binds the land—
the terrible sounds of winter.
Then come want and pallor,
nightshadow darkens,
hail from the thunderhead

flung out of the North–
men driven before it.

All suffer. All is hardship.
The kingdom of earth is
Fate's heavy creature,
World under Heaven.

Artie Gold

[O'HARA DIED LIKE CHRIST]

O'hara died like christ
a blue chrysler struck him down
he died suddenly in a field of white yellow daisies
scattered among grass, he died surreally
in a kitchen wallpaper

he had fallen off a stepladder
awkwardly rehearsing his death
                                                    a daisy
grew among his teeth and one
curved up his ass curiously orphic
he lay there dead hands extended into another life

he might have fallen off a ladder hanging wallpaper
on a Bucks County ceiling
pushed away and twisted to his death
one star torn from a blue mural, bothering
to lightly descend upon his head.

I doubt several friends of his were there
innocently playing with him after
a blue chrysler had tapped the life from him;
I doubt they realized he could be dead
having arrived at a death so ineffectually
that no one had bothered to arrange a thunderstorm
and sandpipers didn't shriek their brains out
for this crushed gentle poet

who turned as he died away from the car
or possibly rolled away after the wheels

294

had contracted his chest and arm;
I doubt anybody knew what he was doing
when he silently tumbled down to earth.

god's love on tenderness, the harbormaster
of Long Island Sound gone
to sleep.

[LIFE.]

                    life.

                In a sense
it is the exact opposite of what we want   and
that opposite isn't death
                            but fence.
somewhere over the rainbow
you see, it's parabolic.
sometimes stretched out on drugs that make me taller
I sway over two kingdoms of sidewalk concrete adjacent
but over the line. clothes vanish through the magic agency
    of drugs
naked to my brain my genitals hang like a child's drawing
    of scissors
open large enough only for the beam of life to shine through
I trap the living photon and aim it down. my friends say:
    Artie,
  you have dropped your handkerchief.

Artie Gold

[I HAVE NO ASTROLOGER–]

I have no astrologer–
and don't believe in falling in love
on any particular August day you could name

I have knapsacks full of knick-knacks
that spread beneath a tree
would suffocate a hermit

and a perpetual cough
that when I've had enough of–
I'll die from.

I came to this city
naked   and from a small town
and have rearranged some of its objects

I will hitch-hike out of here one day
with my hair in my eyes and a good breeze blowing
and cause a little confusion I'm sure–

though no more than a hair
discovered in a gravy.

Leona Gom

There was never gentleness.
All this romantic bullshit
about growing up on farms.
All I remember
are the pain and death.
When pigs were castrated,
their screams all afternoon
and my father coming in,
the guilty blood all over him.
When calves were dehorned,
their desperate bawling
and my mother saying,
"it doesn't really hurt them."
When I saw kittens smashed
against the barn walls,
and dogs shot
when they were too old
to herd the cattle,
and chickens
with their severed heads
throbbing on the bleeding ground,
and horses shipped
when my father bought a tractor,
and I could bus to school.
I learned a lot about necessity,
that things are functional, or die;
and I was not as ill-equipped
as first I thought
to live in cities.

NAZIS

Nazis, the whispers began,
Nazis, when they gathered
and poured over each other
memory of the Old Country
to wash away the dust
of the cold Canadian fields.
Nazis, the voices said
to their backs in the town,
Nazis, to their children
bewildered at school,
Nazis, until they kept alien
to their farms and afraid.

Such relief for us all,
the end of the war,
the enemy now redefined:
the stooped Ukrainians
pausing over their plows.
Communists, we said.
Communists.

UNIVERSITY

*"He's got a scholarship.... Mr. Gates, your son's up into the
middle-class now, and you won't be speaking the same language.
You know that, don't you?"*

> *Lessing*, The Golden Notebook

Education an amulet
against the lives of our parents,
it seals our skins against the touch
of old rituals, presses us

into the corners of family gatherings,
fills our mouths with lumps
of harmless reminiscence.

You are different, they say,
you are changed,
too good for us now, they laugh,
needing our clumsy contradiction,
when we should say,
yes, it is all true,
our tongues unlearn daily
the vocabulary of crops and cattle,
there is less and less here
we can explain.

A head of barley:
what has it to do
with quadratic equations,
with medieval literature?
The day we left
we began to believe it,
and now our knowledge fits our hands
like a manicure
too expensive to soil
with the fact of these farms.
Yes, we should say,
it is all true,
we are no longer your children.

They will watch us leave them
and be afraid,
something they wished for
gone wrong,
like a crop so heavy
it lies down in the field.
That it is no easier for us
is the first
of our educated lies.

Kristjana Gunnars

from *Settlement Poems 1*

[Stefán Eyjólfsson speaks:]

XIV

i'm down to collecting skeletons
bones with deeper relations
than flesh or skin, bones that show
how we live, seven

are dead at fridjón's, two
left, at ólafur's the third
baby swells in the gums
blood streaks the white teeth

scurvy cuts away the flesh
as cleanly as it can, removes
the skin, viscera, bones
too small, too delicate

to be touched hang together
by thin ligaments, tags
of leather separate the segments
the hatchets of disease do

rough work among us
cut the tendons that join
cheek bones, pelvic bones, deep
bones loosen like ribs

i'm buckling under, can't watch
ólafur's third one bruise, swell
thirty five are dead, every
third one of us, a child

a weak adult, the saw
of scurvy picks away
the eyes, scrapes the brain
out of the skull, washes out

the loosened brain, folds
the legs, limbs, ties up
the marrowed bones in rags
bones, deep bleeding bones, see

how we hang in the sun to dry

    xv

i've jotted my notes in the corner
of the newsprint sigtryggur
brought from reykjavík, paper
soiled now with offal

our first battle, first winter
is past: every third man
rolled up, burned or buried
it's a long trip we're taking

we bleed freely like freshly
killed birds, now we lie
for a short time, coagulate
the blood on our feathers

i've learned to leave it at that
the bird, to plug the throat

with a ball of oilcloth, put
wads of string in the nostrils

when the blood continues to creep
out, the bird stiffens
very fast, a tap with the hammer
snaps the wingbones in two

once settled, on our backs
like this we can't fly again
we're mounted into the prairie
pinned by broken promise, by

confusion, each man thinks
for himself now, the feathers parted
with a barren strip, pinned
by the unwilling in winnipeg

who won't make the journey north
with food, our own people
cut off
in the middle of the breast

Diana Hartog

YOU NEVER DID

You never did leave for Japan on that tiny raft
we talked about. I never had the chance
to pack you a lunch or imagine you
bobbing out on the Pacific – our love purer
each day spent apart.

Fate wanted that voyage! She'd made plans, she had in mind
storms of an advanced spiritual nature,
she wanted you tossed on a black poisonous sea
while I on shore would post letters of absolute felicity
– white-winged singing letters
flying low and at a steady pace behind you.

THE COMMON MAN

Spring, and all day today in town I noticed
pregnant women – waxing at different stages
but always that same round belly floating by, like a mote
just beyond focus, something I meant to say

– about last night: the presence that eclipsed us both,
that moved out of sight if we looked – what was it we held
as we held each other? When it left
it left me your face: luminous, blinded

and I remembered how you put down your fork in the
    restaurant

and leaning over, murmured in my ear "I love you for saying
'I hate you for saying that' "
– from our public argument about the common man
when you'd spat out "Well it ain't Rilke!" –

your mouth sad from the side, the way it looked
the night we met, the curve of your forehead
rising above the horizon, legions of deer
leaping to the right across your chest
– I love that sweater, you never wear it anymore.

WHO

If I could stop telling you what's wrong
so you could make it right or untrue

If I could look straight at you without hate
or hope

If I could see us plain and say
Enough!

Who would pick the fluff from your bellybutton?

MATINEE LIGHT   *a movie review*

Bellows, squeals, howls: a cacophony of mating calls
rising from the planet as ants, elephants, ostriches –
    everything else
except us – did it.

I liked the slugs the best, the two flexing like muscles
oh and the swans, they didn't make a wrong move: the
    football star
and his date on prom night – gliding across the gym.

They stuffed in death as filler, a pair of spent salmon
draped from a low-hanging branch, their shredded flesh
trailing in the water, their spines elegantly bent musical
    instruments.

I winced and thought of you as a lady
praying mantis began to munch her suitor's head: the horror
of his body carrying on like that, pulsing, faithful to her still

as we shuffled out: the couple ahead of me
holding hands – meeting matinee light
with that dazed expression of lovers.

Gary Hyland

SCRAWNY'S SUREFIRE ACNE CURE

The thing with acne is your parents
who think it's some modern invention
caused by cokes and chocolate bars.
Truth is it's probably as old as sex.
Think of it. Helen of Troy stayin in
with a big zit on her perfect nose,
Cleopatra before a date rubbin sand
on her cheeks to grind the pimples off,
Lancelot shinin up his best shield
so he can pop a coupala white-tops.
It kinda helps to think all those
heroes went through the same thing.
Okay so I'm crazy but I could be rich
with acne clinics all across Canada
cause I developed a surefire treatment,
scarless, painless and inexpensive.
First apply a cloth dipped in hot water.
The heat draws the gunk to a head
and sterilizes the whole operation.
Then when you got it ready to pop
press a strip of adhesive tape on it
and give it some time and more heat
so it merges real good with the tape,
then rip off the tape fast and, look ma
no pimple – it's stuck onto the tape
and you've just got this little hole
which you dab with another hot cloth.
Well, now you got my secret method
Scrawny's genuine "Zap your Zit Kit"

and I'm not any the richer for it.
Of course, your folks will still nag
about the cokes and chocolate bars
but Lancelot probably had that too.

DEKE AND DANTE

What happened was in our social text
the author says *The Divine Comedy* by Dante
is onea the best books of all time.
With that title I think it's gotta be funny
so I tool on down to the library
and Mrs. Burns falls off her stool
when I ask for it but she gets it
and it looks okay, y'know nice and small
so I head home and open it.
                          Well shit
you never saw such goddamn small print.
Looked like the Lord's Prayer on a dime
with footnotes longer than the story
only it wasn't a regular-type story
but a jeezus poem which if it was printed
the right size would outweigh *The Bible*.
Worse yet it's ten thousand years old
so you can imagine me in grade nine
squinting at sixteen miles of poetry
but I decided I was gonna get some laughs
from this thing come hell or my old lady
which is what does come – a trip to hell
and jeezusmurphyman was it sumthin awful
about as funny as your average math class.

I won't lay the whole scene onya but Dante
gets outa hell and hits purgatory next

then heaven before swingin back to earth
and never a fraction of a joke anywhere
but I stuck her out because to tell the truth
I got so I kinda liked that snazzy lingo
and the sharp way Dante zapped these losers
he decided oughta be dumped in hell
even a coupala popes.
                But most of all
there was this Beatrice babe he loved
who was right-out-of-this-world beautiful
and it was her that inspired and guided him
right up to God's goddamned front porch.
All the time I just kept imaginin Beatrice
was Elaine Wells and I was this Dante guy
and I sailed through that whopper of a book
in I'd say only about two or three months.

August Kleinzahler

Pissed but idyllic
I stew
      in the lilies awhile.
     Logs slosh.
             Mill
lights across the strait
are tentative as stars.

If a certain one,
          a lady
known
to wander this strand

walked past,
whistling a foolish torch song

and found me so

   'Come down
      from the drizzle,'
I would tell her.
         'Come,
muddy your knees a spell.

Dreams are a watery gruel
to fend the day.
        Before gulls,

tugs and Winnebagos
chase off the night

bully my nose with kisses.'

DEJECTION BETWEEN FOOT AND BROW

Mr Moo heard stuff 'round the trough
ah me, dumb
like a yoke.   Iz cumulative
you know
till the hole's plugged
and what it is backs up
to the doors of Penny Palace.
                              The racket, man
in that arcade – those slobs
at toy war go unh, unh night and day.
                                        Remember
the world, Beau
2 miles high
so any chair or bough was bright
like the eye-fur
burnt-off.
                Birds just shot through
the arch
screaming,
                Jeeeeezus, my feathers
my pretty little bones...
                              I remember
where was that
in Troy, I think –
                    or some dry hill
out west.
It's years now.

310

SUMMER'S END

Seven miles through tangled bush and on
to the HoHo outpost.
A steady trickle from spruce boughs above
has us telling thetruththetruth
to tree frogs and slugs.
Weariness, wet socks and a keen deltoid rheum
have turned the world back on us.
Flynn commences to whistle, inhale
and whistle, whistling nothing
but a thread of abuse
at the blameless cedar, or hoping
perhaps, to flush a nervous eagle.
I think not.
And on:

                  whittling maledictions
                  two miles in an afternoon
on to the HoHo outpost.

No sooner had our people sung us
to the forest's edge
than the radio weevil was on them,
leeching the private knowledge.
As for the news ahead –
HoHo is in ruins
and the hamadryads far,   far.

Thus clenches the world
as the sibyl long ago told us it must
long ago under the weaving poplar.
Too far gone to turn around

we journey again for journey's sake.
Sick with woe?
> "HoHo,"
> Flynn shouts to the sun
> and the shout resounds
"Semper HoHo!"

Charles Lillard

RIVERS WERE PROMISES

The rising mist,
Rising above
The Skeena, Fraser, Nass,
Rising from pine shadows,
Rising from a height of land
    At Raven's lair;
The Skeena, Fraser, Nass,
The Dean, Bella Coola, Sombrio,
    Flooding the Pacific's maw;
On my desk, the daybooks:
Here's a lichen-studded fly,
Here's the salmonberry flush,
Here's that first breath of winter,
    In those misted green hills and far passes;
The Chilko, Taseko, Washwash,
              Where I paid my dues.

The Adams, Tuya, Eagle,
Where the stars shot holes in the darkness,
The Noeick, Kimsquit, Raush,
From the muskeg hills, streaming waters,
From the pine ridge's arête,
    A cascade hangs, noiseless, a rainbow;
The Kechika, Alexis, Homathko,
Where our siwashpurps wouldn't brave a spring kill,
Where horseflies and woodticks drove us into the freshet,

Our mules wading, shank-deep in the *cultus chuck*,
                 Where I paid my dues.

The Machmell, at the First Narrows, black with rain,
               The tide twisting...
The Sheemahant, where the second gut narrows, a siamese
    bear
              Walking too quietly...
The Tzeo, where the Owikeno shallows, where we crossed
    to the
              Asseek and ran...
                 Where I paid my dues.

The Nazko, Lillooet, Neechanz,
Draining the twisted mountains,
Draining the green, cedar-spruce stillness,
Draining the damp from the tap-root,
Draining the power of the muskeg,
Draining the land, draining the sky's sap;
The Nitinat, Leech, Quesnel,
Where the ruins sink,
Where the past sleeps beneath tree-line;
The Alsek, Parton, Tahini, Flemmer, Tutshi, Wann,
In a land of dying ice;
The Parsnip and Nation, fragrant willow at sunset,
The Sustut, Otseka and Ingenika,
The Kettle and Omineca – Gun-an-noot country;
    First story, then myth,
In the flattening of a winterlandscape.
                 Out of the minds of men,
Out of campfires, the white-eye's chase;
The truth wrenched: the need to make;
Out of too many campfires, the air's stillness at dusk, lies
    To make history tally;
From the mountained hush, from those poplar at Bowser
    Lake

Simon Gun-an-noot
 The Little Bear That Climbs Trees,
   Rises,
His, the one impeccable story.

The Dease, Kwadacha, Babine,
 Outside a grey drizzle, the forage mouldering,
And I caress these splayed books,
My only receipts.

On the blackwater of the Damdochax, a sweeper,
 I couldn't meet the ante when the owl called . . .
It was my time.
In my time I'd used my time
 In too many places,
Yet I bluffed it through to this house
On the Skeena's floodplain;
 My children, the brown tint high in their skins,
Snarl like cats killing
Over some trifle,
 The house is loud with their noise, my mind is loud,
   Loud,

The Kiteen, Prophet, Sikanni,
 Snow flaking the July weather,
White and white-silver clogging the sky;
The Fulton, Kispiox, Nakina,
Salmon work the eddies, the bright twist of salmon,
 Moving, moving inland, towards the *Mama illahie*,
 The headwaters,
   Raven's lair.

The Dease, Kwadacha, Babine,
 Outside a grey drizzle, the forage mouldering,
And I caress these splayed books,
My only receipts.

Kim Maltman

TINA

Tina comes down to the pumphouse by the river.
In a small backwater where heat is poured out from the
    generators
she watches him, the man she brought here with her.
He swims about lazily, with power, but she stays near the
    shore,
bobbing slowly up and down, letting herself in
each time only to her chin. She knows this place and how
the warmth ends suddenly, you stray a foot too far
and you're in freezing river water. As it
tumbles down to the shore behind her,
the stream from the pumphouse rumbles in the background.
Tina starts to talk. Sometimes it's her father talking,
showing up again after a year or so, in need of money,
or her mother who never drank and always
covered her bruises, and loved her daughters
(and her god) so much she sent them away from it all
to convent schools where the nuns were no better,
strutting around all the time with canes. This
when Tina was 14. Tina had a child at 16, at 18
took too many pills. Now Tina is 21, has been in love
often. She wants not to trust this man, but who could blame
    her if she did.
And the man, he knows there's only so much he is
    capable of
giving, which he thinks of as being honest with her,
so he just listens and says nothing and keeps
paddling around, letting out sporadic yelps as he misjudges
the water for the tenth time, and watching

316

how she dips, each time, exactly to her chin. He is fasc-
   inated,
but Tina mostly stays in one place, never straying from the
   warmth,
not even after dark. It is a beautiful evening, quiet,
she thinks, and stays in one place. Instinctively
she knows the boundaries, she is used to these things.

NIHILISM

By mid-August there's not much left to do.
All the mothers are fed up with having kids around,
underfoot, and so all morning they've been hurrying off
from place to place trying to get things done.
Maybe they'll take the afternoon off, they think,
stay in out of the heat and rest. Even the boy
who's been squealing and tearing about with the other kids
while they drenched one another with garden hoses
is bored stiff by now, just going through the motions.
What difference does it make, he's already tried
everything he could think of, so it's all the same,
it's all waiting. A few more weeks and he'll be
back in school and it'll be cool enough to
run around all day if he wants, nothing to stop him.
He can wait. The sun's too high, he's tired of playing in the
heat. Let the grown-ups push themselves around
from one thing to the next, looking miserable. When you're
growing up you've got all the time in the world. Time to
see things for what they are. Looking around he sees
the women in twos and threes, getting old and trying to
   hide it,
and the men bored with them but afraid of their own
   bodies too,

of ending up with nothing. Not him he thinks.
He's not going to end up like that. The woman next door
with the nervous frightened look, the hard bored
faces of the men out working on the streets. All they want
is to get through the day, and if things are harder than usual
so what? They don't care. They never expected much
    anyway.
It's a bad day all right. The heat's made
everything feel dull and faded. Even the rest of the kids.
Over the last few weeks they've started getting lazy,
sitting around all afternoon half asleep
waiting for things to happen to them.
Now that it's too late he's sick of it, he wants to
take something and shake the hell out of it.
But what's the use, nobody gives a damn anyway.
So maybe he'll just wander off by himself again, he thinks.
Maybe he'll drag out something big and useless from the
    dump
and smash it.

A. F. Moritz

CATALOGUE OF BOURGEOIS OBJECTS

Candle in the form of a white numeral 1 with a green
   monkey on its back
Statuette of bi-sexual Siamese twins, the base of the
   passive's throat joined to the dominant's crotch, her
   nose melting into his navel
Victorian lady and gentleman of black yarn hung by
   their collars
Four shepherds and four shepherdesses on a mahogany
   plain with a flock of hardened gum drops
Frightened hailstorm that attempts to return to the sky
Pond of vertical surface clogged with chartreuse plaster,
   several light switches, half of an oak door
Painting of an inverted tulip with a clipped stem
   touching the keyboard of a rusty shadow
Pair of toilets with blue fur, trained to eat table scraps
Silver tray full of dried tongues (with miniature
   broadsword)
Three-footed wingless bird of prey with desolate
   plateau head dominated by the following obsession:
   a naked woman balancing a blank head on her blank
   head, the topmost head wearing a hat which is a
   burning mainsail
One reedless clarinet among a rattling of dried reeds
Passageway that prevents the rain from touching you
Discreet cupboard which has endured many dinners
   without ever giving its untainted service
Wicker stand full of promises
Several ghosts, singly and in assorted groups, who bear
   striking resemblance to their former bodies at certain

appropriate moments (each with gold safety leash)
Fishbowl with fish of purple waxen balls and the scent
    of vaudeville lilacs
Fire in which a magic log burns without being consumed
Several shrines consisting of cave-like apertures fenced
    with steel net, where dry heat issues from below
Mary with God's only sibling, a tired vine, struggling
    from her belly
Sacred book wherein you are reminded to plant in the
    spring
Star that will descend from the night sky when you want
    to read
One inexhaustible fund of variations on certain themes,
    chiefly that crime does not pay
One room of furniture for a pet dwarf
Birdbath with attached birds of various plumage and in
    various postures of delight
Leafless tree where melodramas roost
Mechanized guillotine with procession of haughty
    blades
Decorative thicket of shy virgins succeeded by dragons
One small fortune in petrified eyeballs
Glass-eyed cabinet of further silence
Rivers of orange flowers everywhere
Six cascades of drummer boys and milkmaids
Statue of the sun with a clock in his womb

WHAT THEY PRAYED FOR

What they prayed for seemed not much,
and already, despite the dusty weeds
extending to the sky, a possession:
a grassy land, lightly wooded,
rolling, with intricate slopes

and crossed by streams, relieved
by lakes, pools and reedy swamps.
Breezes over the water to suggest
music; and, visible from rises,
the ocean, glinting among the trees,
near so that when you are silent
within yourself it can be heard.
Also shade and shadow:
an openness to the sun,
to the sky, that is yet defended
and moistened by fingers of the earth.
Then a few things will follow
from these first conditions: women
singing in full light and at dusk
before reflecting water;
and some way to live together
that is not a scandal and a shame.

PRAYER FOR PROPHECY

May the old women of music, frozen
in days before memory into words
(they cooled and suffered into use
between anvil and hammer), give
my ear a rumor of why the stars
flee and in what directions. Not
how the atoms and the grids of force
assembled like network the inept
sprawling design, but the future,
for which the loose lip of the sea
drools on this beach, sucking down
the dissolving sand. To what
purpose each winter the moaning chords
of night drag out their limp tails

longer, and with reptilian stares
rekindle soot in the day's face.
And if to this depth of nature I
am not destined to reach, then let
the country and the streams of water
that freshen valleys content me, hiding
in their sluggish harmony the cold
springs of the blood that clogs my heart.

Al Pittman

CONFESSION

What is there left
to say, now
that I've lied to you
all night long?

How my fingers curled
too tightly in your hair
was a small lie, hardly
a lie at all, but my hand
quivering in yours
like an egg anxious to give
birth, that was certainly
a lie, and my mouth's
gentle journey across
your breast was a lie,
and my eager hand's slow
search for your flesh
beneath the blankets, that
was a lie, and my holding
you desperately, like my life
depended on it, that was
a lie too.

And now this stark morning
what lies are there left
to tell, except the one lie
I must speak to you with words?

I speak it now, give you
the words without guilt:

I don't ever want to stop
lying to you.

THE ECHO OF THE AX

My father tells me of the time
he put his hand
on the chopping block
and dared his brother
to cut it off

and whack
just like that
he did it
and my father remembers
the blood on the steel blade
and his mangled hand
hanging barely
by a thread of skin
and he remembers too
how his brother looked
after he'd done it
in that moment
when the whack of the ax
still echoed about the yard

and he recalls
with a heavy breath
how he felt inside
having made his brother
a most amazed victim
of his weird and private fantasies

APRIL

The child sits hunched
in the corner of the yard.
The snow floating slowly down
gathers on his knees, his shoulders,
his bowed head. Gathers on the woodpile,
the fence, the chopping block.

The child sits still,
waiting to be erased.

All the voices in the world
could call him now and he
wouldn't hear.

He's discovered
almost what it's like
to be nothing.

The snow floats slowly down.
The child sits hunched in the corner
of the yard. Companion and almost kin
to the woodpile, the fence, the chopping block.

Robert Priest

GOD IN THE MUSEUM

God in the museum didn't seem so miraculous now. They had put stained glass up on it and fooled him. They had fooled him with tape recorded messages and supposed pilgrims lined up outside in black and white. Now there he was under glass with the divine cheese. Still it tasted good to him, that divine cheese, even in the wire cage. Poor old God. How he ranted and he raved in there while the supposed pilgrims walked by him in legions remarking on the odor. Milk Products! they would sigh. Imagine eating Milk Products.

After many years when he was so old they had almost forgotten why somebody said why not let him go, but others said no it would be cruel. He wouldn't remember how to hunt down his own food anymore and besides it was no longer the right weather for him. So poor old God stayed in there with the dinosaurs and tanks and the crystal balls and dreamed up things as usual. After a time they wondered why he hadn't died. Why he was still so much dust – a palaver of old tongues – unable even to crawl now, just a botched lump on a pedestal. Not even ethnic anymore. Just a cheesie reminder of a past no longer significant. In the end when they had completely forgotten they put up a sign that said – "Probably an old turd."

THE KISS I JUST MISSED

The kiss I just missed giving you wound up later on another mouth, but by then it had become a little cold and cruel. It wanted to be just burned off in sunbursts and cleansed of its longing. It imparted only melancholy. Where it goes now I don't know. Probably to be used and used on other mouths. Each time worn down a little more like a coin to its true longing. Perhaps it will reach you then from some impartial lover – from some dispassionate goodbye – like a stem cut from its rose.

That kiss that didn't make it to your mouth made it instead to Toronto, for I could not be rid of it in Palo Alto. It stained my lips even in Mendocino. In a Triumph Spitfire I could not by singing out the window leave a long burning stream of it hissing in the blue air. It has become an irreconcilable wound now. A grand comparer. It lands on lips in a regular autumn but it will never be severed from its mouth. I wash it in water – it is there. I wash it in wine – still it is there. Drunken then, singing your name, mouthing it hot and burning into my mind it has shown me its red edges, its arms and legs that didn't go round. It has talked to me sadly of clothes, of beds it didn't lie down in. What a weeper! It has dragged me under rain. Indelible. Indelible. Wants to go finally to the graveyard of old kisses, each one with its denied rose strolling ghostly over. Each one with its sunset nova quenched in amber on its headstone. O each of its stopped explosions driven down to juice in some white withering berry there.

CHRIST IS THE KIND OF GUY

Christ is the kind of guy
you just can't help hurting
No matter how much you love him
when you walk you stumble into him
you push him accidently from a window
If you back the car out
you will find him squashed behind the wheels
broken on the door – all over the grate
Christ has the kind of skin
that when you hold him it bruises
The kind of face that kisses cut
He is always breaking open
when we go to embrace him
Christ the haemophiliac
even the gentlest people can't help
wounding Jesus Christ
They are always running for a band-aid
and then pulling open his old wounds
on a nail
If there is a cross in your house
you will find yourself bumping up against him
accidently
moving him closer and closer to it
his arms continually more and more
widespread as he talks
Christ is the kind of guy
who can't help falling asleep like that
his arms spread wide as though over the whole world
You have a dream with a hammer
You are making a house
In the morning you awake
and find him up there on the cross beams

one hand nailed to the door-frame
"Look Jesus" you say
"I don't want to be saved like this!"
But then you hurt him extra
even taking him down
You pry at the nails savagely
but it's no use
Christ is the kind of saviour
you can only get off a cross
with a blow torch
"Father forgive them" he says
as you begin to burn his hands

Monty Reid

HER STORY

I was born in a hospital in a small town
      beside a large shallow lake. My mother
said while she lay there, between the spasms of
      pain, she could hear the hard
flights of mallard and pintail, avocets, bittern
      heron, the ragged V's of Canada geese
come flailing in to the mudflats and reed beds
      around the lake. When I cried they may have
heard me there, the birds gathering on the shore
      before migration.

Once I had appendicitis and there were no birds
      but once, when I was getting my tonsils
out, I lay propped up on the pillows and watched
      the gulls, herring and ring-billed and California
even a glaucous, strut around the incinerator
      pecking at scraps of garbage
generals plotting a coup.

Later, my eldest son being born
      prematurely into the world and the birds
were there then. In fact, we had been out hunting
      and it may have been the squatting in the cold
blind while the mist came off the lake like a wool
      sweater, the steel of the shotgun ice

against my cheek, that brought the birth
    on early. Or it may have been the excitement, the
      gun
bruising my shoulder, the weight of ducks
    we carried back to the truck, or it may simply
have been the smallness of my body and its inability
    to carry full term. But he was early.
We weren't sure he would live. And the birds
    were there then too. I dreamt them tumbling
shot out of the sky above the hospital.

I live now near the lake I was born beside.
    The kids aren't that interested in birds.
I watch the herons and cranes and storks
    flap over and my husband yells at the gulls
that shit on the fence he's just painted.
    I sometimes think the birds are crazy
to keep coming back to this lake
    tho I love watching them
and I also know
    they can't help it.

NECKLACE

When the dogs came home
they weren't interested in supper.
We could see them from the kitchen window
lying by the barn.

When we went to check the cattle
we found one dead, stiff
legs in the sky, a red hole

where the dogs had eaten
the udder away.

When we crept up to the house
with whatever had killed the cow
already tearing at their stomachs
we could see how far in
they'd stuck their heads

around their necks
a noose of blood.

Robyn Sarah

FUGUE

Women are on their way
to the new country. The men watch
from high office windows
while the women go.
They do not get very far
in a day. You can still see them
from high office windows.

Women are on their way
to the new country. They are taking
it all with them: rugs,
pianos, children. Or they are leaving
it all behind them: cats,
plants, children.
They do not get very far in a day.

Some women travel alone
to the new country. Some
with a child, or children.
Some go in pairs or groups
or in pairs with a child
or children. Some in a group with
cats, plants, children.

They do not get very far in a day.
They must stop to bake bread on the road
to the new country, and to share
bread with other women. Children

Robyn Sarah

outgrow their clothes and shed them
for smaller children. The women too
shed clothes, put on each other's

cats, plants, children, and at full moon
no one remembers the way to the new country
where there will be room for everyone and
it will be summer and children will
shed their clothes and the loaves will
rise without yeast and women will have come
so far that no one can see them, even from

high office windows.

A VALEDICTION

Declining
frequency.   Sometimes
when we laughed

it was an antler
shaken of snow.
Whole pianos opened

at a phrase.   That's
gone now; the buzz,
too – but I liked

your fingernails, you know,
their curve, the full
spoons of them

334

Robyn Sarah

A MEDITATION BETWEEN CLAIMS

You want to close your hand
on something perfect, you want to say
Aha.   Everything moves towards this,
or seems to move, you measure it
in the inches you must let down
on the children's overalls,
tearing the pages off the wall
each month; a friend phones
with news that another friend
has taken Tibetan vows, meanwhile the
kitchen is filling up with the smell
of burnt rice, you remind yourself
to buy postage stamps tomorrow

The mover
and the thing moved, are they two
or one; if two, is the thing moved
within or without, questions
you do not often bother yourself with
though you should; the corner store
is closed for the high holy days,
and though the air has a smell
not far from snow, your reluctance
to strip the garden is understandable

Laundry is piling up
in the back room, Mondays and Thursdays
the trash must be carried out
or it accumulates, each day
things get moved about and
put back in their places

and you accept this, the shape
that it gives a life, though the need
to make room supersedes other needs

If, bidding your guest goodbye,
you stand too long at the open door,
house-heat escapes, and the oil bill
will be higher next month, the toll
continues, wrapping the green tomatoes
in news of the latest assassination.
The mover
and the thing moved, it all
comes down to this: one wants
to sit in the sun like a stone,
one wants to move the stone; which
is better

David Solway

They are the bane
of ignorant swimmers:
a single brush
is an afternoon of pain.

Shaped shapelessness,
they are a food for nothing –
clutter the shore,
a queasy, languid mess –

that calmly come
coagulate of the depths,
half substance, half
participial jetsam.

Step gingerly,
scoop them out with buckets
to splat on rocks,
spear them with sticks, and see

the jellyfish
dribble into nothing
or close on them-
selves with a gluey squish

as if they felt
no inconvenience
in being dead,
as if they liked to melt.

In appearance
yielding to the elements,
they drift and drift
in aspic tolerance

of wind and wave,
yet cannot be deflected
from the floating
dumb directedness they have.

It's this absence
of desire but perfect
self-extension,
as they flex, expand and tense,

with the sea's will,
this pure ideology
untenanted
by mind yet impregnable,

that puzzles us –
although they have a blind
kind of beauty,
these filaments of sea-pus.

We can see right
through them, we can scoop and spear,
burn them in sun,
ravel their pink and white;

we can avoid
their myriad poisonous shoals
a day or two,
so intricately deployed;

but in the end
the jellyfish encircle

every island,
ring every beach, distend

their colloid net
round every swimmer, and sting
with even less
need or hunger than regret.

APOLOGIA

I understand the times are cool
    to all that discipline
men of the introspective school
    were once accomplished in.

Epigrammatic Frenchmen say,
    if temperate or staid,
that "reculer pour mieux sauter"
    explains the retrograde.

I study that austerity
    the profligate assault,
and I must fast with Emily
    before I feast with Walt.

CAT KILLING

Because solitude breeds mawkishness,
not just pugnacity,
she had in many years upon the island
collected thirty cats

to talk to, care for, rescue from starvation
and allow to be eccentric.

They came in bands, ears twitching with the news,
all nose and belly and strokable fur –
each with a proper name she gave
to chime with temperament –
and multiplied, dynasties of cats and kittens
to grace her insularity.

And because she was, if not a friend,
somewhat more than an acquaintance,
I agreed to ease the trauma of departure
by helping her dispose of cats
who would without her be condemned
to die of hunger, thirst, exposure and neglect.

We chopped the sleeping pills into the meat,
dissolved them in the milk,
fed them to the kittens with syringes,
thirty cats, a regular morning's work,
and after stuffed the living carcasses
into three great burlap sacks.

I never thought ten cats could weigh so much
as I heaved the first sack on my shoulder
and lugged it up the hill
to where I knew a disused well or cistern
plummeted as many feet
into that baking Serifos of earth.

Down they went into the hole,
that narrow up-rushing shaft,
the plop and squilch of cat bodies
drugged in burlap
subsiding in two inches of water –
one of the sounds one must live with:

then back for the next load and up the hill again
to let it drop upon the first;
and back again, this time to the sea,
the sack by now a squirming clutch of cats –
the scratch of claws on jute,
another sound –

to sink from the side of a fishing boat.
I watched the brown sack bulge and flatten
on the sea bottom
till I could not tell the movement
of the sea from the movement of the sack.
Cats take a long time drowning.

Let's say she was a friend in need
of much consideration,
of back-up sympathy and slaughter-help;
recall that Buddha once ate pork
to gratify his host,
setting courtesy above principle –

O, if I've learned anything at all
in these intervening years,
I've learned to place scant credence in
the clamoring of conscience;
and as for the seductions of integrity,
I'd rather lose a friend than kill a cat.

Andrew Suknaski

PHILIP WELL

prairie spring
and i stand here before a tire crimper
two huge vices held by a single bolt
(men of the prairies were grateful to a skilled man
who could use it and fix wooden wheels
when the craft flourished)

i stand here
and think of philip well found in his musty woodshed
this morning
by dunc mcpherson on the edge of wood mountain –
philip well lying silent by his rusty .22

and i ask my village: *who was this man?*
this man who left us

in 1914
well and my father walked south from moose jaw
to find their homesteads
they slept in haystacks along the way
and once nearly burned to death
waking in the belly of hell they were saved by mewling mice
and their song of agony –
a homesteader had struck a match and thought he
would teach them a lesson

well and father lived in a hillside and built fires
to heat stones each day in winter
they hunted and skinned animals to make fur blankets

threw redhot stones into their cellars
overlaid the stones with willows
and slept between hides

father once showed me a picture
nine black horses pulling a gang plough
philip well proudly riding behind (breaking
the homestead to make a home)

well quiet and softspoken
loved horses and trees and planted poplars around his shack
when the land began to drift away
in tough times well bought a tire crimper
and fixed wheels tanned hides and mended harnesses
for people

and later (having grown older and often not feeling well)
moved to wood mountain village
to be near people who could drive him to a doctor
if necessary

today in wood mountain
men's faces are altered by well's passing
while they drink coffee in jimmy hoy's cafe
no one remembers if well had a sweetheart
though someone remembers a school dance near
the montana border one christmas –
well drunk and sleeping on a bench in the corner
while the people danced
well lonelier than judas after the kiss
(the heart's sorrow like a wheel's iron ring
tightening around the brain till
the centre cannot hold and
the body breaks)

JAMES LETHBRIDGE

i love buckin broncos
but love women more he says as he reminisces
about his rodeo days

talks of drinking with pete knight and soak and toata brown
in moose jaw the summer of 1930
and how they were heading west to the calgary stampede
how he wondered whether to return to wood mountain
   rodeo
or travel west with them

and he says: *now here was my problem*
am i going to go to calgary buckin broncos
or am i going to return to wood mountain and my good
   woman?
this was the predicament i was in
now what would you have done?
anyway i said to the fullas in moose jaw
"i'm goin with a woman in wood mountain
and i'm suppose to go back to wood mountain
if i don't go back to wood mountain
maybe she'll disown me"

and so he bought a ring and returned home
married the young woman and lived happily for thirty years
and never has seen the calgary stampede
now lives alone in the village
still makes the odd purse or pocket wallet

he spends most of his afternoons in the trails end
drinking calgary beer or whiskey and water
has all the memories he needs here
to sustain him –

arrives nightly at the town well where the children once
    played
in the playground
slowly pumps a pail of water to make another lonely pot
    of coffee
and slowly ambles coughing all the way home
carrying something more than merely a pail of water

Anne Szumigalski

ANGELS

have you noticed
how they roost in trees?
not like birds
their wings fold the other way

my mother, whose eyes are clouding
gets up early to shoo them
out of her pippin tree
afraid they will let go their droppings
over the lovely olive
of the runnelled bark

she keeps a broom by the door
brushes them from the branches
not too gently
go and lay eggs she admonishes

they clamber down
jump clumsily to the wet ground
while she makes clucking noises
to encourage them to the nest

does not notice how they
bow down low before her anger
each lifting a cold and rosy hand
from beneath the white feathers
raising it in greeting
blessing her and the air
as they back away into the mist

THE DISC

over and over a woman is told that she's not what she seems
to be   at first she fights this *I am* she says *what I seem to
be*:   sand, twigs, stones, and waves of disturbed air through
which a bird has just flown, also light refracted from the lid
of a syrup tin   the disc of light wobbles on the floor and
ceiling

she begins to have second thoughts   perhaps after all she is
not what she seems: a laurel hedge, a butterfly flagging on
the beach, a scale from the wing of that butterfly, a rhubarb
bush, the oiled wheel of a train

she could indeed be something not yet mentioned not yet
named *for always* she tells herself *before you have finished
naming a thing the meaning has changed*   no one can speak
as fast as a thought darts across the mind   no one can speak
faster than the sound of words

I'm not what I seem to be she confesses at last then a warm
subservience floods through her and she becomes the fluent
shadow of any names we may choose to throw at her

SHRAPNEL

shrapnel has torn the man's ribs apart
there is a shabby wound in his breast
his mouth opens innocently upon a cry

he wants to curse his enemies but cannot
for he sees them as striplings lying in the grass
each with a girl beneath him

the long grass full of clover and fieldherbs
waves gently in the heat
the men get up from the women
and buckle on their belts
the women just lie there looking up at the thundery sky
we are wounded with joy they tell each other
we are happy happy happy

the soldier sees this he hears all this
as he lies there asking the earth
is this my final place my own place
he glances upwards to where
the tops of the trees almost meet
there is just a small patch of empty sky showing
it must be spring for a bird with a straw in its beak
swoops down to a low bough   he tries to think
of the name of the bird
he tries to think of his own name
the name of his son who has learned to speak already
so his wife writes   he has seen the child only once
and that was more than a year ago

he tries to remember the colour of his wife's eyes
he sees only her frailty those little narrow birdbones
beneath the soft flesh
he wishes she was another woman
one easier to abandon   one calm and robust
with a wide smooth brow

but who could forget that pitiful teat
in the child's mouth
the curious maze of blue milkveins whose pattern
he traces in the dirt   his hand touches a broken brick
here was a house   now he remembers the collapse
of its walls

he licks his lips tasting for brickdust
he counts his strong teeth with his tongue
they are all there unchipped   he hears the bland
voice of the dentist telling him he has perfect bite

he shuts his eyes against the light but it shines on
through rosy lids which are the same colour exactly
as his wife's secret he wants to part her legs
and touch her glistening vermilion lining
now at last he understands
why he loves the bodies of women
more than the bodies of men   for pale skin covers
a man all over and only a wound can show his lining

carefully he passes his hands over his body
buttoned into its tunic of stiff drab wool
until he finds the hole in his chest
he thrusts in his fist to staunch the blood
a pulse beats close to his folded fingers
it is insistent and strong
it is pushing him away from himself

John Thompson

THE CHANGE

It's in the dark we approach
        our energies, that instant
the tide is all fury, still,
        at the full:

as that time I lost an axe-blade
        in the chopping,
and listened, for days, to the rust
        gathering; and that night

I didn't find it, but came upon
        a cow moose blind, stinking
with heat, moaning, and

hooving the black peat with
        such blood, such fury,
the woods broke open, the earth

        recovered her children,
her silences, her poems.

from *Stilt Jack*

I

Now you have burned your books: you'll go
with nothing but your blind, stupefied heart.

On the hook, big trout lie like stone:
terror, and they fiercely whip their heads, unmoved.

Kitchens, women and fire: can you
do without these, your blood in your mouth?

Rough wool, oil-tanned leather, prime northern goose
    down,
a hard, hard eye.

Think of your house: as you speak, it falls,
fond, foolish man. And your wife.

They call it the thing of things, essence
of essences: great northern snowy owl; whiteness.

XVI

The barn roof bangs a tin wing in the wind;
I'm quite mad: never see the sun;

you like sad, sad songs that tell a story;
how far down on whiskey row am I?

I believe in unspoken words, unseen gods:
where will I prove those?

If I wash my hands will I disappear?
I'll suck oil from Tobin's steel and walnut.

If one more damn fool talks to me about
sweetness and light . . .

I'm looking for the darkest place;
then, only then, I'll raise my arm;

someone must have really socked it to you:
were the lips made to hold a pen or a kiss?

If there were enough women I wouldn't write poetry;
if there were enough poetry

XXI

I know how small a poem can be:
the point on a fish hook;

women have one word or too many:
I watch the wind;

I'd like a kestrel's eye and know
how to hang on one thread of sky;

the sun burns up my book:
it must be all lies;

I'd rather be quiet, let the sun
and the animals do their work:

John Thompson

I might watch, might turn my back,
be a done beer can shining stupidly.

Let it be: the honed barb drowsing in iron water
will raise the great fish I'll ride

(dream upon dream, still the sun warms my ink
and the flies buzzing to life in my window)

to that heaven (absurd) sharp fish hook,
small poem, small offering.

Howard White

THE MEN THERE WERE THEN

It sounds like something that's been
said before too many times
but I want you to know
I mean it, now, when I say
there are no men around today
like the men there were then.
You see those enormous tree stumps
with the notches in, and you don't think.
Those were big trees.
There are no trees like that today.
We think today what we do with machines
is hard work, but our trees are tiny
and they did it all by hand.
They did it all standing on springy, narrow
boards, stuck twelve feet up above the ground
sometimes canyons below them
swinging their axes into that big wood.
To move along they'd give a hop with one toe
held under the springboard, to swing it.
Then they'd stick the axe in the wood
and stoop to reach their saws. I never
heard of one who fell.
But one time one man when he
turned to reach for his saw,
he brushed that razor sharp axe

and it slit his middle
right along the belt line for about eight inches.
It didn't bleed so much but
his intestines came looping down like bunting.
When we came with the stretcher this man
was under the cut crouched on his knees
delicately holding up these gut loops
one by one splashing sawdust off 'em
with water from his waterbag.
There are no men like that
around today.

THOSE BLOODY FISHERMEN

Those bloody fishermen you know
they're not even human
not during fishing season
you know old Scotch John
take a look at
that man's hands if you ever
get the chance
left or right I forget,
one of 'em's got a hole
right through it
'e was running 'is lines out one time
feeling the fathom markers
with the flat of 'is hand, it was
the old bronze type of line, and a loose strand speared 'im
clean through the fingers
threaded 'em tight together

yanked 'im overboard
but 'e hit the gurdy clutch
goin' by   climbed back in
one-handed   cut the fingers apart
with sidecutters
each one separately
went on fishing
holes started stinkin'n goin' green
so he soaked 'em in the bleach bucket
he had there for his spoons
poked out the gunk with a broomstraw, holes got so big
'e could see through 'em
white furry stuff lining 'em
still he couldn't miss any fishing
holes closed up eventually
went bluish black   saw a doctor
end of the season, said
didn't that hurt?
Hurt? he sez, yeah by God it hurt
like a son of a bitch
passed out right there
in the doctor's chair
said later that was the
first time 'e stopped to think about it
and it hit 'im all at once

THESE HERE POETS

Used to be in the woods all you had to
watch for was junkies nodding off
getting caught with their ass in the bight
now it's these Christly poets
scratching away behind every tree
trying to get you to repeat everything
gotta do your job and their job too
babysit the useless bastards
until the first plane goes out
Canada Council gives 'em ten thousand bucks
to write about what it's like
to be a workingman
tiny little book comes out
cost you half a day's pay to buy it
and here's all your own words
all phonied up so you sound like
some fucking Okie or something
everything's all ass-backwards
Jesus it makes me mad
if that guy ever shows up around here again
he'll have a real accident to write about

Biographies and Notes

ROO BORSON, born in Berkeley, California in 1952, has lived mainly in Vancouver and Toronto since 1974, holding such jobs as secretary, administrative assistant, lab technician. Her major collections are *A Sad Device* (1981) and *The Whole Night, Coming Home* (1984).

MARILYN BOWERING was born in Winnipeg in 1949. Now based near Victoria, she has lived in Greece, the Queen Charlotte Islands, and Scotland, and has worked as an editor and teacher of writing. Her selected poems, *The Sunday Before Winter,* appeared in 1984.

"Russian Asylum." The pun on "asylum" is a bitter one. In the Soviet Union, authorities sometimes confine political dissidents to institutions for the insane.

"St. Augustine's Pear Tree." St. Augustine (354–430) recalled how in his teens he had stolen some pears for the sheer joy of stealing, not because he wanted to eat. He analyzed this as a perverted desire to emulate God's omnipotence.

ROBERT BRINGHURST was born in 1946 in California, and grew up in the Canadian Rockies and the western United States. Fluent in half a dozen languages, he has been an editor and book designer in Vancouver, and now writes full time. *The Beauty of the Weapons* (1982) is his selected.

"Deuteronomy." The speaker is the prophet Moses. In the Bible, at the end of the Book of Deuteronomy, he has led the children of Israel from slavery in Egypt to the land promised them by the Lord, yet knows that he himself will die before they enter it. Previous events in the poem are recounted in the Book of Exodus.

"Demokritos." This is from a group of poems in which Bringhurst recreates the teaching of Greek philosophers from before the time of Socrates. He was drawn, he remarks, to the non-compart-mentalized quality in their thinking about what is, a quality very unlike anything in modern thought. They "knew no distinctions between physicist, philosopher, biologist and poet." Demokritos, sometimes called the "laughing philosopher," lived from approximately 460 to 370 B.C.

"Leda and the Swan." Leda, wife of the king of Sparta (or Lakonia), was impregnated by Zeus, who had assumed the form of a swan. She produced two sets of twins; all four children were involved in bloodshed and battle, and one, Helen, was the cause of the Trojan War.

"The Stonecutter's Horses." The speaker is the Italian poet Petrarch (1304–74); the poem is an imagined version of the first draft of his will (which survives only in the final draft). Petrarch had an illegitimate daughter. Since he could not publicly explain his affection for her, he eventually dealt with the problem by adopting her husband as his own son. This is the "Brossano" to whom veiled instructions are given in the will.

"Saraha." Saraha was a Buddhist sage in North India, probably of the ninth century, who composed the philosophic poems on which Bringhurst draws here.

DON COLES was born in 1928 in Woodstock, Ontario; from 1952 to 1964 he lived in Europe, periodically working as a translator. He teaches literature at York University in Toronto, and has directed its creative writing program. His most recent book is *The Prinzhorn Collection* (1982).

"Ah! Qu'ils sont pittoresques..." The title echoes a line by the nineteenth-century French poet, Jules Laforgue: "Ah, qu'ils sont pittoresques, les trains manqués."

"Major Hoople." Coles remembers the title figure from "reading the funnies" daily in the *Woodstock Sentinel-Review*. The comic strip portrayed a portly, self-important gentleman who presided over the dinner table in a boarding house, with a motley crew of boarders subjected to his harangues, and a nagging, overburdened wife in the background.

JENI COUZYN was born in South Africa in 1942, lived in England for a decade after 1965, and then settled in Toronto till

1978. At present she is a freelance writer and editor in London, England. *Life by Drowning,* her selected poems, appeared in 1983.

LORNA CROZIER, born in Swift Current, Saskatchewan in 1948, has spent most of her life on the Prairies, where she has been a teacher and a director of communications for the Saskatchewan government. Her new and selected poems *The Garden Going on Without Us,* came out in 1985.

"The Flowers of Georgia O'Keefe." Georgia O'Keefe: a mid-twentieth-century American painter known for her depictions of animal skulls and sensuous flowers.

CHRISTOPHER DEWDNEY was born in 1951 in London, Ontario, to a family with strong scientific and literary interests. He currently teaches part time at York University in Toronto; he is also a visual artist. His selected poems, *Predators of the Adoration,* appeared in 1983.

A reader intrigued by the unique challenge of Dewdney's poetry will want to explore *Predators of the Adoration,* which includes a statement by the author, a glossary, and an Afterword by Stan Dragland. Of his ongoing major work, "A Natural History of Southwestern Ontario," Dewdney writes there: "In a sense, this book is the voice of the land and the creatures themselves, speaking from the inviolate fortress of a primaeval history uncorrupted by humans. It is a codex of the plants and animals whose technology is truly miraculous, and for whom I am merely a scribe."

And Stan Dragland makes an observation on Dewdney's language which might serve as a more general invitation: "The language suddenly seems very roomy.... What to do with fright at what is on the other side, or between the words? One possibility is to withdraw.... The other is to bake a cake, set the table. A new universe is beginning to appear through rents in the old. Why not greet it hospitably?"

PIER GIORGIO DI CICCO was born in Italy in 1949, and after 1952 lived in Montreal, Toronto, and Baltimore. He returned to Toronto in 1967, where he has worked as a bartender and editor. Among his collections are *The Tough Romance* (1979) and *Flying Deeper into the Century* (1982).

"Letter to Ding an Sich." "Ding an sich," or "thing in itself," is a term from Kantian philosophy, and refers to any thing that is – not as known by the human mind, but as it exists in itself. Di Cicco is not concerned with technical terminology, however; he posits a time when people did know "things-in-themselves" through direct experience, and mourns its loss.

MARY DI MICHELE left her native Italy in 1955, at six, to come to Canada. She lives in Toronto, and has been poetry editor of *Toronto Life*. Recent books are *Mimosa and Other Poems* (1981) and *Necessary Sugar* (1983).

DON DOMANSKI was born in Sydney, Cape Breton Island in 1950, and now lives in Wolfville, Nova Scotia. His latest books are *Heaven* (1978) and *War in an Empty House* (1982).

DAVID DONNELL was born in 1939 in St. Marys, Ontario, and lives in Toronto. He has held factory and office jobs but now writes full time, working in fiction and non-fiction as well as poetry. His new and selected poems, *Settlements,* won the Governor General's Award for 1983.

PAUL DUTTON works in publishing in Toronto, where he was born in 1943. He writes fiction and poetry for the page (as in the 1979 volumes *Right Hemisphere, Left Ear* and *The Book of Numbers*); he also writes sound or "voice" poems which he performs live and on records, often as one of The Four Horsemen.

"From *So'nets*." There are eight "so'nets" in all; these are numbers 7, 5, 3, and 6 respectively. Dutton's re-exploration of the sonnet form is playfully conceptual; the results are intended as sound poetry and visual poetry simultaneously.

BRIAN FAWCETT, born in 1944, moved to Vancouver in 1965 from his native Prince George. He has worked as a logger, truckdriver, community organizer, planner, and teacher. Recent volumes are *Tristram's Book* (1981) and *Aggressive Transport* (1982), as well as two collections of stories.

"From *Tristram's Book*." Fawcett locates the speaker in both the contemporary world and the realm of heroic legend. From the latter perspective he is Tristram, who fell in love with Isolde, the bride-to-be of his uncle, the King of Cornwall. Their love was intense and illicit; they were frequently separated, but Tristram never ceased his longing for Isolde.

RAYMOND FILIP, born in Germany in 1950 to Lithuanian parents, came with them to Montreal the following year. He is a full-time writer and musician; his books include *Somebody Told Me I Look Like Everyman* (1978) and *Hope's Half-Life* (1983).

JUDITH FITZGERALD was born in Toronto in 1952. She has worked as a cab driver, university teacher, and journalist (winning the Fiona Mee Award for literary journalism in 1983), and is now a book editor. Her selected is *Given Names* (1985).

JON FURBERG, born in Vancouver in 1944, teaches at Vancouver Community College. His collections include *Prepositions for Remembrance Day* (1981) and *Anhaga* (1983). He also writes songs.

"From *Anhaga*." These poems are from a sequence inspired by the mood, sound, and themes of the Anglo-Saxon elegy *The Wanderer* (in Anglo-Saxon, *Ānhaga*), which dates from roughly 700 A.D. Of the speaker of the original elegy, Furberg comments in his foreword: "He may be the oldest written European example of the sole survivor. In some battle... his fellowship has been wiped out. Instantly, he becomes an outcast, since his provider-lord is dead. Despite the arguments of memory and will, he is utterly forsaken."

The phrase "Midden Yard" puns on the Anglo-Saxon term for the world (which translates as "middle earth" – midway between heaven and hell) and the contemporary meaning, "refuse heap." "The Wall" adheres closely to the corresponding passage in the Anglo-Saxon.

ARTIE GOLD was born in Brockville, Ontario in 1947, but has lived for many years in Montreal, working at times as a draftsman, geology lab instructor, bookstore manager. A recent volume is *before Romantic Words* (1979).

"[O'hara died like christ]." Frank O'Hara, a central poet in the "New York School," was killed in 1966 at the age of forty.

LEONA GOM was born in 1946, and grew up on an Alberta farm; in 1972 she moved to British Columbia. Of various jobs she has held, her favourite was that of tombstone cutter in Edmonton; she now teaches at a community college. Her selected poems, *NorthBound,* appeared in 1984.

KRISTJANA GUNNARS, born in Iceland in 1948, was raised there and in Denmark. She came to Canada in 1969, and works in Winnipeg as a freelance writer and translator. Among her books are *Settlement Poems 1* and *2* (1980), and *Wake-Pick Poems* (1981).

"From *Settlement Poems.*" The volumes of this name recreate the experience of Icelandic immigrants as they settled parts of Manitoba in the late nineteenth century.

DIANA HARTOG was born in California in 1942, and immigrated to Canada in 1971. She works in New Denver, B.C. as a house renovator and sometime electrician. Her first collection was *Matinee Light* (1983).

GARY HYLAND, born in Moose Jaw in 1940, teaches English at a high school there. His books include *Just Off Main* (1982) and *Street of Dreams* (1984).

PAULETTE JILES was born in Missouri in 1943. She came to Canada in 1969, and from 1973 to 1983 practised and taught journalism in native communities in the North. She now lives in Nelson, B.C. Her new and selected poems, *Celestial Navigation,* appeared in 1984.

AUGUST KLEINZAHLER was born in New Jersey in 1949. From 1971 to 1978 he lived in Victoria and Montreal; he now works in San Francisco as a locksmith. Among his books are *A Calendar of Airs* (1978) and *Storm over Hackensack* (1985).

ROBERT KROETSCH was born in Alberta in 1927. After two decades studying and teaching in the United States, he is now a professor at the University of Manitoba. One of his seven novels, *The Studhorse Man,* won the Governor General's Award in 1969. He started publishing poetry in 1975; the poems collected in *Field Notes* (1981) form part of an ongoing work. His essays on poetics are collected in *Open Letter* (Series 5, No. 4, 1983).

CHARLES LILLARD was born in California in 1944, and lived in Alaska for fourteen years before coming to British Columbia in 1967. He worked for many years as a logger, machine operator, and university lecturer; he is now an historian and editor in Victoria. His collections include *Voice, My Shaman* (1976) and *A Coastal Range* (1984).

"Rivers Were Promises." The rivers and creeks named are in British Columbia. The speaker, Lillard has observed, is projecting his present sense of inertia into the future, in a mood of depression. He imagines himself looking back on a life in which he has "paid his dues," but has never risen any further above the immediate circumstances which both nourish him and hem him in.

Simon Gun-an-noot was an heroic exception to the entropy which the speaker fears. An Indian from the Hazelton area, he was accused of murder in 1906; knowing he was unlikely to receive fair trial, he fled into the mountains – where he lived as a fugitive for thirteen years, refusing to harm anyone during the manhunts launched against him. In 1919 he surrendered, and was tried and acquitted.

KIM MALTMAN, born in Medicine Hat in 1950, describes himself as an itinerant physicist; in the course of his education he has lived in Calgary, Vancouver, Toronto, and Berkeley. Among his books are *Branch Lines* (1982) and *Softened Violence* (1985).

DON MCKAY was born in Owen Sound, Ontario in 1942. Studies took him to Saskatoon and Wales; he now lives near London, Ontario, where he teaches literature at the University of Western Ontario. *Lependu* (1978) is a sequence; *Birding, or Desire* (1983) is his new and selected shorter poems.

"Alias Rock Dove, Alias Holy Ghost." "Rock dove" is another name for the North American pigeon; the European white dove is a traditional symbol of the Holy Ghost.

"Adagio for a Fallen Sparrow." The epigraph is from "Mid-Winter" by Christina Rossetti.

"Notes Toward a Major Study of the Nose." A vibrissa is a stiff hair-like projection; here, a nostril hair.

ALFRED FRANK MORITZ was born in Ohio in 1947, and moved to Toronto in 1974. He has worked in journalism, advertising, and publishing; he now writes full time. His collections include *Black Orchid* (1981) and *The Visitation* (1983).

ERIN MOURÉ was born in Calgary in 1955, and moved to Vancouver in 1974. She has worked for the CNR, and since 1978 for VIA Rail, most recently in Montreal. Among her books are *Wanted Alive* (1983) and *Domestic Fuel* (1985).

"Paradisical Vallejo." César Vallejo (1892–1938) was a Peruvian poet.

SUSAN MUSGRAVE was born in California in 1951, to Canadian parents. She has spent periods in Ireland, the Queen Charlottes, Panama, and Colombia, but returns to Vancouver Island where she was raised. Her new and selected poems, *Tarts and Muggers,* appeared in 1982; her latest collection is *Cocktails at the Mausoleum* (1985).

"Sir Lionel Luckhoo. . . . " Sir Lionel was one of the lawyers for the cult leader Jim Jones. After the 1978 massacre in Jonestown, Guyana, Sir Lionel became a Born-Again Christian. The title reproduces an autobiographical note in his pamphlet, *To My Muslim Friends.*

AL PITTMAN, born a Newfoundlander in 1940, found himself a Canadian citizen on April 1, 1949. He teaches English at

Grenfell College in Corner Brook, and writes plays, fiction, and children's stories. His latest volume of poetry is *Once When I Was Drowning* (1978).

ROBERT PRIEST was born in England in 1951, immigrating here with his family in 1955. He makes his living as a songwriter and rock singer in Toronto, with albums out for adults and children. Among his books are *Sadness of Spacemen* (1980) and *The Man Who Broke Out of the Letter X* (1984).

MONTY REID was born in Saskatchewan in 1952, and writes and edits for the Tyrrell Museum of Palaeontology in Drumheller, Alberta. His collections include *The Life of Ryley* (1981) and *The Dream of Snowy Owls* (1983).

ROBYN SARAH was born in New York City in 1949, to Canadian parents, but has lived in Montreal from the age of four. Since leaving an incipient career in classical music, she has taught college English and co-directs the Villeneuve Press. Her newest volume is *Anyone Skating on That Middle Ground* (1985).

DAVID SOLWAY was born in Montreal in 1941. He has done freelance broadcasting and scriptwriting for the CBC, and alternates between living in Greece and teaching English at John Abbott College. His *Selected Poems* appeared in 1982; *Stones in Water* came out in 1983.

ANDREW SUKNASKI was born in 1942, to Polish and Ukrainian parents, on a homestead near Wood Mountain, Saskatchewan – his "eternal forwarding address." He studied art, and has founded several small presses. His selected, *The Land They Gave Away,* appeared in 1982. He and his work have been featured in several films.

ANNE SZUMIGALSKI was born in London, England in 1922, came to Canada in 1951, and now lives in Saskatoon. She has worked as a translator, interpreter, editor, teacher, and mother. Her books include *A Game of Angels* (1980) and *Doctrine of Signatures* (1983). With Terrence Heath, she has written four voice poems for the CBC.

SHARON THESEN was born in Saskatchewan in 1946; she moved to British Columbia at the age of six, and since 1966 has lived in Vancouver. Her varied jobs have included those of dental assistant, cab driver, and record librarian; she is now an instructor at Capilano College. Her most recent books are *Holding the Pose* (1983) and *Confabulations: Poems for Malcolm Lowry* (1984).

"Praxis." The title is a term from Marxist thought; its various shades of meaning include "purposeful social action, directed by a sound theoretical understanding." The word was widely adopted in the New Left during the late sixties and seventies.

"From *Confabulations*." The Englishman Malcolm Lowry (1911–57) wrote the celebrated novel *Under the Volcano*. He lived in Mexico and British Columbia with his wife, Margerie, and died in the village of Ripe in Sussex, England. Thesen's sequence conflates material from Lowry's fiction and letters, and from Douglas Day's biography.

COLLEEN THIBAUDEAU was born in Toronto in 1925, and since 1961 has lived in London, Ontario. Of her work history she remarks, "When you are a grandmother, you've done about everything." Her books include *My Granddaughters Are Combing Out Their Long Hair* (1978) and *The Martha Landscapes* (1984).

JOHN THOMPSON, born in England in 1938, moved to New Brunswick in 1966 to teach at Mount Allison. His first collection, *At the Edge of the Chopping There Are No Secrets* (1973), was followed by *Stilt Jack* (1978), published after his death at thirty-eight.

"From *Stilt Jack*." The poetic form here is that of the "ghazal," which originated in Persia, probably in the ninth century. A ghazal is written in couplets (five, in the Persian convention) which are related by startling intuitive leaps, rather than by a safer, more orderly logic of developing theme or narrative. "The ghazal allows the imagination to move by its own nature," Thompson wrote in his preface. "It is the poem of contrasts, dreams, astonishing leaps. The ghazal has been called 'drunken and amatory' and I think it is."

PETER VAN TOORN was born in Holland in 1944, and has lived in Montreal since 1954. He played tenor sax in the Albert Faille Blues Band, and now teaches English at John Abbott College. *Mountain Tea and Other Poems* (1984) is his selected.

van Toorn's translations are "imitations" or "versions"; he writes that his aim is to "produce what the poet whose work is being translated might have done had he been writing in English in Canada at the present time." Albius Tibullus (54?–18 B.C.) was Roman; François Villon (1431 – ?), French; Heinrich Heine (1797 – 1856), German; Matsuo Basho (1664–94), Japanese.

BRONWEN WALLACE, born in 1945, lives in her hometown of Kingston, Ontario; at present she works as counsellor in a centre for battered women and children. Her books include *Signs of the Former Tenant* (1983) and *Common Magic* (1985). She has collaborated with Chris Whynot on several films.

TOM WAYMAN was born in eastern Ontario in 1945, grew up in British Columbia, and studied and taught for three years in California and Colorado. He has worked at a wide variety of jobs, from factory hand to university teacher. His many books range from *Waiting for Wayman* (1973) to *Counting the Hours* (1983).

"The Interior." The poem refers to places in Chile and British Columbia. Concerning "The Chilean Elegies," Wayman has written: "In the fall of 1973 the human race suffered a setback when the elected government of Salvador Allende was overthrown by the Army.... The new regime quickly imposed the customary brutalities of a Latin American military dictatorship.... I wrote the five elegies to the slaughter in Chile which intend to touch also on the condition of our own life."

HOWARD WHITE was born in Abbotsford, B.C. in 1945. He has been a heavy-equipment operator and a construction-company owner, as well as a writer and editor for periodicals. He is the proprietor of Harbour Publishing; his first collection is *The Men There Were Then* (1983).

DALE ZIEROTH was born in 1946 in Neepawa, Manitoba. From 1970, he spent eight years in the eastern part of the Rockies, working as a naturalist and freelance writer for the National Parks. Latterly he has studied and taught in Vancouver. His books are *Clearing: Poems from a Journey* (1973) and *Mid-River* (1981).

Bibliographies

This is a bibliography of all the books written, and some of the books edited, by each poet. Collections of poetry are listed first; other volumes are designated by genre. A chapbook (here, a book of under 48 pages) is indicated with the symbol †, a volume of selected poems, or new and selected poems, with the symbol *. Pamphlets, broadsides, and ephemera are not noted here. Among books edited, only those having to do with literature are included. (Where the poet has served as editor for another writer's book, the credit is not listed.) For presses outside Canada, and for lesser-known or defunct presses within Canada, place of publication is given when the press is first mentioned in each bibliography.

ROO BORSON: *Landfall* (Fiddlehead, 1977). *In the Smoky Light of the Fields* (Toronto: Three Trees, 1980). †*Rain* (Moonbeam, Ont.: Penumbra, 1980). †*Night Walk* (Toronto: Missing Link, 1981). *A Sad Device* (Quadrant, 1981). *The Whole Night, Coming Home* (M&S, 1984). *The Transparence of November/Snow* (Quarry, 1984; with Kim Maltman).

MARILYN BOWERING: †*The Liberation of Newfoundland* (Fiddlehead, 1973). *One Who Became Lost* (Fiddlehead, 1976). *The Killing Room* (Sono Nis, 1977). *Sleeping with Lambs* (Porcépic, 1980). *Giving Back Diamonds* (Porcépic, 1982). ** The Sunday Before Winter* (General, 1984). [stories:] *The Visitors Have All Returned* (Porcépic, 1979). [co-editor:] *Many Voices: Contemporary Canadian Indian Poetry* (Vancouver: J. J. Douglas, 1977).

ROBERT BRINGHURST: *The Shipwright's Log* (Bloomington, Ind.: Kanchenjunga, 1972). *Cadastre* (Bloomington, Ind: Kanchenjunga, 1973). †*Deuteronomy* (Sono Nis, 1974). †*Eight Objects* (Vancouver:

371

Kanchenjunga, 1975). *Bergschrund* (Sono Nis, 1975). †*Jacob Singing* (Kanchenjunga, 1977). †*The Stonecutter's Horses* (Vancouver: Standard Editions, 1979). *Tzuhalem's Mountain* (Oolichan, 1982). **The Beauty of the Weapons* (M&S, 1982). [catalogue of book exhibition:] *Ocean/Paper/Stone* (Vancouver: William Hoffer, 1984). [tales:] *The Raven Steals the Light* (Douglas & McIntyre/ University of Washington Press, 1984; with Bill Reid). [co-editor:] *Visions: Contemporary Art in Canada* (Douglas & McIntyre, 1983).

DON COLES: *Sometimes All Over* (Macmillan, 1975). *Anniversaries* (Macmillan, 1979). *The Prinzhorn Collection* (Macmillan, 1982).

JENI COUZYN: *Flying* (London, Eng.: Workshop, 1970). *Monkey's Wedding* (London, Eng.: Cape, 1972; London, Eng.: Heinemann/ Douglas & McIntyre, 1978). *Christmas in Africa* (Heinemann/ Vancouver: J. J. Douglas, 1975). *House of Changes* (Heinemann/ Douglas & McIntyre, 1978). **Life by Drowning* (Anansi/South Africa: David Philip, 1983; rev. ed., London, Eng.: Bloodaxe, 1985). [story:] *The Happiness Bird* (Sono Nis, 1978). [editor:] *Twelve to Twelve* (London, Eng.: Poets' Trust, 1970). *The Bloodaxe Book of Contemporary Women Poets* (Bloodaxe, 1985).

LORNA CROZIER [until 1981, L. C. published as Lorna Uher.]:†*Inside Is the Sky* (Thistledown, 1976). *Crow's Black Joy* (NeWest, 1978). *No Longer Two People* (Turnstone, 1979; with Patrick Lane). *Humans and Other Beasts* (Turnstone, 1980). *The Weather* (Coteau, 1983). **The Garden Going on Without Us* (M&S, 1985).

CHRISTOPHER DEWDNEY: †*Golders Green* (Coach House, 1971). *A Palaeozoic Geology of London, Ontario* (Coach House, 1973). *Fovea Centralis* (Coach House, 1975). *Spring Trances in the Control Emerald Night* (Berkeley: The Figures, 1978). *Alter Sublime* (Coach House, 1980). *Spring Trances in the Control Emerald Night & The Cenozoic Asylum* (The Figures, 1982). *The Cenozoic Asylum* (Manchester, Eng.: Délires, 1983). **Predators of the Adoration* (M&S, 1983).

PIER GIORGIO DI CICCO: †*We Are the Light Turning* (Toronto: Missing Link, 1975; Birmingham, Alabama: Thunder City Press, 1976). †*The Sad Facts* (Fiddlehead, 1977). *The Circular Dark* (Borealis, 1977). *Dancing in the House of Cards* (Toronto: Three Trees, 1978). *A Burning Patience* (Borealis, 1978). †*Dolce-Amaro* (Tuscaloosa, Alabama: Papavero, 1979). *The Tough Romance* (M&S, 1979). †*A Straw Hat for Everything* (Birmingham, Alabama: Angelstone, 1981). *Flying Deeper into the Century* (M&S, 1982). *Dark to Light: Reasons for Humanness* (Vancouver: Intermedia, 1983). *Women We Never See Again* (Borealis, 1984). *Post-Sixties Nocturne* (Fiddlehead, 1985). *Twenty Poems* (Mexico: University of Guadalajara, 1985). [editor:] *Roman Candles: An Anthology of Seventeen Italo-Canadian Poets* (Hounslow, 1978).

MARY DI MICHELE: *Bread and Chocolate* (Oberon, 1980). *Mimosa and Other Poems* (Mosaic, 1981). *Necessary Sugar* (Oberon, 1983). [editor:] *Anything Is Possible: A Selection of Eleven Women Poets* (Mosaic, 1984).

DON DOMANSKI: *The Cape Breton Book of the Dead* (Anansi, 1975). *Heaven* (Anansi, 1978). *War in an Empty House* (Anansi, 1982).

DAVID DONNELL: †*Poems* (Thornhill, Ont.: Village, 1961). *The Blue Sky* (Black Moss, 1977). *Dangerous Crossings* (Black Moss, 1980). *Settlements* (M&S, 1983). [prose:] *Hemingway in Toronto* (Black Moss, 1982). [stories:] *The Blue Ontario Hemingway Boat Race* (Coach House, 1985).

PAUL DUTTON: †*So'nets* (Toronto: Ganglia, 1976). *Right Hemisphere, Left Ear* (Coach House, 1979). *The Book of Numbers* (Porcupine's Quill, 1979). *spokesheards* (Longspoon, 1983; with Sandra Braman; case, postcards). †*The Plastic Typewriter* (Toronto: Underwhich, 1985). [as a member of The Four Horsemen, with Rafael Barreto-Rivera, Steve McCaffery, bp Nichol:] *Horse d'Oeuvres* (General, 1975). †*A Little Nastiness* (Toronto: grOnk, 1980; envelope, unbound pages). *The Prose Tattoo: Selected Performance Scores* (Milwaukee, Wisc.: Membrane, 1983). [P.D. solo LP recording:] *Blues, Roots, Legends, Shouts and Hollers* (Starborne Productions, 1980). [LP recordings, with The Four Horsemen:] *Canadada* (Griffin House, 1973). *Live in the West* (Starborne Productions, 1977).

BRIAN FAWCETT: *Friends* (poetry and prose) (Vancouver: New Star, 1971). †*Five Books of a Northmanual* (Vancouver: Beaver Kosmos Folio, 1973; same as *Imago*, no. 18). *Permanent Relationships* (Coach House, 1975). †*Cottonwood Canyon* (Prince George: Caledonia Writing Series, 1976). †*The Fall of Saigon* (Vancouver: private printing, 1976). †*Three Revolutionary Poems* (Vancouver: William

Hoffer/NMFG, 1976). †*The Second Life* (Caledonia Writing Series, 1977). *Creatures of State* (Talonbooks, 1977). *Tristram's Book* (*Capilano Review,* no. 19, 1981). *Aggressive Transport* (Talonbooks, 1982). [prose:] *The Opening* (New Star, 1974). [stories:] *My Career with the Leafs and Other Stories* (Talonbooks, 1983). *Capital Tales* (Talonbooks, 1984).

RAYMOND FILIP: *Jaws in a Fishbowl* (Montreal: Ecowi, 1976; with Robert Tembeck). *Somebody Told Me I Look Like Everyman* (Pulp, 1978). *Hope's Half-Life* (Véhicule, 1983).

JUDITH FITZGERALD: †*City Park* (Bracebridge, Ont.: Northern Concept, 1972). *Victory* (Coach House, 1975). *Lacerating Heartwood* (Coach House, 1977). *Easy Over* (Black Moss, 1981). *Split/Levels* (Coach House, 1983). †*The Syntax of Things* (Toronto: Prototype, 1984). *Beneath the Skin of Paradise: The Piaf Poems* (Black Moss, 1984). *Given Names (Black Moss, 1985). [prose:] *Journal Entries* (Dreadnaught, 1975). [children's poem:] *I'm Gonna Be a Poet* (Black Moss, 1985). [editor:] *Un Dozen: Thirteen Canadian Poets* (Black Moss, 1982).

JON FURBERG: †*Jonas* (Pulp, 1972). †*Prepositions for Remembrance Day* (Pulp, 1981). *Anhaga* (Pulp, 1983).

ARTIE GOLD: †*cityflowers* (Montreal: Delta Can, 1974). †*Mixed Doubles* (Berkeley: The Figures, 1975; with Geoff Young). *Even Yr Photograph Looks Afraid of Me* (Talonbooks, 1975). †*5 Jockeypoems* (Montreal: The Word, 1977). †*Some of the Cat Poems* (Montreal: CrossCountry, 1978). †*Poo Comix* (Montreal: private printing, 1978). *before Romantic Words* (Véhicule, 1979). †[prose:] *Golden Notes/Living on Gold* (Montreal: private printing, 1981). [co-ordinating editor:] *The Véhicule Poets* (Montreal: Maker, 1979).

LEONA GOM: †*Kindling* (Fiddlehead, 1972). *The Singletree* (Sono Nis, 1975). *Land of the Peace* (Thistledown, 1980). *NorthBound (Thistledown, 1984).

KRISTJANA GUNNARS: *Settlement Poems 1* (Turnstone, 1980). *Settlement Poems 2* (Turnstone, 1980). *One-Eyed Moon Maps* (Porcépic, 1980). *Wake-Pick Poems* (Anansi, 1981). [stories:] *The Axe's Edge* (Porcépic, 1983).

DIANA HARTOG: *Matinee Light* (Coach House, 1983). [prose poems:] *Taking Candy* (Coach House, 1985).

GARY HYLAND: †*Poems from a Loft* (Wood Mountain, Sask.: Sundog, 1974). †*Home Street* (Coteau, 1975). *Just Off Main* (Thistledown, 1982). *Street of Dreams* (Coteau, 1984). [co-editor:] *Number One Northern: Poetry from Saskatchewan* (Coteau, 1977). *100% Cracked Wheat* (Coteau, 1983).

PAULETTE JILES: *Waterloo Express* (Anansi, 1973). **Celestial Navigation* (M&S, 1984). [juvenile:] *The Golden Hawks* (Lorimer, 1978).

AUGUST KLEINZAHLER: †*The Sausage Master of Minsk* (Montreal: Villeneuve, 1977). *A Calendar of Airs* (Coach House, 1978). *Storm Over Hackensack* (New York: Moyer Bell, 1985). [editor:] *News and Weather: Seven Canadian Poets* (Brick, 1982).

ROBERT KROETSCH: †*The Ledger* (London, Applegarth Follies, 1975; Brick/Nairn, 1979). **The Stone Hammer Poems* (Oolichan, 1975). *Seed Catalogue* (Turnstone, 1977). *The Sad Phoenician* (Coach House, 1979). *The Criminal Intensities of Love as Paradise* (Oolichan, 1981). *Field Notes (General, 1981). †*Letters to Salonika* (Toronto: Grand Union, 1983). *Advice to My Friends* (General, 1985). [book-length interview:] *Labyrinths of Voice* (NeWest, 1982; with Shirley Neuman and Robert Wilson). [essays, on poetics:] *Open Letter* (Spring 1983, fifth series, no. 4). [novels, Canadian cloth editions only:] *But We Are Exiles* (Macmillan, 1965). *The Words of My Roaring* (Macmillan, 1966). *The Studhorse Man* (Macmillan, 1969). *Gone Indian* (New Press, 1973). *Badlands* (New Press, 1975). *What the Crow Said* (New Press, 1978). *Alibi* (Stoddart, 1983). [travel:] *Alberta* (Macmillan, 1968). [journals:] *The Crow Journals* (NeWest, 1980).

CHARLES LILLARD: †*Cultus Coulee* (Sono Nis, 1971). *Drunk on Wood* (Sono Nis, 1973). †*Jabble* (Vancouver: Kanchenjunga, 1975). *Voice, My Shaman* (Sono Nis, 1976). †*Poems* (Victoria: Islomane, 1979). *A Coastal Range* (Sono Nis, 1984). [history:] *Paths Our Ancestors Walked* (Victoria: Indian Cultural Centre, 1977). [co-editor:] *Volvox: Poetry from the Unofficial Languages of Canada* (Sono Nis, 1971).

KIM MALTMAN: *The Country of the Mapmakers* (Fiddlehead, 1977). †*For Nobody Else, Should They Ask* (Toronto: Missing Link, 1981). *The Sickness of Hats* (Fiddlehead, 1982). *Branch Lines* (Thistledown, 1982). *The Transparence of November/Snow* (Quarry, 1984; with Roo Borson). *Softened Violence* (Quadrant, 1985).

DON MCKAY: †*Air Occupies Space* (Windsor: Sesame, 1973). *Long Sault* (London: Applegarth Follies, 1975). *Lependu* (Brick, 1978). *Lightning Ball Bait* (Coach House, 1981). *Birding, or Desire* (M&S, 1983).

A.F.MORITZ: †*New Poems* (Boston: Swan Song, 1974). *Here* (Portland, Maine: Contraband, 1975; rev. ed., 1980; with cassette). †*Catalogue of Bourgeois Objects* (New York: Some, 1977). †*Water Follies* (London: Killaly, 1978). †*Signs and Certainties* (Montreal: Villeneuve, 1979). †*The Death of Francisco Franco* (White Rock, B.C.: Blackfish, 1979). †*Keats in Rome* (Montreal: L1 Editions, 1980). †*Music and Exile* (Dreadnaught, 1980). *Black Orchid* (Dreadnaught, 1981). *Between the Root and the Flower* (Blackfish, 1982). *The Visitation* (Toronto: Aya, 1983). [translations:] *Children of the Quadrilateral: Selected Poems of Benjamin Péret* (Syracuse, N.Y.: Bitter Oleander, 1976). *In the Country of the Antipodes: Poems 1964–79*, by Ludwig Zeller (Mosaic, 1979; with Susana Wald and John Robert Colombo). *Testament for Man: Selected Poems of Gilberto Meza* (Dreadnaught, 1983; with Theresa Moritz).

ERIN MOURÉ: *Empire, York Street* (Anansi, 1979). †*The Whisky Vigil* (Harbour, 1981). *Wanted Alive* (Anansi, 1983). *Domestic Fuel* (Anansi, 1985).

SUSAN MUSGRAVE: *Songs of the Sea-Witch* (Sono Nis, 1970). *Entrance of the Celebrant* (Macmillan/London, Eng.: Fuller d'Arch Smith, 1972). *Grave-Dirt and Selected Strawberries* (Macmillan, 1973). *The Impstone* (M&S, 1976; London, Eng.: Omphalos, 1978). *Kiskatinaw Songs* (Victoria: Pharos, 1977; with Sean Virgo). *Selected Strawberries and Other Poems* (Sono Nis, 1977). *Becky Swan's Book* (Porcupine's Quill, 1978). *A Man to Marry, a Man to Bury* (M&S, 1979). *Tarts and Muggers* (M&S, 1982). *Cocktails at the Mausoleum* (M&S, 1985). [children's poetry:] *Gullband* (Vancouver: J.J. Douglas, 1974). [novel:] *The Charcoal Burners* (M&S, 1980; Totem, 1981). [juvenile:] *Hag Head* (Clarke Irwin, 1980).

AL PITTMAN: *Through One More Window* (Breakwater, 1974). *Once When I Was Drowning* (Breakwater, 1978). [drama:] *A Rope Against the Sun* (Breakwater, 1974). [children's poetry:] *Down by Jim Long's Stage* (Breakwater, 1976). [children's story:] *One Wonderful Fine Day for a Sculpin Named Sam* (Breakwater, 1983). [stories:] *The Boughwolfen and Other Stories* (Breakwater, 1984). [co-editor:] *Thirty-one Newfoundland Poets* (Breakwater, 1979).

ROBERT PRIEST: *The Visible Man* (Toronto: Unfinished Monument, 1979). *Sadness of Spacemen* (Dreadnaught, 1980). *The Man Who Broke Out of the Letter X* (Coach House, 1984). [recording:] *The Robert Priest E.P.* (Airwave Records, 1982). [children's LP recording:] *Summerlong* (G-Tel Records, 1984).

MONTY REID: *Fridays* (Camrose, Alta.: Sidereal, 1979). *Karst Means Stone* (NeWest, 1979). *The Life of Ryley* (Thistledown, 1981). *The Dream of Snowy Owls* (Longspoon, 1983). *The Alternate Guide* (Red Deer: rdc, 1985).

ROBYN SARAH: †*Shadowplay* (Fiddlehead, 1978). †*The Space Between Sleep and Waking* (Montreal: Villeneuve, 1981). †*Three Sestinas* (Villeneuve, 1984). *Anyone Skating on That Middle Ground* (Véhicule, 1985).

DAVID SOLWAY: *In My Own Image* (Montreal: McGill Poetry Series, 1962). †*The Crystal Theatre* (Fiddlehead, 1971). †*Paximalia* (Fiddlehead, 1972). †*The Egyptian Airforce* (Fiddlehead, 1973). *Anacrusis* (Fiddlehead, 1976). *The Road to Arginos* (Montreal: New Delta, 1976). †*Twelve Sonnets* (Montreal: Mansfield Book Mart, 1978). *Mephistopheles and the Astronaut* (Mosaic, 1979). *Selected Poems (Montreal: Signal, 1982). *The Mulberry Men* (Signal, 1982). *Stones in Water* (Mosaic, 1983). [editor:] *4 Montreal Poets* (Fiddlehead, 1973).

ANDREW SUKNASKI: †*This Shadow of Eden Once* (Lake Louise, Alta.: Deodar Shadow, 1970). †*Circles* (Deodar Shadow, 1970). †*In Mind or Xrossroads or Mythologies* (Wood Mountain, Sask.: Anak, 1971). †*Rose Way in the East* (Toronto: Ganglia, 1972). †*Old Mill* (Blewointment, 1972). †*The Nightwatchman* (Anak, 1972). †*The Zen Pilgrimage* (Anak, 1972). †*Y th Revolution into Ruenz* (Anak, 1972). *Four Parts Sand: Concrete Poems* (Oberon, 1972; anthology with A.S., Birney, bissett, and Copithorne). *Wood Mountain Poems*

(Anak, 1973; rev. ed., edited by Al Purdy, Macmillan, 1976). *Suicide Notes, Book One* (Wood Mountain, Sask.: Sundog, 1973). †*Phillip Well* (Prince George: Caledonia Writing Series, 1973). †*These Fragments I've Gathered for Ezra* (Edinburg, Texas: Funch Press, 1973). *Leaving* (Prince George: Repository, 1974). †*On First Looking Down from Lion's Gate Bridge* (Anak, 1974; rev. ed., Black Moss, 1976). †*Blind Man's House* (Anak, 1975). †*Leaving Wood Mountain* (Sundog, 1975). †*Writing on Stone: Poem Drawings, 1966–76* (Anak, 1976). *Octomi* (Thistledown, 1976). *The Ghosts Call You Poor* (Macmillan, 1978). †*Two for Father* (Sundog, 1978: with George Morrissette). *East of Myloona* (Thistledown, 1979). *Montage for an Interstellar Cry* (Turnstone, 1980). *In the Name of Narid* (Porcupine's Quill, 1980). **The Land They Gave Away* (NeWest, 1982; edited by Stephen Scobie). *Silk Trail* (Toronto: Blewointment, 1985). [translator:] *The Shadow of Sound,* by Andrei Voznesensky (Caledonia Writing Series, 1975).

ANNE SZUMIGALSKI: *Woman Reading in Bath* (Doubleday, 1974). *Wild Man's Butte* (Coteau, 1979; with Terrence Heath). *A Game of Angels* (Turnstone, 1980). *Doctrine of Signatures* (Fifth House, 1983). *Risks* (Red Deer: rdc, 1984). *Instar* (rdc, 1985).

SHARON THESEN: *Artemis Hates Romance* (Coach House, 1980). †*Radio New France Radio* (Vancouver: Slug, 1981). *Holding the Pose* (Coach House, 1983). †*Confabulations: Poems for Malcolm Lowry* (Oolichan, 1984).

COLLEEN THIBAUDEAU: †*Ten Letters* (Coach House, 1975). *My Granddaughters Are Combing Out Their Long Hair* (Coach House, 1977). *The Martha Landscapes* (Brick, 1984). [The Vancouver magazine *Air* devoted issue 3 (1971) and issue 14–15–16 (1973) to poetry by C. T.]

JOHN THOMPSON: *At the Edge of the Chopping There Are No Secrets* (Anansi, 1973). *Stilt Jack* (Anansi, 1978).

PETER VAN TOORN: †*Leeway Grass* (Montreal: Delta Canada, 1970). *In Guildenstern County* (Montreal: Delta Can, 1973). **Mountain Tea and Other Poems* (M&S, 1984). [editor:] *Lakeshore Poets* (Montreal: The Muse's Company, 1982). [co-editor:] *Cross/cut: Contemporary English Quebec Poetry* (Véhicule, 1982). *The Insecurity of Art: Essays on Poetics* (Véhicule, 1982).

BRONWEN WALLACE: *Marrying into the Family* (Oberon, 1980). *Signs of the Former Tenant* (Oberon, 1983). *Common Magic* (Oberon, 1985). [films, co-directed with Chris Whynot:] *All You Have to Do,* 1982; *That's Why I'm Talking,* 1985.

TOM WAYMAN: *Waiting for Wayman* (M&S, 1973). *For and Against the Moon: Blues, Yells and Chuckles* (Macmillan, 1974). *Money and Rain: Tom Wayman Live!* (Macmillan, 1975; with cassette). *Free Time* (Macmillan, 1977). *A Planet Mostly Sea* (Turnstone, 1979). **Introducing Tom Wayman* (Princeton, N.J.: Ontario Review Press, 1980). *Living on the Ground: Tom Wayman Country* (M&S, 1980). *The Nobel Prize Acceptance Speech* (Thistledown, 1981). *Counting the Hours: City Poems* (M&S, 1983). [essays:] *Inside Job: Essays on the New Work Writing* (Harbour, 1983). [editor:] *Beaton Abbot's Got the Contract: An Anthology of Working Poems* (NeWest, 1974). *A Government Job at Last: An Anthology of Working Poems* (Vancouver: MacLeod, 1976). *Going for Coffee: Poetry on the Job* (Harbour, 1981).

HOWARD WHITE: *The Men There Were Then* (Pulp, 1983). [biography:] *A Hard Man to Beat* (Pulp, 1984). [editor:] *Raincoast Chronicles: First Five* (Harbour, 1975). *Raincoast Chronicles: Six/Ten* (Harbour, 1983).

DALE ZIEROTH: †*Poems for Friends* (Invermere, B.C.: private printing, 1973). *Clearing: Poems from a Journey* (Anansi, 1973). *Mid-River* (Anansi, 1981). [prose:] *Nipika: The Story of Radium Hot Springs* (Calgary: Minister of Supply and Services for Parks Canada, 1978).

Acknowledgments

ROO BORSON: "Talk," "Flowers," "Jacaranda," "Grey Glove," "The Midwest Is Made of Appleblossoms," "Now and Again," "At Night You Can Almost See the Corona of Bodies" are from *A Sad Device* (1981). Reprinted by permission of Quadrant Editions. All other poems are from *The Whole Night, Coming Home* (1984). Reprinted by permission of The Canadian Publishers, McClelland and Stewart Limited, Toronto. MARILYN BOWERING: "Armistice," "Night Terrors," "Too Happy," "St. Augustine's Pear Tree" are from *The Sunday Before Winter: The New and Selected Poetry of Marilyn Bowering* (1984). Reprinted by permission of General Publishing Co. Limited, Toronto, Canada. "Wishing Africa," "Russian Asylum" are from *Sleeping with Lambs* (1980). Reprinted by permission of Press Porcépic Limited. "Grandangel," "Well, it ain't no sin to take off your skin and dance around in your bones," are from *Giving Back Diamonds* (1982). Reprinted by permission of Press Porcépic Limited. ROBERT BRINGHURST: "Saraha" is used by permission of the author. All other poems are from *The Beauty of the Weapons: Selected Poems 1972–82* (1982). Reprinted by permission of The Canadian Publishers, McClelland and Stewart Limited, Toronto. DON COLES: "Photograph," "Sometimes All Over" are from *Sometimes All Over* (1975). "Codger," "On a Bust of an Army Corporal . . ." are from *Anniversaries* (1979). All other poems are from *The Prinzhorn Collection* (1982). The above poems by Don Coles are reprinted by permission of Macmillan of Canada, A Division of Canada Publishing Corp. JENI COUZYN: Both poems are taken from *Life by Drowning: Selected Poems* (1983). Reprinted by permission of House of Anansi Press, Toronto. LORNA CROZIER: "Animals of Spring," "Marriage: Getting Used To," "This One's for You," "We Call This Fear" are from *Humans and Other Beasts* (Turnstone Press, 1980). Reprinted by permission of the author. "Even the Dead," "The Child Who Walks Backwards," "Stillborn" are from *The Weather* (1983). Reprinted by permission of Coteau Books. All other poems used by permission of the author. CHRISTOPHER DEWDNEY: All poems are from *Predators of the Adoration: Selected Poems 1972–82* (1983). Reprinted by permission of The Canadian Publishers, McClelland and Stewart Limited, Toronto. PIER GIORGIO DI CICCO: "Canzone," "The Head Is a Paltry Matter," "The Man Called Beppino," "Remembering Baltimore, Arezzo," "Willing," "The Jump on Death" are from *The Tough Romance* (1979); "Flying Deeper into the Century," "Male Rage Poem," "Relationships" are from *Flying Deeper into the Century* (1982). The above are reprinted by permission of The Canadian Publishers, McClelland and Stewart Limited, Toronto. Other poems used by permission of the author. MARY DI MICHELE: "As in the Beginning," "Poem for My Daughter" are from *Necessary Sugar* (1983). Reprinted by permission of Oberon Press. "False Analogies 2" is used by permission of the author. DON DOMANSKI: All poems are from *Heaven* (1978). Reprinted by permission of House of Anansi Press, Toronto. DAVID DONNELL: "Abattoir" is used by permission of the author. All other poems are from *Settlements* (1983). Reprinted by permission of The Canadian Publishers, McClelland and Stewart Limited, Toronto. PAUL DUTTON: All poems are from *Right Hemisphere, Left Ear* (Coach House, 1979). Reprinted by permission of the author. BRIAN FAWCETT: "Lament," "The Hand," "The City" are from *Aggressive Transport* (1982). Reprinted by permission of Talonbooks. Poems from *Tristram's Book* (1981) are reprinted by permission of the author. RAYMOND FILIP: Both poems are from *Somebody Told Me I Look Like Everyman* (1978). Reprinted by permission of Pulp Press Book Publishers. JUDITH FITZGERALD: "Past Cards 21" is from *Split/Levels* (Coach House, 1983). Reprinted by permission of the author. JON FURBERG: "Into Goes In," from *Prepositions for Remembrance Day* (1981), and poems from *Anhaga* (1983) are reprinted by permission of Pulp Press Book Publishers. ARTIE GOLD: "[O'hara died like christ]" is from *cityflowers* (Montreal: Delta Can, 1974). Reprinted by permission of the author. "[life.]," "[I have no astrologer–]" are from *before Romantic Words* (1979). Reprinted by permission of Véhicule Press. LEONA GOM: All poems are from *NorthBound* (1984). Reprinted by permission of Thistledown Press. KRISTJANA GUNNARS: Both poems are from *Settlement Poems 1* (1980). Reprinted by permission of Turnstone Press. DIANA HARTOG: All poems are from *Matinee Light* (Coach House, 1983). Reprinted by permission of the author. GARY HYLAND: Both poems are from *Just Off Main* (1982). Reprinted by permission of Thistledown Press. PAULETTE JILES: "Waterloo Express," "The Tin Woodsman," "Conversation," "Far and Scattered Are the Tribes . . . ," "Body" are from *Waterloo Express* (1973). Reprinted by permission of House of Anansi Press, Toronto. All other poems are from *Celestial Navigation* (1984). Reprinted by permission of The Canadian Publishers, McClelland and Stewart Limited, Toronto. AUGUST KLEIN-

Acknowledgments

ZAHLER: "Minstrelsy, a Penny's Worth" is from *A Calendar of Airs* (Coach House, 1978). It and "Dejection Between Foot and Brow" and "Summer's End" are used by permission of the author. ROBERT KROETSCH: "Stone Hammer Poem," "How I Joined the Seal Herd," "Sketches of a Lemon" are from *Field Notes* (1981). Reprinted by permission of General Publishing Co. Limited, Toronto, Canada. CHARLES LILLARD: "Rivers Were Promises" is from *Voice, My Shaman* (1976). Reprinted by permission of Sono Nis Press. KIM MALTMAN: "Tina" is from *Branch Lines* (1982). Reprinted by permission of Thistledown Press. "Nihilism" is used by permission of the author. DON MCKAY: "Notes Toward a Major Study of the Nose" and "Territoriality" used by permission of the author. All other poems are from *Birding, or Desire* (1983). Reprinted by permission of The Canadian Publishers, McClelland and Stewart Limited, Toronto. A. F. MORITZ: "Catalogue of Bourgeois Objects" is from *Black Orchid* (1981). Reprinted by permission of Dreadnaught, Toronto. "What They Prayed for," and "Prayer for Prophecy" are from *The Visitation* (1983). Reprinted by permission of Aya Press, Toronto. ERIN MOURÉ: "Fusillade" and "Paradisical Vallejo" are used by permission of the author. All other poems are from *Wanted Alive* (1983). Reprinted by permission of House of Anansi Press, Toronto. SUSAN MUSGRAVE: "Fishing on a Snowy Evening," "Night and Fog," "Right Through the Heart," "Boogeying with the Queen" are from *Tarts and Muggers: Poems New and Selected* (1982). All other poems are from *Cocktails at the Mausoleum* (1985). The above poems by Susan Musgrave are reprinted by permission of The Canadian Publishers, McClelland and Stewart Limited, Toronto. AL PITTMAN: Both poems are from *Once When I Was Drowning* (1978). Reprinted by permission of Breakwater Books Ltd. ROBERT PRIEST: "God in the Museum" and "The Kiss I Just Missed" are from *Sadness of Spacemen* (1980). Reprinted by permission of Dreadnaught, Toronto. "Christ Is the Kind of Guy" is from *The Man Who Broke Out of the Letter X* (Coach House, 1984). Reprinted by permission of the author. MONTY REID: Both poems are from *The Life of Ryley* (1981). Reprinted by permission of Thistledown Press. ROBYN SARAH: "Fugue" is from *The Space Between Sleep and Waking* (Villeneuve, 1981). Reprinted by permission of the author. "A Valediction," "A Meditation Between Claims" are from *Anyone Skating on That Middle Ground* (Véhicule Press, 1984). Reprinted by permission of the author. DAVID SOLWAY: All poems are from *Selected Poems* (1982). Reprinted by permission of Véhicule Press (Signal Editions). ANDREW SUKNASKI: Both poems are from *Wood Mountain Poems* (1976). Reprinted by permission of Macmillan of Canada, A Division of Canada Publishing Corp. ANNE SZUMIGALSKI: "Angels" is from *A Game of Angels* (Turnstone Press, 1980). Reprinted by permission of the author. "The Disc," "Shrapnel" are from *Doctrine of Signatures* (1983). Reprinted by permission of Fifth House. SHARON THESEN: "Loose Woman Poem," "Po-It-Tree," "Dedication" are from *Artemis Hates Romance* (Coach House, 1980). "Evocation," "Spiritual," "Praxis," "'Til Then," "From Long Distance: An Octave" are from *Holding the Pose* (Coach House, 1983). Selections from *Confabulations: Poems for Malcolm Lowry* (Oolichan Books, 1984). The above poems by Sharon Thesen are reprinted by permission of the author. COLLEEN THIBAUDEAU: "My Grandmother's Sugar Shell ...," "Into the Trees" are from *The Martha Landscapes* (1984). Reprinted by permission of Brick Books. All other poems are from *My Granddaughters Are Combing Out Their Long Hair* (Coach House, 1977). Reprinted by permission of the author. JOHN THOMPSON: "The Change" is from *At the Edge of the Chopping There Are No Secrets* (1973). Selections from *Stilt Jack* (1978). The above poems by John Thompson are reprinted by permission of House of Anansi Press, Toronto. PETER VAN TOORN: All poems are from *Mountain Tea and Other Poems* (1984). Reprinted by permission of The Canadian Publishers, McClelland and Stewart Limited, Toronto. BRONWEN WALLACE: "The Woman in This Poem" is from *Signs of the Former Tenant* (1983). Reprinted by permission of Oberon Press. All other poems are from *Common Magic* (Oberon, 1985). Reprinted by permission of the author. TOM WAYMAN: "The Interior," "The Death of the Family" are from *Money and Rain: Tom Wayman Live!* (1975). "Highway 16/5 Illumination," "Kitchen Poem" are from *Free Time* (1977). The above poems are reprinted by permission of Macmillan of Canada, A Division of Canada Publishing Corp. "Life on the *Land Grant Review*," "Wayman in Love" are from *Waiting for Wayman* (1973). Reprinted by permission of The Canadian Publishers, McClelland and Stewart Limited, Toronto. "A Cursing Poem" is from *For and Against the Moon: Blues, Yells and Chuckles* (Macmillan of Canada, 1974). Reprinted by permission of the author. HOWARD WHITE: All poems are from *The Men There Were Then* (1983). Reprinted by permission of Pulp Press Book Publishers. DALE ZIEROTH: "The Hunters of the Deer," "Father," "Beautiful Woman" are from *Clearing: Poems from a Journey* (1973). "Baptism," "Coyote Pup Meets the Crazy People...," "The Truck That Committed Suicide" are from *Mid-River* (1981). The above poems by Dale Zieroth are reprinted by permission of House of Anansi Press, Toronto. "The Boat" is used by permission of the author.